MALTA

C000009765

How to use this book

Following the tradition established by Karl Baedeker in 1846, sights of particular interest are distinguished by either one ★ or two ★★.

To make it easier to locate the various sights in the "A to Z" section of the Guide, their coordinates on the large map of Malta are shown in red at the head of each entry.

Coloured strips along the outside edge of the right-hand pages make it easy to find the different sections of the guide. Blue indicates the introductory articles, red the descriptions of sights and yellow the practical information at the end of the book.

Only a selection of hotels and restaurants can be given: no reflection is implied, therefore, on establishments not included.

In a time of rapid change it is difficult to ensure that all the information given is entirely accurate and up to date, and the possibility of error can never be completely eliminated. Although the publishers can accept no responsibility for inaccuracies and omissions, they are always grateful for corrections and suggestions for improvement.

Preface

This guide to Malta is one of the new generation of Baedeker guides.

These guides, illustrated throughout in colour, are designed to meet the needs of the modern traveller. They are quick and easy to consult, with the principal places of interest described in alphabetical order, and the information is presented in a format that is both attractive and easy to follow.

This guide is devoted to the island republic of Malta, which consists of the main island of Malta with its many treasures of art and architecture, the smaller island of Gozo with its charming scenery and the tiny rocky islet of Comino. The guide is in three main parts. The first part gives a general account of Malta, its climate, flora and fauna, population, government and society, economy, history, famous people, art and culture. A number of suggested routes for visitors provide a lead-in to the second part, in which the principal sights are described; and the third part contains a wealth of practical information designed to help visitors to find their way about and make the most of their stay. Both the sights and the practical information are listed in alphabetical order.

Among the scenic and archaeological highlights of Malta are the Blue Grotto and the Neolithic temple complex of Hagar Qim

The new Baedeker guides are noted for their concentration on essentials and their convenience of use. They contain numerous specially drawn maps and colour illustrations; and at the end of the book is a large map making it easy to locate the various places described in the "A to Z" section of the guide with the help of the coordinates given at the head of each entry.

Contents

Baedeker Specials

Navel of

The Maltese archipelago, a group of rocky islands with a sparse growth of vegetation, has for many millennia been a bridgehead between Europe and Africa, with magnificent natural harbours. In the course of its eventful history it has had two cultural high points. The first was between 4000 and 2500 BC, when an advanced culture developed on the islands which built the oldest free-standing religious architecture in the world. There are still many unsolved riddles about the early inhabitants of Malta, and most mysterious of all is the meaning of the underground cult complex of Hal Saflieni. Was it the place of burial of the priestesses who ruled the islands?

Then in the early modern period the islands gained fresh importance as the strategically situated stronghold of the Knights of St John, whose rule lasted almost 270 years. Impressive evidence of the power and splendour of the Knights is provided by the fortress town of Valletta, laid out on a regular plan in the late 16th century, which is now the capital of the independent republic of Malta. Equally impressive as a synthesis of art and architecture, with its palaces and churches, is the old town of Mdina, the city of the Maltese nobility.

But Malta has much to offer apart from its art and culture. For many people its climate is sufficient inducement for a visit. The first green shoots of spring appear in Malta when elsewhere in Europe it is still winter, and the islands which had seemed stony and inhospitable are transformed into a sea of blossom. Bathing is possible until well into autumn, and even in winter the warming rays of the sun are never far away, with

Temple

built to honour the Magna Mater

Grand Harbour

the port between Valletta, Senglea and Vittoriosa has always had major economic importance

Mighty

fortress – the citadel in Victoria, on Gozo

the Ocean

day temperatures which are frequently around 15°C. Truly, Malta is a good place for a holiday at any time of year!

The Maltese are proud also of some of their natural features, such as the Blue Grotto, which can stand comparison with its celebrated counterpart on Capri, and the imposing Dingli Cliffs. And visitors can relax after their sightseeing by bathing or sunbathing on beautiful beaches which for the most part have not been spoiled by over-development.

Most visitors to Malta only see the smaller island of Gozo on a day trip. This is a pity, for Gozo is not merely Malta's junior partner: it is an island with its own distinctive characteristics. It is greener and more rural than the larger island – ideal country for long walks which will reveal its beauties. The villages of the island of Gozo are scattered about among fields marked out by stone walls, with the citadel of Victoria rising majestically above them all.

Views
are free – the Vedette in Senglea

Finally visitors who want to get away from the noise and hectic bustle of towns will enjoy a holiday on Comino, a tiny rocky islet with two hotels offering a wide range of sports facilities for more energetic visitors.

It is not surprising, therefore, that this happy combination of natural beauty and cultural interest, together with the natural friendliness of the Maltese, is attracting increasing numbers of visitors. Those who come here with an open mind will realise how much Malta has to offer – particularly, perhaps, to those who like rocks and stones!

Siesta
in Great Siege Square in Valetta, after a hard day's work

Tourism
dominates the scenery in Spinola Bay in St Julian

**Nature, Culture
History**

Facts and Figures

The island republic of Malta (officially Repubblika ta'Malta, Republic of Malta), situated in the western Mediterranean, consists of the two main islands of Malta and Gozo, together with the smaller islands and islets of Comino, Cominotto, Filfla and St Paul's Islands.

The Maltese archipelago extends between latitude 35°48' and 36°00'N and between longitude 14°10' and 14°35'E at the narrowest point in the Mediterranean, 95 km from Sicily and 290 km from the coast of Tunisia. It lies almost exactly half way between the western and eastern ends of the Mediterranean, roughly 1800 km from Gibraltar at one end and Lebanon at the other. This central situation gives Malta enormous strategic importance as a bridgehead between Europe and Africa and an area of passage between the western and the eastern Mediterranean.

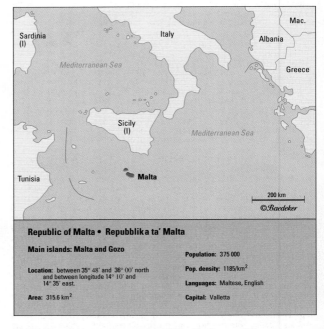

Republic of Malta • Repubblika ta' Malta

Main islands: Malta and Gozo

Location: between 35° 48' and 36° 00' north and between longitude 14° 10' and 14° 35' east.

Area: 315.6 km^2

Population: 375 000

Pop. density: 1185/km^2

Languages: Maltese, English

Capital: Valletta

◀ The Megalithic temple complex of Mnajdra is one of the most impressive sights on Malta. Even its situation close to the southern coast is grand.

The total **area** of the Maltese islands is 315.6 sq. km – the main island of Malta 245.6 sq. km, Gozo 67 sq. km, Comino 2.5 sq. km and the other small islets 0.5 sq. km. Malta is 27 km long by 15 km across, with a total coastline of 136 km. Gozo, separated from the main island by the 5.5 km wide Comino Channel, is 14.5 km long by 7 km across, with a coastline of 43 km.

The name Malta is derived from the Phoenician word *mlt* (probably pronounced malet), meaning a safe haven or anchorage. It was used as such by the Phoenicians on their long trading voyages from the 9th c. BC onwards. During the Roman period the island was called Melita, a name often thought to be associated with *mel*, the Latin word for honey, which was one of the island's principal products. The name Malta first appears in written sources in the late 4th century AD as a possession of the Eastern Roman Empire. During the period of Arab rule this became Mâlitah; then after the conquest of the island by the Normans at the end of the 11th century the name reverted to Malta.

Origin of name

Geology

The Maltese islands are, geologically, part of the base structure of the European continent. After the Mediterranean came into being and mountain folding movements took place during the Tertiary era the islands were linked with Sicily and Africa until the ice ages of the Quaternary, as animal bones found in the Ghar Dalam cave show. When the masses of ice began to melt and the sea level rose the land bridge between Europe and Africa was covered by the sea and Malta became an island, on which an endogenous flora and fauna then developed.

The islands consist almost exclusively of marine sedimentary rock formed from the calcareous deposits left by myriads of tiny sea creatures. Five different strata can be distinguished: at the lowest level coralline limestone and then globigerina limestone, followed by blue clays, greensands and finally an upper layer of coralline limestone. The limestone has been used as a building material for many thousands of years, the upper and lower coralline limestones being much superior in quality and hardness to the softer and more easily worked globigerina limestone, which is used in sculpture and craft products.

The main island of **Malta** seems at first glance a featureless rock plateau, which as a result of the slight inclination of the strata to the south-east and the varying hardness of the rock has developed a stepped profile. Four different topographical regions can be distinguished. In the west is a high plateau of upper coralline limestone falling away in steps on all sides. On the seaward side is a cliff-fringed coast of lower coralline and globigerina limestones remarkable for its sheer drop and for the varied colouring of the rock, ranging from red by way of yellow to white. On the north the plateau is bounded by an escarpment caused by the Great Fault (Victoria Lines). On the east the scarped edge of the plateau is indented by a number of small valleys. These lower-lying areas with their good alluvial soils are intensively cultivated with the help of irrigation, while the karstic plateau provides only sparse grazing for sheep and goats. To the north of the plateau is a landscape of ridges and depressions formed from hard karstic limestone, a fault system which is continued in Comino and Gozo. Bare karstic terrain alternates with fertile alluvial and intensively cultivated basins, notable among which is Pwales Valley, with springs which provide an easily accessible water supply. Between the Great Fault in the south-east, the steep-sided Wardija Ridge to the south-west and the sea to the north are the Il-Ghasel lowlands, formerly an area of marsh and alluvial land. The south

Topography

11

and south-east of Malta consist of gently undulating uplands of globigerina limestone, in which most of the population live.

The coastal topography of Malta ranges from the imposing cliffs in the south-west by way of a series of shallow bays in the north-west with beautiful bathing beaches (Ghajn Tuffieha Bay, Golden Bay) and the wide bays in the north (Mellieha Bay, St Paul's Bay) to the much indented low-lying coasts on the north-east and south-east. Marsamxett Harbour and the Grand Harbour are parts of a drowned valley system, separated by the ridge of Mount Sciberras. The Grand Harbour in particular, a natural deep-water harbour with a depth of 25 m, has been since time immemorial of great economic as well as strategic importance.

The landscape of **Gozo** is less varied. The island consists mainly of a ridge tilted slightly to the north-east, with its highest point (176 m) in the west. It has fewer bays and inlets than the main island, but it too has cliffs up to 100 m high falling vertically down to the sea, with beautiful bathing beaches on the north coast (Ramla Bay, San Blas Bay) and the wide expanse of Mgarr Harbour to the south-east. In the interior are flat-topped hills and wide valleys. Less affected by karstic action and with deeper soils, the land on Gozo is intensively cultivated.

Water supply

The Maltese islands are poorly supplied with water. There are no rivers or lakes, and only in winter is there much rain, which quickly seeps away into the porous limestone or flows down dry valleys into the sea. The islands do, however, have underground stores of fresh water which until recently met the needs of the population. This groundwater is on two levels. The high level springs are easily accessible supplies of water under the Mdina plateau formed by rainwater filtering through the globigerina limestone which then accumulates on an underlying bed of blue clays. While the Stone Age inhabitants collected water in cisterns, the Knights of St John, needing larger supplies

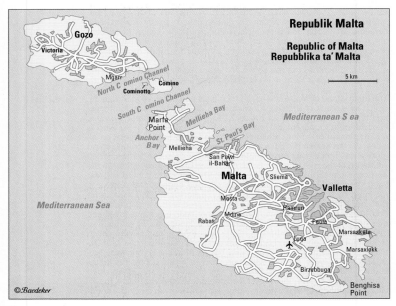

A landscape in western Malta: fruit and vegetables are grown on small terraced fields.

of water, tapped these underground resources and conveyed the water, using an aqueduct for part of the way, to Valletta. From 1856 onwards the lower water table was also tapped to provide a public water supply. In the east central part of the island rainwater and seawater accumulate in cavities in the lower coralline and globigerina limestones, with fresh and salt water forming separate layers because of their difference in gravity. As a result of over-use of the fresh water without adequate replacement by water seeping down from the surface the water has become increasingly saline. The continually increasing demand for water for domestic use, agriculture, industry and the ever greater numbers of visitors has led to recurrent shortages. Since 1982 efforts have been made to meet the demand by the establishment of seawater desalination plants (Ghar Lapsi, Tigné Point, Cirkewwa), though at high cost in the use of energy.

Climate

The climate of Malta is basically Mediterranean, with hot, dry summers and mild, wet winters, influenced by subtropical zones of aridity and the trade winds.

During the summer months (May to September) there is little rain, there are between 10 and 12 hours of sunshine daily and temperatures average 23.5°C (see climatic table on p. 212). The minimum temperature in August is 22.9°C, the maximum 29.3°C.

The first showers of rain come at the end of September. In December and January, the rainiest months, they are very heavy but do not usually last long. The sun keeps breaking through, so that even during the coldest part of the year, from December to February, temperatures average around 13°C. In February the minimum is 10.3°C, the maximum 14.7°C.

Frost and ice are unknown, and there are only very occasional brief snow showers.

Sea temperatures fall from a maximum of 25.6°C in August to a minimum of 14.5°C in February.

Thanks to the exposed situation of the islands winds of varying strength blow throughout the year. In winter the prevailing wind is the north-easterly grigal, a cold and stormy wind coming from the European mainland, while in spring and summer the north-westerly majjistral brings a refreshing coolness to alleviate the heat. Less tolerable is the sultry warm and humid air brought by the xlokk, which blows over Malta from North Africa, particularly in late summer and autumn.

Flora and Fauna

Flora

With their relatively uniform surface structure, the Maltese islands have no differentiated vegetation zones. In general the vegetation on these rocky islands is fairly sparse.

Influence of human activity

In the time of the Neolithic temple-builders Malta was still partly forest-covered. Archaeologists have found evidence of pines, ashes, Judas trees, olives, figs and whitethorn between 4000 and 2500 BC. Heavy felling began in the Bronze Age and continued on a greater scale during the periods of Carthaginian and Roman rule. Timber was needed mainly for shipbuilding, but the forests were also cleared to make room for agriculture. As a result many areas were eroded by karstic action.

After the fall of the Roman Empire in the 5th century agriculture declined and the mulberry trees, evergreen holm-oaks and juniper bushes disappeared, leaving the soil exposed to erosion by wind and rain.

During the 220 years of Arab rule the land was brought back into intensive cultivation. Terraced fields were laid out and irrigated, and carob-trees were planted to provide protection from wind erosion. In the 13th century, however, economic decline again set in, with extensive destruction of the cultivated areas, so that even the commissioners of the Knights of St John who were sent to survey Malta in 1524 were horrified at the desolate state of the land, reporting that on this treeless island wood was so scarce that it was sold by the pound and that the inhabitants used dried animal dung as fuel.

From the late 16th century onwards the Knights brought the land back into cultivation, intensified wine-growing, planted olive-trees and laid out fields of cotton. They also imported the Aleppo pine and the oleander. In order to get humus for their gardens they brought in good soil as ballast in their ships in exchange for stones. Hedges of agaves and opuntias (prickly pears) as well as stone walls were used to mark out and provide shelter for their fields. By the 18th century olive-trees had almost returned to their former numbers, and place-names such as Zebbug ("olive-grove"), Birzebbuga ("olive spring") and Zejtun ("olive-press") still bear witness to the importance of the olive-tree in the life of the islands. In spite of this almost 80,000 olive-trees were felled during the period of British rule in the 19th century to make room for the more lucrative cotton fields. Then, when after only a few decades cotton-growing proved uneconomic, the fields were abandoned and left as waste land.

It was only after the Second World War, in the 1950s, that a beginning was made with the replanting of olive-trees, pines and eucalyptus trees. This is a laborious and expensive process which will take many years to

View towards Verdala Palace: in spring the barren countryside of Malta becomes a sea of blossom.

alter the landscape of Malta – if only the contemporary building boom does not frustrate these hopes.

In place of the earlier forest cover a thin layer of natural vegetation has, over the centuries, spread over the stony soil, consisting of plants and shrubs adapted to the Mediterranean climate, particularly those that can do with little water or have the ability to store it. They include heather, hard grasses, mastic bushes, spurges, various types of thistle, thyme, rosemary and the Malta onion, which is used to cure coughs. During the few rainy months there is a magnificent show of blossom – wild orchids, red poppies, tamarisks, narcissus, meadow saffron, geraniums and anemones.

Mediterranean vegetation

Fauna

In the time of the Knights there were still the larger kinds of game on the islands. Now there are only a few small mammals – rabbits (fenek), which feature frequently on Maltese menus, weasels, hedgehogs, various rodents and bats.

Mammals

There is a wider range of reptiles than of mammals. Five endemic species of lizard have been identified, one of which, the dark green Lacerta filfolensis, is found only on the uninhabited rocky islet of Filfla. Geckoes are common, but snakes and scorpions are rare. There are three non-poisonous species of snakes, found almost exclusively on Gozo and Comino.

Reptiles

Conditions on the Maltese islands are not favourable to birds. Among the twelve breeding species are the short-toed lark, the grey bunting,

Birds

the merill, a member of the thrush family which is Malta's national bird, the yellow-billed and black-billed shearwaters and the stormy petrel, which nests in the Buskett Gardens and on the sheltered rocky islet of Filfla.

The islands are also, however, an important staging-point for migrant birds flying between Europe and Africa. According to estimates made by the Maltese Ornithological Society, which has campaigned for more than 25 years for the protection of Malta's birds, the islands are visited annually by more than a million finches, half a million songbirds and thousands of birds of prey and herons.

Bird-shooting

Many birds who come to Malta meet their end there, since, exhausted after their long flight, they are an easy prey for Maltese shooting enthusiasts (see Baedeker Special). Another popular Maltese occupation is bird-catching. Drop-nets are used to catch the birds – mainly songbirds, chaffinches and greenfinches – which are enticed into the trap by captive members of their species. In many parts of Malta can be seen groups of low stone towers which are used to support the net. On the towers are set cages containing the decoy birds. Birds caught in this way are sold in the Valletta market and spend the rest of their lives in tiny cages on balconies, kiosks and fast food stalls and in restaurants for the pleasure of passers-by and customers.

Insects

The insects of the Maltese islands include various species of butterflies and moths, crickets, dragonflies and bees, which produce an excellent thyme-flavoured honey.

Marine fauna and flora

Maltese coastal waters have always had relatively few fish because of their lack of plankton, but various Mediterranean species can occasionally be encountered, among them sea bass, barbel, dorado, amber jack, sardines, cod and swordfish. Tunnies appear off the coasts of Malta only during their spawning season in June. Dolphins are common visitors.

For scuba divers the coastal waters of Malta offer nothing particularly spectacular – no tropical luxuriance or richness of colour – but they nevertheless contain a rich variety of underwater life: meadows of sea grass which are home to many small sea creatures, striped learned rockfish, greenish wrasse, brightly coloured sea peacocks, various types of sponge, zoantharian anemones and cup corals. And perhaps occasionally a St Peter's fish may come up from the great depths where it normally lives.

Unfortunately Malta's marine fauna also faces threats to its existence – from untreated sewage discharged into the sea, from oil pollution from tankers and oil-drilling platforms and also from the illicit trade in turtleshells. Every year some 2000 of the seriously endangered loggerhead turtle are caught in fishermen's nets, and instead of throwing them back into the sea the fishermen leave them to dry and to die a painful death in the sun, and then sell their shells in the local market. (Visitors should not under any circumstances buy one of these shells, since apart from anything else this would make them liable to penalties when taking it home).

Useful animals

Donkeys and mules have traditionally been used as pack animals on Malta. Goats and sheep have long been kept for their milk, cheese and meat; and more recently cattle and pigs, kept in stalls and sties, have contributed in a small way to the islands' food supply.

Domestic animals

Favourite domestic pets, in addition to songbirds, are dogs and cats. The Maltese dog, a type of lapdog with white silky hair, standing around 25 cm high, has been known since ancient times. Still bred in Malta, it may well be descended from an Egyptian breed of dog.

A Cruel Sport

Pembroke beach is quiet and peaceful on this early morning in October. We are enjoying the mild autumn air, waiting for the sun to rise. We are not the only ones to rise early, though: a small songbird already sings in competition with others of his species. With a cheerful song, it lifts off to fly away – when a loud bang shatters the air, and the little bird flaps past us, wounded by the shot. A man jumps out from behind a pile of stones, aims and shoots again. This time he has more success – the little finch is dead. The man picks up the tiny bird and proudly carries it off with the rest of his prey.

year, hundreds of thousands of birds fall prey to the shooting rage of such sportsmen. Most of the birds that die under a hail of bullets are not native, they are itinerant species from Northern and Central Europe, such as song thrushes, turtle doves, larks, hoopoes, birds of prey, herons and others who have chosen Malta as an ideal stopping point on their long and exhausting trek from their homeland to their winter residence in Africa. Many of these species are endangered which is, however, of little interest to the amateur hunters on Malta. The only thing that counts for them is the beauty or the size of the bird, because, after shooting them down the birds are stuffed and displayed as trophies that decorate their living rooms. And if the bird is not worth showing off, it just ends up in a rubbish bin or it is left lying dead on the ground.

The bird hunters of Malta are not universally loved by all their compatriots, however. The Ornithological Society of Malta, founded in 1962, has been

Birds on Malta are not only hunted by the gun; many are also caught alive in the nets of the bird-catchers and then sold, on the market in Valletta.

Unfortunately our observations are not an isolated incident. There are about 11,000 men – and it is only men – on Malta who are licensed to kill birds. Hunting birds is one of the most popular pastimes, at least as popular as football. According to estimates, 12 million shots are fired every year, the equivalent of about 250 tons of lead. Tough luck for our feathered friends! And so, every

trying to promote awareness amongst the Maltese bird hunters, for example through demonstrations. In 1980 a law was passed to protect endangered birds, prescribing close seasons and protected areas. But the bird hunters who insist on their "habitual rights" do not take much notice and (so far) are left unchecked, for they are potentially important as voters.

Population

As a result of successive periods of foreign rule over the past six thousand years Malta has a population which is ethnically very mixed. The present inhabitants are mainly the descendants of North African/Arab and Italo-Sicilian population groups. Since the 19th century, when Malta came under British colonial rule, there has also been a British minority, and in addition there are smaller numbers of Greeks, Syrians and Indians.

Saint's day in Zabbar: spectators watch from their balconies

Emigration

For many years now, as a result of over-population and unemployment, many Maltese (153,260 between 1940 and 1989) have been emigrating to neighbouring Mediterranean countries as well as to Britain, Canada, the United States and above all Australia. Since the early 1990s, emigration numbers have decreased dramatically; only around 100 people decided to move to another country in the last few years. In addition, there has been an increasing move back to Malta since 1975.

Demographic structure

As in all western countries, the rate of population growth in Malta has fallen. In the 1990s, population growth has averaged 0.9%. Over the last two decades the proportion of under-20s in the population has fallen from over 40% to around 30%, while the proportion of over-65s has risen slightly. Life expectancy at present averages 77 years. Malta has a working population of 140,000, or about 38% of the total population. Considerable effort has been devoted to school and vocational education, but 4% of the population are still illiterate.

Religion

The overwhelming majority of the population (93%) are Roman Catholics, with only small minorities of Protestants and Jews. Over many centuries the pattern of life on the islands has been moulded by religion; but its influence is now being progressively reduced by the adoption of a secularised western way of life.

Of the islands' total population of around 375,000 92.5% live on the main island of Malta, 7.5% on Gozo and Comino, with some 90% of the population living in towns. Population density, at 1181 to the sq. km, is one of the highest in Europe.

Pattern of settlement

The highest concentration of population is in the urban belt extending along the central section of the north-east coast from the tourist centres of St Julian's and Sliema by way of Birkirkara to the capital, Valletta, and from there to the historic "Three Cities" (Senglea, Cospicua and Vittoriosa), which are now working-class districts. In some parts of this agglomeration there is a population density of 8000 to the sq. km. The largest town is Birkirkara with nearly 20,000 inhabitants, followed by Sliema which, together with neighbouring St Julian's also has 20,000 residents.

In the interior are a number of small country towns. North-western Malta and the cliff-fringed southern coast are relatively sparsely populated. The population of Gozo lives mainly in villages scattered over the island.

Typical Maltese terraced houses are mostly of two storeys with a flat roof. They have narrow fronts on the street but extend farther back. A characteristic feature taken over from the Arabs is a wooden oriel window on the first floor. The windows have shutters which in summer are frequently kept closed all day. The houses often have double doors, a massive outer wooden door and an inner glass door with just enough space for one person to sit down between the doors.

House types

Since the Second World War numerous modern housing estates have been built, with the help of government subsidies, to meet the needs of the country's increasing population. There are, however, practically no high-rise blocks of flats.

Over the last thirty years the built-up area on the islands has risen from 6% to 17% of their total area. Since there is little in the way of development plans or regulation of development many built-up areas have expanded without control, destroying much of the countryside. Although official statistics show that 20% of all houses in Malta are unoccupied this over-building continues remorselessly.

Government and Society

After more than 150 years of British colonial rule Malta became independent on September 21st 1964 but remained in the Commonwealth, with the Queen as head of state. On December 13th 1974 Malta declared itself a parliamentary republic, although it remains in the Commonwealth. The head of state is the President, who is elected by Parliament for a five-year term. His functions are mainly representational. He appoints the prime minister and invites him to form a government. The government is responsible to Parliament, which consists of a single chamber of 65 or a maximum of 69 members elected for five years by universal democratic suffrage; the voting age is 18. Valetta is the capital and seat of government.

The national colours of the Republic of Malta are white and red – the heraldic colours of the Norman Duke Roger II of Sicily, who granted them to the island in 1091. The Maltese national flag has two vertical fields of white and red, of equal size. In the top left-hand corner of the white field is the George Cross, which was awarded to Malta by King George

National flag

Government and Society

VI in 1942 for its bravery and fortitude under German and Italian air attack and blockade during the Second World War.

Coat of arms

The Maltese coat of arms consists of a shield parti-coloured white and red flanked by two branches and surmounted by a five-towered mural crown; below it is a scroll bearing the official name of the Republic.

Administration

Because of the country's small area and a centuries-old tradition of central rule, there is no sharp distinction between national and local government, and all the country's affairs are run centrally. Only Gozo has had a minister of its own in the Cabinet since 1987. For administrative purposes the country is divided into six regions – the Inner Harbour, Outer Harbour, South-Eastern, Western and Northern regions and Gozo and Comino.

Foreign policy

Under conservative governments from 1964 to 1971 Malta retained its traditional links with the western alliance (NATO and the European Community) and its close relationship with Britain as a member of the Commonwealth. From 1971 to 1987 the Socialist government followed a policy of non-alignment and neutrality and established economic and cultural contacts with the Arab world, the countries of the Eastern bloc and China. Links with Western Europe became looser. NATO's naval command was transferred from Malta to Naples in 1971, and in 1974 Malta gave notice of termination of the treaty on the stationing of British troops on the island with effect from 1979. Between 1987 and 1996 the conservative government sought to establish closer relations with the rest of Europe and applied for full membership of the European Union. Between 1996 and 1998 the ruling socialist considered the withdrawal of the application, but after the return of a conservative majority to government in September 1998, the new Maltese president, Fench Adami, reaffirmed Malta's application for membership.

International organisations

Malta is a member of the United Nations and an associate member of the European Union. It is the seat of the Regional Oil Combating Centre (ROCC), a UN organisation established in 1976, with the 17 states bordering the Mediterranean as members, to combat oil pollution.

Defence

As a non-aligned state, Malta is a member of no military alliances and, under an amendment to the constitution in 1987, is committed to neutrality in the event of an international conflict. Its defence forces consist of an army of 1000 volunteers, the Malta Land Force, together with various pioneer corps, a naval group and a small air group.

Parties

Since Malta became independent the earlier multi-party system has given place to a two-party system. The two parties are the Malta Labour Party (Partit tal-Haddiema; socialist) and the Nationalist Party (Partit Nazzjonalista; middle-class, conservative). After a general election the leader of the majority party is, in accordance with parliamentary tradition, appointed prime minister. From 1964 to 1971 the government was conservative, from 1971 to 1987 socialist, from 1987 to 1996 conservative. After a brief socialist interval the conservatives have been back in power since September 1998 with 35 out of 65 seats.

Both parties were originally established in the last quarter of the 19th century and since 1921, when Malta was granted limited self-government, have won increasing political influence. Traditionally the Labour Party has had close links with the trade unions, finds its main support among workers and the lower income groups and has a higher number of registered members than the Nationalist Party. Since reforming its structure in 1977 the Nationalist Party has a paid-up membership of just under 33,000 members and has transformed itself from a party of the better-off to a broad-based people's party with a high proportion of women, white-collar workers and skilled workers in its membership. There is bitter competition between the two parties, and this has sometimes led to violent confrontations during elections.

Malta's single unified trade union is the powerful General Workers Union (GWU), which first showed its strength in the strikes and rebellions by shipyard and dock workers against the British colonial government in 1919. Since then it has continually worked for the improvement of the working and living conditions of its members. It finds its strongest support in the working-class districts in the eastern part of the area round the Grand Harbour. In 1975 the organised dock workers gained the right to participate in the management and administration of the state-owned dockyard authority. They have since also won extensive job guarantees. **Trade unions**

The dominance of the Roman Catholic church in Malta is made evident by the number of churches – around one church for every square kilometre of territory. An archbishop has his seat in Valletta and the old cathedral city of Mdina, and there is a bishop on Gozo, with his seat in Victoria. Lacking any other sense of national identity during centuries of foreign rule, the Maltese were at least unified and strong in their religious faith. The village priest, in the past one of the few literate members of the community, acquired over the centuries various secular functions in addition to his religious role. He was responsible for the education of children, mediated in disputes between the poor rural population and landowners or the state, represented his parishioners in court, strengthened the village's sense of community through the various festivals in the ecclesiastical year and cared for the needs of the poor. **Church**

Times have changed, and the priests have lost much of their former influence. In the late seventies there was a bitter conflict between the Roman Catholic church and the socialist government over the private schools run by religious bodies. The anti-clerical Malta Labour Party sought, with partial success, to exclude the clergy from concern with social affairs and confine them to their religious duties. The church cannot, in any event, prevent the changes which are taking place in Maltese society through the adoption of freer western ways of life and leisure which is undoubtedly a consequence of the development of the tourist trade. The provision of social services by the state, too, is reducing the role of the church in this field. And the church's position as a final judge on moral issues is increasingly being questioned, particularly by young people, whose views on marriage and the family are often out of line with the prescriptions of the church.

Incomes and living costs in Malta are reasonably well matched, enabling the majority of the population to enjoy a satisfactory standard of living. The state-provided social services such as unemployment insurance, health insurance, pensions, maternity leave, education and children's allowances are in line with European standards. The health services, partly state-run and free of cost at time of use, together with privately provided facilities largely meet the needs of the population. The role of women has changed substantially during the last few decades: they are no longer confined to running the household and bringing up children but are increasingly taking on jobs of their own. The progressive legislation introduced by the socialist government has given women equal pay with men and facilitated their return to working life after pregnancy and the bringing up of their children. **Standard of living**

School attendance is compulsory between the ages of 6 and 15. State schools charge no fees and books and teaching materials are free. **Education**

Teaching is in Maltese and English. Private schools (some 25% of all secondary schools), many of which are run by the Roman Catholic church, also abolished fees in 1985; in these schools teaching is exclusively in English. They are generally considered to be better than the state schools.

The six years of primary school (attended by 89% of the appropriate age group) are followed by five years of secondary school (with a 72% attendance rate), with the alternative, after three years, of moving to a commercial school (two to four years). A further two years in the New Lyceum, with alternate semesters in specialist instruction and work experience (the "pupil-worker system"), lead to a qualification for university entry.

The University of Malta, at which currently 7000 students are enrolled, grew out of a Jesuit college established in 1592. It has all normal university faculties. There is also a College of Technology.

Media

The forests of aerials on Malta's house roofs demonstrate the enthusiasm of the Maltese for television. Programmes are usually in two languages, Maltese and English. About half the output is locally produced by state-run and private channels. Also available in Malta are Italian television and British satellite television. Two radio programmes broadcast mainly in Maltese.

For a small country Malta is well provided with newspapers and periodicals. There are two Maltese-language dailies, "In-Nazzjon Taghna" (circulation 20,000) and "L'Orizzont" (circulation 25,000), and one English-language daily, "The Times" (circulation 22,000), with a Sunday edition, "The Sunday Times" (circulation 29,000), covering both local and international news.

Economy

After 150 years of economic dependence on Britain as a major naval base Malta has devoted its efforts over the last 35 years to the rapid development of industry and tourism in order to make up for the loss of income after the complete withdrawal of the Royal Navy. From an initial high unemployment rate of almost 9% and an inflation rate of around 6% in the mid-seventies the economic situation has greatly improved. In the 1990s, the inflation rate averaged only 2.9% and the unemployment rate settled down at 5%. In recent years Malta has increasingly encouraged foreign investment.

In 1996 Malta's gross domestic product was US$9635 per head of population, putting it at the lower end of the economic scale in Europe. Between 1980 and 1992 the economy grew at an average rate, in real terms, of 4.1%.

Energy and raw materials

Apart from limestone and sea salt (annual output 600 tons), and recently also some oil, Malta has no natural resources. Raw materials and sources of energy for its processing industries must, therefore, be imported. Since the oil crisis of the 1970s imports have mainly been of coal, which is transformed into energy in power stations; but lacking as they do modern filtering systems, these coal-fired power stations contribute through their sulphurous emissions to air pollution, while practically no use is made of abundantly available "clean" sources of energy such as sun and wind. Raw materials are needed particularly for the two most important branches of the economy, steel production and textiles.

Industry

Industry plays a major part in the economy of Malta, contributing 27% of the gross domestic product and employing 27% of the working population.

The mining of globigerina limestone near Mqabba – since time immemorial the Maltese have been using this soft rock as building material. It hardens quickly when exposed to air.

The traditional industrial zone is round the Grand Harbour, with the docks, shipyards, tanker-cleaning installations and steelworks, but a new industrial area has now developed between Marsa and Valletta, with light industry and textile and leatherworking plants producing for the European market, while the opening of a new industrial port in Marsaxlokk Bay, in 1991, with a container terminal and deep-water wharves, has given Malta another industrial zone and made it still more attractive as a centre of international trade.

Malta's largest industrial employers are the state-owned Malta Drydocks, with 4300 employees, and its subsidiary Malta Shipbuilding (2300 employees). The other 1500 firms engaged in the processing industries have a total of around 26,000 employees; half of them have no more than five workers.

Thanks to the generally low wage levels in its labour-intensive processing industries Malta is favoured as an industrial site by foreign firms, particularly in the supply industries. The government has also sought, by investment in the country's infrastructure – the telephone system, the road network, a new power station which came on stream in 1991 – to increase the attractiveness of Malta as an industrial base, particularly to firms in the high-tech sector.

Since the cultivable land in Malta and Gozo, amounting to 13,000 hectares, accounts only for a third of the country's total area and produces good crops only with the help of irrigation, agriculture plays only a minor role in the Maltese economy, employing only 2% of the total work force and contributing only 3% of the gross domestic product.

Agriculture

Some 80% of the total cultivable area is worked by dry farming methods: that is, the fields are planted only during the rainy winter months and only one harvest in the year is possible. During the dry

Lack of water confines agriculture on Malta. Wind turbines are increasingly used to extract brackish water from the ground.

summer months the fields remain uncultivated but are ploughed and kept clear of weeds. Only 8% of cultivable land can be irrigated, producing good yields and three harvests a year. The rest of the land lies fallow. The main irrigated areas are in the Pwales Valley, in the Ghadira depression and on Gozo, which supplies almost half the country's agricultural produce, the principal crops being tomatoes, cabbages, onions, strawberries and cut flowers. Other crops are wheat, barley and potatoes, and in some areas wine and citrus fruits are grown. The output of olive oil is low, at an average of 20 tons a year. Although Malta's agriculture does not produce enough to meet its own needs, some types of produce are exported, mainly potatoes, vegetables and cut flowers to the European Union.

The land, much fragmented and divided into numerous small holdings, is mostly let out on long lease by large landowners and the church, which is Malta's largest landowner. It is worked by small farmers, four-fifths of whose holdings are less than 5 hectares. For most of them farming is only a part-time occupation and their produce is sold in local markets. Since the flight from the land is continuing, with many young people leaving to get better paid jobs in industry, the importance of agriculture to the economy is likely to decline still further.

Stock-farming

Sheep and goats are are grazed on the sparse steppe grass of the plateaux; elsewhere they are kept in sheepcotes. There are some cattle farms, and on Gozo cows' milk provides the basis for the ricotta cheese produced there. On Comino pigs are reared. Over all, however, Malta cannot produce all the meat it needs.

Fishing

Although Malta is surrounded by the sea, fishing plays only a very minor role in its economy. Only about 1100 Maltese are fishermen, and for two-

Idyllic fishing boats can still be found on Malta

thirds of them it is only a part-time occupation. Since no rivers flow into Malta's coastal waters they contain little plankton and thus offer little food for fish. Moreover Maltese fishing methods are antiquated. With their small motorboats and rowing boats the fishermen cannot go far out to sea and usually cast their nets close inshore, where they catch mainly dorado (dorado) and swordfish (pixxispad). The total catch is only about 1000 tons. This is not enough for domestic consumption, and more than half Malta's needs must be imported.

Malta's balance of trade continues to show a deficit, with imports worth US$1025 million far exceeding exports worth $631 million. Of the imports 58% are industrial goods, 24% consumer goods, a tenth agricultural produce and the remainder fuel and chemicals. Three-quarters of the imports come from the countries of the European Union, mainly Italy, France, Britain and Germany; imports from Libya and the United States are of lesser importance. Exports consist almost exclusively of finished industrial products, principally ship repairs, shipbuilding, automobile parts, textiles and electronic apparatus. 75% of exports go to the countries of the European Union, mainly to France, Italy, Britain and Germany as well as the USA.

Foreign trade

Investment in the infrastructure of the tourist trade and Europe-wide publicity campaigns since the early seventies have brought rich dividends, increasing the number of visitors to Malta from 20,000 in 1960 to 700,000 in 1987. In 1992, for the first time, more than 1 million tourists visited Malta. In 1997, 1.1 million foreign visitors provided 250 million MTL, about 40% of Malta's national income and employment for 30,000 people. Visitors usually spend between 10 and 12 days on the island. Fully half of them come from the United Kingdom and Ireland.

Tourism

Economy

It is planned to develop tourism still further in the upper price ranges by improving the facilities for leisure and recreational activities and by catering for conferences and congresses. The negative consequences of tourism, however, have appeared in the form of supply difficulties and an uncontrolled building boom.

Transport

Shipping traffic is, of course, of great importance to this island state. Malta's ports handle almost all the country's imports and exports. Sea Malta runs services between Malta and all the major European and North African ports, and there are regular ferry services to and from Naples, Sicily and Tunis. There are also domestic ferry services between Malta (Valletta and Cirkewwa) and Gozo (Mgarr).

Malta has **no railways**. The island's only railway line, the 13 km long stretch from Valletta to Mdina where steam engines built in Britain ran between 1883 and 1931 has long since closed down. At the turn of the 20th c. about 1 million passengers were transported every year. Today, only the Old Railway Station Garden which surrounds the former station in Birkirkara as well as the restaurant "Stazzjon" in the old railway station of Mdina and Rabat remind of Malta's brief railway history.

Public passenger transport is provided exclusively by **buses**. The hub of Malta's bus services is the City Gate Bus Terminal in Floriana, at the gates of Valletta, from which any place in Malta can be reached within an hour.

Malta's 1500 km of **road network** is in general good, though some roads in the interior of the island are narrow and bumpy. The number of cars using the roads has trebled over the last 20 years, and this gives rise to problems, with traffic jams and pollution from exhaust gases at the rush hours when thousands of commuters travel to and from work.

The reconstruction and extension of the international **airport** at Luqa, which lies conveniently near Valletta, in the early seventies gave it the capacity to handle charter flights as well as the scheduled services of the national airline Air Malta. During the last few years this has been steadily expanded. In 1996 a heliport opened on Gozo, with an ultra-modern terminal.

Environmental problems

Unfortunately concern for the environment has not kept pace with Malta's economic progress. Bus services and the increasing numbers of private cars pollute the atmosphere with their exhaust gases, as do the coal-fired power stations with their sulphurous emissions, and the lead content of the air and the soil is steadily increasing. Recent investigations have shown that the concentration of lead in the blood of the Maltese is three times higher than in the blood of the Swedes. There are, for example, no special arrangements for the disposal of poisonous waste from battery factories. Malta's waste is either tipped in remote valleys or burned on rubbish dumps (two on Malta and one on Gozo) in the open air; there are no separate dumps for different kinds of waste. Ground-water – a rare and precious commodity in Malta – is increasingly polluted by nitrates and pesticides as a result of the excessive use of fertilisers in fields. There is only one plant for the treatment of waste water on Malta and none on Gozo; much of it still goes untreated into the sea. The cost of environmental protection measures, long neglected, will continue to be a burden on Malta's economy. A beginning was made, on a small scale, in 1995 with arrangements for the separation of different types of waste (glass, paper, plastics) so that they could be recycled.

History

First settlement of Malta by incomers from Sicily. Skeletons and simple everyday objects recovered by excavation give evidence of human settlement in the Ghar Dalam area. Men live a largely nomadic life in the numerous caves on the islands, gaining a subsistence by fishing, hunting in the forests which still existed in their day and a primitive form of farming.	5200 BC
Malta's isolated island situation leads to the development of an endogenous megalithic culture. This finds visible expression in large stone temples in which earth mother goddesses are worshipped. There are simple forms of social organisation. The building of temples, using only tools fashioned from stone, is a communal activity. The builders show considerable artistic skills, demonstrated in a variety of ornamental features on the stones. The inhabitants live a semi-nomadic life in family groups, sheltering in caves or simple huts, and practise primitive farming and the rearing of useful animals. The temples are served by priestesses, who sacrifice animals, make burnt offerings and offer libations to their deities. Later come the practice of incubation (healing by sleeping in a sacred place) and oracles. Since neither weapons nor evidence of violence have been found, it seems that this was a peaceable culture.	4000–2500 BC
Sudden collapse of the megalithic culture around 2500 for reasons unknown, presumably as the result of a devastating epidemic or a catastrophic drought. For several centuries the islands remain uninhabited.	2500 BC
Bronze Age settlers come to Malta from Sicily and southern Italy. They bring metal tools, build defensive strongholds and store-rooms, carry on a certain amount of trade and leave mysterious "cart ruts" in the rock. They live as communities in fortified villages – evidently fearing enemy attack.	2000–1000 BC
The Phoenicians, in the course of their long trading voyages from their base in Asia Minor, use Malta as a base and a wintering harbour. They give it the name Mlt (probably pronounced Malet), meaning "place of refuge" or "anchorage". Some elements in the Maltese language, for example marsa, meaning "sheltered harbour", in such place-names as Marsaxlokk and Marsaskala and the name of the Maltese boat, the dghajsa, are relics of the period of Phoenician and Carthaginian rule in Malta.	1000–800 BC
The Carthaginians (inhabitants of the Phoenician colony of Carthage in North Africa) seize control of Malta, and from 650 onwards built it up into a bulwark against the expansion of Greek colonies into the western Mediterranean. This is why Malta shows no traces of the Greek culture which was predominant in its near neighbour, Sicily. Instead, Phoenician and Carthaginian culture establishes itself in Malta, which in the great shrine of Astarte (a goddess of fertility and war from Asia Minor) near the island's principal harbour of Marsaxlokk has an attraction drawing seafarers from all over the Mediterranean. Thanks to its trade and its agriculture Malta develops into a flourishing Carthaginian colony.	800–218 BC
In 218, during the Second Punic War, the Roman consul Titus Sempronius Longus, setting out from Sicily, conquers Malta, which under the treaty of Zama in 201 BC finally becomes a Roman possession and henceforth is called Melita. However there is little change in conditions on the islands. The temple of Astarte becomes a temple of Juno, the principal Roman goddess, and the harbour remains an important staging-point for trade between Africa and Italy, where most local prod-	218–201 BC

ucts such as honey, linen, olive oil and wheat find a ready market. The capital, Melita, stands on a hill in the centre of the island, on a site now occupied by Mdina and Rabat. Much of Malta's forest cover is felled to provide timber for shipbuilding.

45 BC   After his victory at Munda over Pompey's sons Caesar reorganises the Roman state and distributes land to his soldiers. Thereafter Roman veterans settle on Malta.

AD 59   The Maltese believe – and until the late eighties theologians of international reputation and all denominations agreed – that during his voyage from Crete to Rome in the autumn of AD 59 the Apostle Paul was shipwrecked on Malta, the Melita of Antiquity. Thereafter he is said to have spent three months on the island and converted the population to Christianity (see Baedeker Special).

1st–4th c. AD   In the prosperous Roman colony of Melita (a name perhaps derived from Latin mel, "honey", after the island's principal product) the towns grew in size, the economy flourished and the harbour was improved. Roads were constructed all over the island, and public baths, handsome villas with beautiful mosaics and fortifications to protect the population against attack were built. Carthaginian and Roman cultures increasingly merged. Around the middle of the 4th century Christianity seems to have flourished particularly, to judge by the many catacombs dating from this period.

395   In the division of the Roman Empire Malta falls into the eastern half and becomes part of the Byzantine (East Roman) Empire. From the late 4th century onwards the name Malta increasingly appears in the written sources.

c. 440   During the great migrations the Vandals are believed to have occupied Malta for a time. After the fall of the Western Roman Empire in 476 the island falls under a succession of foreign rulers.

6th century   The conflict between Theodoric's Ostrogothic kingdom in Italy and the Byzantine Empire leads to wars in southern Italy and finally to the conquest of Malta (533), which along with Sicily now returns to Byzantine rule. A garrison with a small fleet looks after the interests of the Byzantine Emperor. The island still, however, maintains its traditional links with the Latin church in Rome.

7th/8th c.   The increasing loss of Byzantine territory in the Mediterranean to the advancing Arabs leads to the economic decline of many islands and coastal regions and their ports. Malta too is hit by this decline.

870   Arab forces of the Aghlabid dynasty, sailing from Tunisia, capture Malta in spite of Byzantine resistance and hold it for two hundred years, repelling repeated Byzantine attempts to recover it. It becomes an important base and staging-point for maritime trade (including the slave trade) between Tunis, Syracuse and Alexandria. The old capital of the island is renamed Mdina (Arabic Medina), and the island, renamed Mâlitah, is ruled by a Muslim governor. The native population is offered the choice between remaining Christian, on payment of a poll tax, or converting to Islam. With an efficient administration, a productive agriculture is developed with the help of irrigation systems and terraced fields, so that even citrus fruits and cotton can now be grown.

1091   The Norman ruler of Sicily, Roger I (1031–1101), conquers Malta, meeting no significant resistance, and exacts tribute from the Arab population and Muslim governor. Christianity is restored. Roger grants the island his heraldic colours of white and red as a symbol of his rule, and these become the island's national colours.

When the Muslims in Malta refuse to pay tribute Roger II (1095–1154) mounts a renewed campaign of conquest on Malta.   1122–27

Along with southern Italy and Sicily Malta becomes part of the new kingdom of Sicily which the Pope grants to Roger II. The island is now ruled from Sicily.   1130

At the Assizes of Ariano Roger II gives his kingdom a new constitution and thus lays the foundations of a modern state administered by officials. Malta is granted local self-government by a council of nobles, the Consiglio Popolare. The villages are given rights of self-government and the government of the council of nobles is made subject to law. Malta enjoys a period of economic and social prosperity.   1140

First mention of a bishop of Mdina, residing in Sicily.   1168

The bishop of Strasbourg visits Malta and finds Christians and Muslims living peaceably together. Arabs are still in a majority.   1175

On the death of Tancred, the last male scion of the Norman dynasty, the kingdom of Sicily falls into the hands of the Hohenstaufens as a result of the marriage of Roger II's daughter Constance, heiress to the kingdom of Sicily, to Henry VI, son of the Emperor Frederick I Barbarossa.   1194

After the death of Henry VI and Constance their son Frederick (1194–1250), having renounced the German crown, becomes king of Sicily and is put under the guardianship of Pope Innocent III. Hohenstaufen rule over Sicily and Malta is thus maintained.   1197–98

After much political turmoil Frederick II, now also king of Germany, reorganises the kingdom of Sicily, cuts out intermediate feudal levels of authority and creates a strictly centralised state, efficiently run by officials and with sound finances (direct and indirect taxes). The new system is given a formal legal basis in the Constitutions of Melfi (1231).   1220–31

Frederick II resettles the rebellious inhabitants of the Calabrian town of Celano on Malta as a punishment. The Muslim population of the island are compelled to convert to Christianity.   1224

After Frederick II's death in 1250 the Hohenstaufen empire falls to pieces under his successors Conrad IV and Manfred. Pope Clement IV grants Charles of Anjou, brother of King Louis XI of France, the fief of Naples, Sicily and Malta.   1265

Conrad IV's 15-year-old son Conradin, the last of the Hohenstaufens, is defeated and executed in Naples on the orders of Charles of Anjou. Sicily and Malta now suffer under a despotic regime and heavy taxation which arouses popular resentment.   1268

The rising known as the Sicilian Vespers puts a bloody end to French rule. Manfred's son-in-law Peter III of Aragon, the "heir of the Hohenstaufens", is greeted with jubilation in Palermo as the new ruler of Sicily. Soon afterwards Aragonese forces under the leadership of Admiral da Loria drive the French garrison and fleet out of Malta.   1282

The kings of Aragon grant Malta as a fief to Sicilian nobles, along with the title of Count or Duke of Malta. The constant change of feudal overlords, most of them only concerned to collect taxes, leads to unrest   1350 among the local ruling class and the population as a whole. Finally Louis of Aragon, at their request, puts Malta under direct rule by the crown.

1372	After Genoese attacks which cause heavy destruction on the island Frederick III of Aragon visits Malta to show his concern for its wellbeing.
1393–97	Under King Martin of Aragon Malta is again granted as a fief to a feudal ruler with the title of Duke of Malta. Fighting between rival Sicilian noble families for predominance leads to much devastation. In a charter of 1397 Malta is finally proclaimed a crown estate which cannot be granted as a fief, and thereafter is administered by royal officials who change every year. The self-government of the island, known as the Università, is strengthened.
1419	King Alfonso V of Aragon, finding himself in financial straits, disregards the rights guaranteed to Malta by treaty and mortgages the islands for a large sum to the Viceroy of Sicily, who thereafter rules them with absolute power.
1427–28	The Maltese contrive, with great effort, to raise the money to buy the islands back, and again come under direct royal rule on the basis of their ancient rights. This is confirmed in a charter of 1428. Malta's rights of self-government (the Università) are also officially recognised. The chief officer is the capitano della verga, with four giurati as assessors. There are also a number of judges, a treasurer, a notary and an engineer responsible for the island's fortifications. The Consiglio Popolare continues to operate as a communal decision-making body.
1429	Raids by pirates cause severe devastation.
1432	King Alfonso V visits Malta. He had previously, in 1428, described the islands as a "precious jewel" (jocale notabile) in his crown, and the capital, Mdina, is now given the style of Città Notabile.
1479	After the marriage of Isabella of Castile and Ferdinand of Aragon in 1469 a Spanish national state comes into being. Malta is now merely an outpost of the expanding Spanish world empire, a potentially useful base for defence against the Turkish danger in the Mediterranean.
1516	The Spanish crown passes to Charles I, a Habsburg who from 1519 is also king of Germany as Charles V and later Holy Roman Emperor. The Ottoman Empire now controls almost the whole eastern Mediterranean, and after the fall of Constantinople in 1453 poses an increasing threat to south-western and central Europe.
1524	Commissioners appointed to look for a new home for the Order of the Knights of St John, driven out of Rhodes by the Turks in 1522, come to Malta but are not impressed, except by the excellent natural harbours. Years of drought, pirate raids and high taxation have impoverished the inhabitants and left the villages and towns in a state of decay.
1530	The Emperor Charles V grants the Knights of St John the islands of Malta and Gozo and the fortress of Tripoli as "perpetual fiefs", with plenary sovereign powers, in return for the symbolic annual presentation of a falcon (1529). Led by Grand Master Philippe Villiers de l'Isle Adam, the Knights, now known also as the Knights of Malta, establish themselves with their fleet in the fishing village of Birgu (now Vittoriosa), on the Grand Harbour.
from 1540	Repeated raids by pirates, particularly the notorious corsair Dragut, are repelled with only minor losses, but make clear the deficiencies in Malta's defences.

Pirates devastate the island of Gozo and carry off more than a thousand of the inhabitants into slavery. The dilapidated forts on the Grand Harbour, particularly Fort St Elmo, are now repaired and strengthened. | 1551

The Great Siege. From May to September an Ottoman fleet of some 200 vessels commanded by Grand Admiral Piali Pasha, General Mustafa Pasha and the corsair Dragut, now allied with them, besiege Malta and blockade the Grand Harbour. After four months of fighting, with heavy losses on both sides, the Ottoman forces withdraw. Grand Master Jean de la Valette considers abandoning Malta and moving to Sicily with the surviving knights. | 1565

In gratitude for the Knights' success in throwing back the Turks the European powers contribute large sums of money for the development of Malta into a military stronghold to check the western expansion of the Ottoman Empire. Grand Master Jean de la Valette founds the town of Valletta as the massively fortified headquarters of the Order. The architect is an Italian, Francesco Laparelli, the leading military engineer of his time. | 1566

The ships of the Order play a major part in the defeat of the Turkish fleet at Lepanto, in the Gulf of Corinth. The Turkish threat is for the time being removed. The outer fortifications of Valletta are completed in the same year, and the town now officially becomes the seat of the Order. | 1571

Foundation and construction of the Order's church, dedicated to St John the Baptist, during the reign of Grand Master Jean l'Evàque de la Cassiäre. Also built during this period, to the design of the Maltese architect Gerolamo Cassar, are the Grand Master's Palace, the houses (auberges) of the various "tongues" of the Order, the Hospital of the Order and various private houses and parish churches. | 1572–77

Inquisitors appointed by the Pope come to Malta for the first time to keep a vigilant watch on the teaching of the faith and to punish heresy, and thereafter reside in Vittoriosa until 1798. This frequently leads to conflicts with the Grand Master and the bishop of Malta. | 1574

Under Grand Master Alof de Wignacourt art (Caravaggio) and science (construction of an aqueduct from Rabat to Valletta) flourish. | 1601–22

The Order's increasing wealth (income from its extensive possessions, lavish donations from many knights) is used by Grand Master Jean de Lascaris Castellar and his Spanish successor Martin de Redin (1657–60) to build warehouses, granaries, workshops and shipyards. The Maltese find employment as members of the militia, craftsmen, labourers and servants, but only a few of them achieve a modest degree of prosperity. | 1636–57

A landing by Turkish forces is repelled without difficulty. | 1641

Establishment of a quarantine station on Manoel Island in Marsamxett Harbour to prevent infectious diseases from being brought into Malta. The crews of ships returning to the island were required to spend 40 days in quarantine. | 1643

Under the Aragonese Grand Master Nicolas Cotoner, between 1670 and 1680, the "Three Cities" (Cospicua, Senglea and Vittoriosa) are linked by a massive ring of walls some 4.5 km long, the Cottonera Lines, behind which, in the event of an enemy attack, around 40,000 people could take refuge. | 1663–80

Outbreak of plague in which almost 10,000 people die . | 1676

A 17th century view of Valletta

1693	A severe earthquake causes great damage in Sicily and Malta. The 12th century Norman cathedral in Mdina is completely destroyed.
1741–73	Under the Portuguese Grand Master Manuel Pinto de Fonseca the secularisation of the Order continues. With no military tasks to occupy them, the knights live a life of luxury and splendour rivalling that of any European court. Prostitution, gambling and drinking are rife. Pinto de Fonseca's absolutist methods of rule lead to the disappearance of the last remains of Maltese self-government. Although oppressed by heavy taxation, the population has increased from around 15,000 in 1530 to almost 100,000.
1749	Captured Muslim galley slaves conspire against the Order, intending to kill the Grand Master and the knights and hand over Malta to the Turks. The plot is discovered in time and ruthlessly repressed.
1769	With the Pope's agreement Grand Master Pinto expels the Jesuits from the island, confiscates their property and converts their college (founded 1592) into a public University, in which the medical institutes of the Hospital of the Order are incorporated.
1775	Long-continued tensions between the Order and the Maltese population come to a head with a priests' rebellion against the unpopular Grand Master Francesco Ximenes de Texada. The priests are rebelling against a tax on bread, the Maltese population's staple food, and the ban on churchmen taking part in worldly activities such as sport and hunting. The rebellion collapses because it receives little support from the population and the ringleaders are executed.

Grand Master Emmanuel de Rohan de Polduc promulgates a new legal code, the Code Rohan, regulating the political and social life of the Maltese state.	1782

The Knights of St John, under Grand Master Ferdinand von Hompesch, surrender without a fight to Napoleon's troops, partly because many French knights are sympathetic to the ideas of the French Revolution and are disloyal to the Order.
   The Knights are compelled to leave Malta, and do not return in spite of the provisions of the treaty of Amiens (1803) for the restoration of the Order's independence. After looting by French troops Malta comes under French occupation. — 1798

In the course of the war between Britain and France in the Mediterranean Malta is blockaded by the Royal Navy. The French troops evacuate Malta, which is then occupied by British forces. — 1800

Under the treaty of Paris Malta is recognised by the European powers as a British colonial possession. It is now ruled by a British governor and English becomes its official language. — 1814

Governor Sir Frederic Cavendish Ponsonby appoints a Maltese advisory council to assist him. The freedom of the press which is now permitted leads to the spread of liberal political ideas. — 1835

The "Carnival riots" against British rule are repressed by troops. — 1845

Malta's first constitution is promulgated. It gives the Maltese little say in political matters. — 1849

After the construction of a dry dock and other developments the Grand Harbour becomes the main British naval base in the Mediterranean and is of great military importance during the Crimean War (1853–56). — around 1850

Malta becomes the see of an archbishop, with his seat in Mdina and in Valletta. From 1889 the post can be filled only by a Maltese. — 1858

The opening of the Suez Canal leads to busy trading activity in Maltese harbours. Many Maltese are employed in the Grand Harbour and British naval dockyards. — 1869

Malta is given a new constitution which marks a further step towards self-government. Maltese representatives elected to the legislature and the executive gain increased influence. — 1887

King Edward VII becomes the first British monarch to visit Malta. Over the past 60 years the population has increased from 70,000 to 185,000, largely as a result of the economic boom brought about by British investment and the accompanying improvement in living standards. — 1903

As a result of price rises and higher taxes after the First World War there are bloody "bread riots" directed against the British colonial administration. — 1919

In the run-up to the election of Malta's first Parliament political parties are formed. The new constitution establishes the principle of dyarchy, under which the Maltese get their own government with restricted powers of decision. Foreign affairs, defence and the regulation of language questions are "reserved matters" for which Britain is responsible. — 1921

The Second Great Siege

"**T**he destruction in towns and villages was horrendous. Where once houses stood there were now only piles of stones and rubble. Many roads were impassable, blocked by rubble, some areas completely rubbed out" (G. Hogan, Malta: The Triumphant Years, 1978). J. Attard, too, describes the extent of the destruction during the war, "the once beautiful harbour now resembles a pond with shipwrecks lined up next to each other . . . Of the quays and storage sheds only piles of rubble remain, dusted with the powder of exploded shells; the formerly white-washed walls of the houses are riddled with bullet holes, and where the bombs had been dropped, giant holes now gape" (The Battle of Malta, 1980).

On June 10th Fascist Italy entered the Second World War as an ally of Germany. The next morning, on June 11th, Mussolini's first act of war was an attack on Malta. Italy's strategic position was excellent: it ruled the straits between Sicily and North Africa; only the British presence on the tiny group of islands in front of the Sicilian coastline was a thorn in the side of the Fascist dictator. Completely isolated in the Mediterranean by the Italian declaration of war and having suffered military neglect for many years, Malta seemed an easy target from Sicily. It was, after all, only half an hour by plane from its neighbouring island, and it only had a few anti-aircraft missiles and three old Gloucester bi-planes of the "Gladiator" type with which to fight its enemy – the Maltese has sarcastically named these three old-timers "Faith", "Hope" and "Charity". Even so, despite its repeated attempts, the mighty Italy's air force did not succeed in forcing Malta to capitulate. The island with its garrison of 30,000 soldiers valiantly defended itself until reinforcements

from the Royal Air Force arrived in the form of additional aircraft.

In December 1940 Germany answered its Italian fellow axis power's requests for military support and sent the Tenth Flight Corps of the *Luftwaffe* to Sicily. This Flight Corps soon considered Malta to be England's dangerous stronghold which had to be destroyed as soon as possible. Relentless air raids on the islands and on the British supply convoys followed. The Germans scored the greatest successes with their *Stukas* and *Ju 88* in January 1941, when they managed to inflict heavy damage on the aircraft carrier "Illustrious" which protected supply convoys to Malta. But even a second wave of attacks could not sink the carrier – the ship slipped into the safety of Valletta Harbour just in time. Six days later the German bombers were again on the attack. The "Illustrious" was only hit by one bomb which did not cause any major damage. Valletta, meanwhile, suffered the greatest devastation up to that point. A few days later, the aircraft carrier was able to leave Malta in the direction of Alexandria – the German *Luftwaffe* had lost 30 planes in their battle over this ship.

In March 1941, the German Afrika-Korps under the leadership of Field Marshall Rommel joined in the war events in North Africa. The greatest problem for the troops in Africa was the question of re-supplies. Food, weapons, munitions, vehicles, spare parts and so on – everything had to be brought in by sea. Ship convoys coming from Italy were under continuous enemy attack from heavy units, submarines and torpedo flights. The base for these convoy hunters was the British island of Malta. German bomber commands were now flying day and night to attack the island, even on Sundays, which was considered especially blasphemous on Malta, as Nicholas Monsarrat explains in his Second World War novel "The Chaplain of Malta".

When the *Luftwaffe* was needed in the Russian campaign, Malta was able to sigh a breath of relief for the time being. British fleet and flight units stationed on the island subsequently alone managed to sink almost half of the supply ships for Rommel's troops in November 1941. According to German assessment of the situation, Malta definitely needed to fall, or else the Afrika-Korps would be lost. Air raids on the island intensified again. In March and April 1942 alone, twice as many bombs were dropped on Malta as within an entire year during the air

people were given strictly rationed portions by soup kitchens in the street. For their heroic endurance, King George VI awarded the Maltese people the George Cross – it still features today in the red-white national flag, and the official name of the island is "Malta G.C." (George Cross).

On August 15th 1942, a British convoy managed to get through to Valletta despite heavy bombing by German and Italian planes. Malta was saved; without this convoy the islanders would only have lasted another two weeks. The naval blockade of the island was lifted after the British victory over the Germans at El Alamein in North Africa. In June 1943, Allied forces launched their invasion of Italy from Malta. Malta's role in the war was finished when Allied troops landed on Sicily.

During the Second Great Siege (an allusion to the First Great Siege, in 1565, by the Turks) about 35,000 houses on Malta were destroyed in approximately 3000 air raids dropping some 14,000 tons of bombs; Valletta,

A refinery in Grand Harbour being bombarded by the German Luftwaffe in 1942.

battle of London in England. The island was bombarded for 154 consecutive days. The inhabitants were hardly ever able to escape from their underground air-raid shelters. 40,000 habitations were destroyed during this time. Between spring and August of 1942, Malta was completely cut off from any supplies, and feeding the population became ever more difficult – the starving

the harbour area and all the villages on the central plateau where the military airports were based had been devastated. Around 1500 British and Maltese citizens lost their lives during the air raids. Some 1250 German and Italian planes were shot down while the Royal Air Force, who kept on supplying the island with more fighter planes, only lost 500 of their own machines.

History

1940–42	During the battle for Malta between the Allies and the Axis powers the islands suffer heavy destruction in Italian and German air raids. 85 per cent of the area of Valletta is destroyed and 1500 people are killed. For many months Malta's supplies are cut off by the Axis blockade. This comes to be called Malta's second Great Siege (see Baedeker Special). After the war Valletta is rebuilt in its original style.
1947	After being ruled by a governor between 1933 and 1947 Malta recovers its powers of internal self-government on the basis of the old constitution.
1954	Over-population and unemployment lead almost 11,000 Maltese to emigrate in a single year.
1955–58	In a referendum held by Dom Mintoff's socialist government in 1955 74 per cent of the population vote for the incorporation of Malta in the United Kingdom. When the proposal is rejected by the British government there are calls for Maltese independence. Discussions on the subject end without result.
1959	Change of government: the socialists are replaced by the conservatives.
1962	Under a new constitution the island finally gains self-government as the "state of Malta". George Borg Olivier, leader of the conservative Nationalist Party (Partit Nazzjonalista) becomes prime minister.
1964	Following a change in Britain's colonial policy Malta becomes independent on September 21st but remains a member of the Commonwealth, with Queen Elizabeth II as head of state. In 1967 the Queen pays a state visit to Malta.
1967	The closing of the Suez Canal leads to economic problems in Malta when shipping traffic in the Mediterranean rapidly falls.
1971	The socialist Malta Labour Party led by Dom Mintoff wins a narrow election victory over George Borg Olivier's conservative government. Mintoff's government introduces a series of social and economic reforms (nationalisations, planned economy), leading to conflicts with the traditional ruling elite, including the Roman Catholic church, which resists the closing of church schools.
1974	Malta is declared a parliamentary republic with a President as head of state. In accordance with Malta's policy of non-alignment the Maltese government gives notice of termination of the agreement with Britain for the stationing of troops in Malta.
1979	The transfer of NATO's Southern Europe Command to Naples in 1971 is followed by the departure of British troops under the 1974 agreement on the closing of military bases. The last troops leave on March 31st.
1981	The Labour Party wins a general election only as a result of a manipulation of constituency boundaries which enables them to win 34 seats, while the Nationalist Party, with almost 51 per cent of votes cast, has only 31. This leads to domestic political tensions.
1982	Agatha Barbara becomes President of Malta, the first woman to hold the post. A seawater desalination plant at Ghar Lapsi comes into operation. This has a daily output of some 20 million litres of drinking water, thus alleviating Malta's chronic shortage of water.

A wage and price freeze introduced by Mintoff's government in 1983, the 1984 expropriation of church property and various social abuses aggravate the domestic political crisis and lead to the resignation of Prime Minister Dom Mintoff in December 1984. His successor is Carmelo Mifsud Bonnici (b. 1933), a socialist and practising Catholic.

After a sometimes violent election campaign a new government is 1987 formed by the Nationalist Party with Edward Fenech Adami (b. 1934; president of the party since 1977) as prime minister.
  Malta's policy of neutrality is now enshrined in the constitution.

In July Malta applies for admission to the European Community. 1991

In an election in February the ruling Nationalist Party wins a convincing 1992 victory. Edward Fenech Adami remains prime minister.

In June the European Union approves Malta's admission but makes it 1993 conditional on various economic reforms (particularly in taxation law).
  Ugo Mifsud Bonnici (Nationalist Party) becomes President of Malta on April 4th.

In an election in October the Labour Party wins 50.7 per cent of the 1996 votes. The new prime minister is Alfred Sant.

The Nationalist Party wins the September elections. The new govern- 1998 ment led by Edward Fenech Adami reaffirms its intention to join the European Union.

The Knights of St John (Knights of Malta)

The Sovereign Military Order of the Hospital of St John of Jerusalem, Rhodes and Malta, the oldest religious knightly order, has existed continuously, with some interruptions in the 19th century, from its foundation in the 11th century to the present day. Its origins go back to a hospice in Jerusalem founded by merchants from Amalfi, a trading city south of Naples, for members of their community and pilgrims to the Holy Land. It is first mentioned in a document of 1048, when the Muslim Caliph granted permission for the building of a hospital to be run by a brotherhood associated with the Benedictine monks of Santa Maria Latina. When Jerusalem was taken by Godfrey of Bouillon in 1099 during the first Crusade the hospital cared for many wounded monks, who showed their gratitude by generous donations, mainly of land on their estates in Europe. These financial resources made it possible to improve the hospital's facilities for caring for the sick and the organisation of the brotherhood. Its leader Gérard de Martigues, a Provençal, organised it on the model of the monastic orders and in 1113 obtained from Pope Paschal II recognition of its status as the Order of Hospitallers of St John of Jerusalem. The Order was directly subject to the authority of the Pope, paid no dues to the Church, and elected its own superior. The hospital was staffed by both religious and lay brothers, who took vows of poverty, chastity and obedience and devoted themselves to the care of the sick and the poor. They wore a black habit with a white cross.

After Gérard de Martigues' death in 1120 a French noble, Raimond du Puy, became head of the Order. He built daughter hospices in ports such as Marseilles, Bari and Messina from which pilgrims sailed to the Holy Land and gave the Order the new task of giving military protection to pilgrims making their way to Jerusalem. In the new Rule of the Order promulgated in 1137 religious and knightly duties were combined, so that the members of the Order became **soldier-monks**, (milites Christi), who threw themselves into battle with the infidel as Knights of the Hospital of St John of Jerusalem. The knights built castles in the Holy Land and from these bases fought the Muslim occupiers, who reacted with fanatical hatred to the Christians' massacre of Muslims in Jerusalem.

During this period developed the division of the Order into **three categories**: the knights of justice, of noble blood, whose main duty was to fight but who also cared for the sick; the chaplains of obedience, who had purely religious duties; and the serving brothers, who cared for the sick and on military campaigns acted as servants to the knights. The widely scattered possessions of the Order, known as commanderies, were managed by a commendator or commander, who transmitted the net income from the land to the treasury of the Order. A group of commanderies formed a priory and the priories were grouped in grand priories. The knights were organised, according to their country of origin, in langues or "tongues", of which there were eight: Provence, Auvergne, France (Paris and north-eastern France), Italy, Aragon (including Catalonia and Navarre), Castile and Portugal, Germany (including Bohemia and Austria) and England. The eight points of the Maltese cross, which is believed to have been derived from the St Andrew's cross of the maritime republic of Amalfi, symbolise these eight "nations", while the four main arms of the cross symbolise the virtues of fortitude, justice, prudence and temperance.

During the Crusades the knights of the Order fought in the forefront of the battle and successfully defended the Holy City until 1187, when they were compelled by the superior force of Saladin, Sultan of Egypt and Syria, to withdraw to Acre, on the coast of Palestine, which became their headquarters for the next hundred years. The life of the soldier-monks, however, was not always in accord with Christian ideals. Complaints began to make themselves heard about their behaviour, particularly in the 13th century, as appears from a papal brief of 1238 banning members of the Order from any contact with Muslims, pillorying their breaches of the vows of chastity and poverty and rebuking them for their immoral and extravagant way of life.

After the fall of Acre in 1291 the Knights were compelled to leave the Holy Land. They moved to Cyprus, where the Order had lands and a castle, to continue the fight against the infidel from there. Conscious also of the Order's responsibility for the care of the sick, they built a new hospital in which many knights served in between their military duties. They thus escaped the attentions of the Christian rulers who, after the end of the Crusades, cast covetous eyes on the enormous wealth of the knightly orders – leading, for example, to the downfall of the Templars in France.

The Order on Cyprus

In Cyprus the Knights were relatively secure, but in the long run they came to dislike the place. In 1306, therefore, they contrived, with papal agreement and the help of Genoese pirates, to drive out the Byzantine governor of Rhodes. Then after three years of fighting, against fierce resistance, they captured the island and in 1310 established their headquarters there, the legitimacy of their possession of the island having been confirmed by the Pope. They now called themselves the Knights of Rhodes.

The Order on Rhodes

Thereafter Rhodes – a Christian island in the Islamic world – developed into a mighty fortress, within which were the Grand Master's Palace, the auberges (lodgings) of the knights and, of course, a hospital, which continued in use into the 19th century. At the same time there was a major change in the role of the Order, which now became a **naval force**. The "Navy of the Religion" ranged over the Mediterranean with its well-armed and manoeuvrable galleys, seeking out and seizing Muslim naval ships and trading vessels, capturing booty, freeing Christian galley slaves and taking Muslim prisoners, who were then chained to the rowers' benches of their own galleys. These expeditions, known as "caravans", served to fill the Order's coffers, give the knights battle experience and maintain the Christian claim to the holy places in Palestine.

On Rhodes the **structures of the Order** took the form which was to endure for centuries. It was headed by a Grand Master, elected for life from among the knights of justice. Under him were the heads of the eight langues (known as Pillars), the prior of the conventual church, who had the rank of a bishop, the bailiffs (chief officers) of the langues and bearers of the grand cross of the Order (awarded for outstanding feats of valour), who together deliberated and decided on the affairs of the Order. The langues were assigned particular functions: Provence supplied the Grand Commander (treasurer), Auvergne the Marshal, with overall command of the armed forces, France the Hospitaller, in charge of medical services, Italy the Admiral, Aragon the Conservator (quartermaster), Germany the Grand Bailiff (oversight of fortifications and officials), Castile the Chancellor and England the Turcopolier (originally commander of the cavalry). The conventual church, the Grand Master's Palace and the eight auberges express in architectural terms the corporative organisation of the Order on Rhodes and later in Valletta.

The Knights of St John (Knights of Malta)

The knights considered themselves an **exclusive elite community**, to which only few men could be admitted by resolution of the chapter of the Order. Young men who desired to become knights of justice had to prove noble descent over four generations on both sides; they could not marry; they must serve no other master or order; and they must have no debts. They committed themselves, after payment of an admission charge, known as "passage money" (from the payment made by pilgrims travelling to the Holy Land), to living in the service of the Order in chastity and without possessions and to respecting the poor and the sick as their "lords and masters". Novices first spent several probationary years, partly on the Order's ships and partly on its European possessions, so as to be trained in both military and administrative skills. After this, usually at the age of 20 to 23, they became knights of justice and thereafter could rise in the hierarchy of the Order. In order to become Grand Master a knight must have had three years of command at sea, three years in the convent and another thirteen years of high office (as pillar or bailiff).

The **number of knights** was always small, usually ranging between 500 and 600. Although of different nationalities they communicated freely in French and Italian. Even in difficult times (for example, during the Great Schism of 1378) they maintained their position as a supra-national community whose sole aim was to defend the Christian faith against Islam.

The **strict rules** of the Order and the resultant suppression of natural impulses served to strengthen the military zeal and ferocity of the knights. Instead of ruling Rhodes in peace they constantly launched commando-style raids on Muslim territory, provoking reprisals from the Turks, against whom they were able to hold Rhodes until the early part of the 16th century. One of their **great successes** was to defeat a Turkish fleet which laid siege to Rhodes in 1480 but was compelled by the knights, under the shrewd leadership of Grand Master Pierre d'Aubusson, to withdraw. D'Aubusson also contrived, with great diplomatic skill, to conciliate the Sultan and secure a treaty which gave the Order forty years' respite.

Then in 1521 Sultan Suleiman (Suleiman the Magnificent) ascended the throne and called on the Order to recognise his sovereignty over Rhodes. In the following year the newly elected Grand Master Philippe Villiers de l'Isle Adam, who belonged to one of the noblest families in France, turned down the Sultan's demand, and the result was war. In July 1522 a Turkish fleet carrying some 50,000 men arrived off Rhodes and laid siege to the Knights' stronghold. The 500 or 600 knights, a few hundred serving brothers and several thousand mercenaries put up a heroic resistance for over five months, but on December 26th 1522 Grand Master de l'Isle Adam was forced to **surrender**. The Turks allowed him and his knights an honourable withdrawal with their treasures, relics and weapons.

The Order on Malta

The Order was now homeless. The knights found temporary accommodation in Messina, Viterbo, Marseilles and Nice, while Grand Master de l'Isle Adam went round the European courts seeking their support in finding a new home for the Order. Possibilities considered were Sicily, Corsica and Sardinia. Since the European powers were at war with one another, however, they showed little interest in the Order's problems. Finally the Order sent commissioners to Malta, a barren rocky island between Sicily and North Africa which had good natural harbours but little else to offer. The chief town, Mdina, and the few villages had a neglected and dilapidated air, the population lived in poverty, there was only sparse vegetation and little water. The knights, spoiled by their stay in Rhodes, were not impressed by Malta.

However in 1530, the year of his coronation as Emperor, Charles V presented Malta and the port of Tripoli in North Africa to the Order as perpetual fiefs, subject only to the obligation to send one Maltese falcon

The Ottomans are blockading Malta with 200 ships, but after four months of fighting and heavy losses, they withdraw. These events enter Malta's history as "The First Great Siege".

annually to the Spanish court. This generous gift was not at all altruistic: Malta was an outpost which in the hands of the Knights would protect his possessions in Sicily.

In the summer of 1530, led by Grand Master de l'Isle Adam, the knights sailed into the Grand Harbour in their galleys. They were henceforth to be known as the Knights of Malta (though they will still be referred to in this guide as the Knights of St John in order to avoid confusion with the Maltese population). They stayed briefly in the island's capital, Mdina, and then established themselves on a promontory adjoining the wretched village of Birgu (now Vittoriosa). There, under the mistrustful eyes of the local population, they erected within a few years all the main buildings of the Order. To improve the defences of the harbour the knights renovated a number of dilapidated forts, notably Fort St Angelo at the tip of the promontory. Under Grand Master Juan de Homedes Fort St Michael was built on the next promontory and the most important defensive structure on the island, Fort St Elmo (named after the patron saint of seamen), was built at the tip of the Sciberras peninsula. Repeated attacks by small Muslim forces and by corsairs showed how necessary these defences were. Their strength was put to a severe test during the Great Siege of 1565.

On May 18th 1565 a mighty **Turkish fleet** of some 200 vessels, carrying 35,000 men, appeared off Malta and engaged the knights in almost four months of bitter fighting. The defenders were hopelessly inferior to the Turks in numbers: the knights had only some 550 of their own people, together with 2000 Spanish foot soldiers and 6000 men of the Maltese militia. The relief army from Sicily that the knights had appealed for was slow in coming. The Turks first anchored in Marsaxlokk Bay and then moved north to bombard Fort St Elmo and force an entrance into the Grand Harbour. After 31 days' fighting the fort fell into their hands: not one of the defenders survived. The Turkish fleet then anchored in Marsamxett Harbour and bombarded Fort St Angelo and Fort St Michael from Mount Sciberras. But all their attempts to enter the Grand Harbour failed. The knights, led by Grand Master Jean Parisot de la Valette, a man of intelligence and courage and a skilful tactician, heroically withstood the constant bombardment, suffering heavy losses. Then on September 6th the Turkish fleet began to withdraw, and at the same time the Sicilian relief force landed in Mellieha Bay in the north of the island; and on September 8th 1565 the bells of St Angelo signalled the victory of the Cross over the Crescent.

It was not only the valour of the knights that won the day. Discord between the 70-year-old Mustafa Pasha, commander of the army, and the young Piali Pasha and the independent action of the cunning old corsair Dragut, now over 80, contributed to the Turkish defeat, as did their tactical errors, for example their failure to take Mdina and thus cut off supplies to the knights, their over-estimate of the strength of the relief force from Sicily, supply problems and anxiety about the safety of their ships in the early autumn storms.

After suffering such heavy losses in gaining victory Grand Master de la Valette considered with the surviving knights whether they should withdraw to Italy, in view of the possibility that the Turks might return next spring. But now, unexpectedly, help came to the Order from all over Europe. Weapons and money flowed in, and praise was lavished on the Knights of Malta as a bulwark for the defence of the Christian West against the Ottoman Empire.

Encouraged by this support, de la Valette decided to stay in Malta. He had also been won over by the persuasive arguments of Francesco Laparelli, Europe's leading military engineer, who had been sent to Malta by the Pope. In December 1565 he laid before the Grand Master detailed plans for an imposing fortified town on Mount Sciberras. On March 28th 1566 Jean de la Valette laid the foundation stone of the town which now bears his name, Valletta. The fortifications were built in great haste with the help of Sicilian and Maltese masons and Turkish slaves. The fear of a further Turkish attack, however, receded when Sultan Suleiman died in September 1566 and an explosion in the arsenal in Istanbul destroyed much of the Turkish fleet. The Knights and the European powers thus gained a few years' respite to rebuild their strength, until in 1571 the decisive Christian victory in the naval battle of Lepanto, in the Gulf of Corinth, destroyed the Ottoman Empire's naval power in the Mediterranean. In the same year the Order's headquarters were transferred from Birgu to the fortified town of Valletta, which remained its military, political and cultural centre until Napoleon's invasion in 1798.

The Order's **activities and structures** remained largely unchanged during their stay on Malta. The knights continued to mount expeditions to capture Turkish vessels, free Christian galley slaves, care for the sick and give help in areas hit by earthquakes. Since they were vowed to poverty they made rich donations to the Order's new stronghold. Palaces were built, churches richly decorated, gardens laid out and festivals celebrated with great splendour. During the 17th and 18th centuries lack of military tasks – for the Ottoman Empire was no longer a threat to Europe – and the lavish way of life which the knights brought with them from the courts of Europe led to the increasing secularisation of the Order. Prostitution, gambling and drinking flourished. The ideas of the Enlightenment and later the French Revolution, the rise of the nation-states, the desire for liberty and personal self-fulfilment increasingly led men to question the purpose of the communal spiritual life of the knights.

Since the Grand Master of the day supported the cause of Louis XVI of France, all the Order's French properties were confiscated by the Revolutionary government in 1792. Increasingly, too, French knights, who made up the majority of the Order, sympathised with the aims of the social reforms proposed by Napoleon Bonaparte. Understandably, too, they were not prepared, as Christians, to fight against other Christians or, as Frenchmen, to fight against other Frenchmen. Thus the last Grand Master of the Order, Ferdinand von Hompesch, a German, had no alternative but to surrender without a fight when in June 1798 Napoleon's troops, on their way to Egypt, occupied Malta without further ado when the Grand Master refused their request for supplies of drinking water. Von Hompesch went into exile in France, where he officially abdicated and in 1805 died in Montpellier. Napoleon seized the Order's treasures and his troops plundered the island.

Some of the knights went to Russia, where Tsar Paul I styled himself Grand Master of the Order – though without papal recognition – until his death in 1801. The treaty of Amiens (1802) provided for the reestablishment of the Order on Malta, but the plan foundered because of differences of view between Britain and France. After Grand Master Giovanni Battista Tommasi, who had resided in Sicily since 1803, died in 1805 the office of Grand Master remained vacant. The headquarters of the Order was transferred to Rome in 1834. It was given a new lease of life in 1879, when Pope Leo XIII approved the appointment of a new Grand Master. Since then the Order, now a sovereign state without any territory, has devoted itself to the care of the sick and other social services all over the world.

The Order after leaving Malta

The Protestant branch of the Order, which after the Reformation continued to call itself the Order of St John to distinguish it from the Roman Catholic Order of Malta, was re-founded in Berlin in 1852. It too devotes itself to national and international charitable work.

Grand Masters of the Order on Malta

Philippe Villiers de l'Isle Adam (French)	1521–1534
Pierino del Ponte (Italian)	1534–1535
Didier de Saint Jaille (French)	1535–1536
Juan de Homedes (Spanish)	1536–1553
Claude de la Sengle (French)	1553–1557
Jean Parisot de la Valette (French)	1557–1568
Pietro del Monte (Italian)	1568–1572
Jean l'Evàque de la Cassiäre (French)	1572–1581
Hugues de Loubenx Verdale (French)	1581–1595
Martin Garzes (Spanish)	1595–1601
Alof de Wignacourt (French)	1601–1622
Luiz Mendez de Vasconcellos (Portuguese)	1622–1623
Antoine de Paule (French)	1623–1636
Jean de Lascaris Castellar (French)	1636–1637
Martin de Redin (Spanish)	1657–1660
Annet de Clermont-Gessant (French)	1660
Rafael Cotoner (Spanish)	1660–1663
Nicola Cotoner (Spanish)	1663–1680
Gregorio Caraffa (Italian)	1680–1690
Adrien de Wignacourt (French)	1690–1697
Ramon Perellos y Roccaful (Spanish)	1697–1720
Marc'Antonio Zondadari (Italian)	1720–1722
Antonio Manuel de Vilhena (Portuguese)	1722–1736
Raymond Despuig (Spanish)	1736–1741
Manuel Pinto de Fonseca (Portuguese)	1741–1773
Francesco Ximenes de Texada (Spanish)	1773–1775
Emmanuel de Rohan de Polduc (French)	1775–1797
Ferdinand von Hompesch (German)	1797–1798

Famous People

This section contains brief biographies of notable people who were born, lived or worked in Malta or died there.

Agatha Barbara
President of Malta
(b. 1924)

Agatha Barbara, the daughter of a working-class family in Zabbar, joined the Labour Party at an early age. She was elected to the Maltese Parliament in 1947 – the first election in which women had the vote – and was Minister of Education from 1955 to 1958, the first woman to become a member of the Cabinet. She became Minister of Education again in 1971 as a member of Dom Mintoff's government, which carried out a series of important social reforms. In 1982 she was elected by Parliament to the Presidency and held this post until 1986, representing Malta on many national and international occasions.

Giuseppe Cali
Painter
(1846–1930)

Giuseppe Cali painted more than 600 works for the churches and palaces of Moscow. He was a typical representative of the Romantic school, influenced by Delacroix and later by the Impressionists. In addition to altar paintings and ceiling paintings, for example in St Francis in Valetta, he painted landscapes, genre scenes and portraits of Maltese notabilities. Among works by Cali in the Museum of Fine Arts are "The Death of Dragut" (an impressive portrait of the dying famous corsair who was killed during the Great Siege of 1565) and two atmospheric nature scenes, "Sunset" and "Girl by the Stream".

Gerolamo Cassar
Architect
(1520–86)

Born in Birgu (now Vittoriosa), Gerolamo Cassar worked between 1566 and 1568 as assistant to the Italian military engineer Francesco Laparelli. On Laparelli's suggestion, and with help from the Italian langue of the Order, he went to Italy to study architecture. In Rome he became familiar with the work of Michelangelo and Vignola and was greatly attracted by Mannerism. After Laparelli left Malta in 1569 Cassar succeeded him, and was responsible for all the important public buildings erected by the Order – the Grand Master's Palace, the conventual church of St John and the auberges (lodgings) of the various langues of the Order. Characteristic features of his buildings are the fortress-like rusticated cornerstones, the plain asymmetrical façades and the richly decorated main doorways. They reflect the sober military taste of the Order. Cassar is buried in the Augustinian church in Rabat which he himself designed.

Manuel Pinto de
Fonseca
Grand Master of
the Order of St
John 1741–73

Under the Portuguese Grand Master Manuel Pinto de Fonseca the Order of St John reached the peak of its splendour and political importance. He was the longest serving of all Grand Masters. His coat of arms, surmounted by a closed royal crown, has crescents and crosses in alternate quarters, in an ironic reference to the mutability of fortune. An English visitor described him in the following terms: "For fully thirty years he has headed his unique little state. He received us with great politeness . . . Although he is over 90 years old, he has preserved all his mental faculties. He has no ministers, but directs everything himself and is fully informed about the smallest details . . . His house and his court are princely, and as Grand Master of Malta he is more absolute and endowed with greater power than many another sovereign."

Pinto maintained diplomatic relations with European royal houses, strengthened the Order's fleet and enlarged its army. Through lavish donations he made the Maltese nobility submissive to his will, requiring them to attend his court and reducing their authority. He was also a patron of art, particularly favouring the French knight and painter Antoine de Favray (1706–c. 1798), who painted his portrait and also treated religious subjects and Maltese genre scenes. He left a worthy architectural memorial in the

Auberge de Castille, Léon et Portugal (by Domenico Cachia, 1744), now the seat of the prime minister of Malta. He also promoted education, dissolving the traditional Jesuit college and founding a public University in 1769.

Lorenzo Gafà, born in Mdina in 1630, left his mark on the architecture of Maltese towns and villages over half a century. Well schooled in Roman Baroque architecture, he applied its complex formal canon, in simpler form, to Maltese churches. St Lawrence's Church in Vittoriosa has a delicate order of pilasters and volutes on the façade. St Catherine's in Zejtun is an elegant, well-balanced Baroque church crowned by an imposing dome. A severe earthquake in 1693 destroyed Mdina's Norman cathedral and Gafà was commissioned to rebuild it. After studies in Rome, particularly of the work of Borromini, he built between 1697 and 1702 the mature work of his old age, Mdina Cathedral, with an imposing twin-towered façade and a mighty dome. Victoria Cathedral on Gozo, with a two-storey show front on a stepped base, was also his work.

Lorenzo Gafà
Architect
(1630–1704)

Born Carmelo Psaila, born in modest circumstances in Zebbug, he began at the age of 18 to write poems in Italian, the language then spoken by the educated classes in Malta. After studying in a seminary in Mdina he was ordained as a priest at the age of 23. He continued writing poetry, now increasingly in Maltese, his mother tongue, as well as in Italian. His first novel, "El-Habib" ("The Friend"), written in Maltese, was published in 1912 and was well received by the critics. Dun Karm thereupon resolved to write only in Maltese in future.

His poems and prose works quickly became popular for their rhythmic musicality and visionary expressive power, which was in tune with the Maltese people's aspirations for cultural independence and national identity. His main themes were love, religion and his homeland, showing the influence of existentialism in his treatment of them. He is now regarded as as Malta's national poet; one of his poems became the Maltese national anthem.

Dun Karm
Writer
(1871–1961)

Dominic (Dom) Mintoff, the son of a cook, grew up in the working-class town of Cospicua. Although brought up as a Catholic, he was attracted to socialist ideas at an early age, and at the age of 20 became secretary-general of the Malta Labour Party. While studying architecture in Oxford he came under the influence of the Fabian Society, which sought to combine the ideas of Marx and Lassalle.

Dominic Mintoff
Prime Minister
(b. 1916)

After working briefly as an engineer Mintoff returned to Malta at the end of the Second World War and served in the government several times between 1947 and 1958. He also became president of the Malta Labour Party. In 1955 his plan for the incorporation of Malta in the United Kingdom came to nothing, as did his aspirations for Maltese independence. In 1958 he left the government and went into opposition. In 1971, however, he made a comeback when his party won a general election by a narrow majority and he became prime minister. During his 13 years in government the political and social face of Malta was transformed by a series of economic and social reforms. The conflict with the Catholic church over private schools and the suppression of opposition parties were not to his credit. His foreign policy made Malta increasingly isolated, seesawing unpredictably between requests for western industrial aid, rapprochement with the countries of the Eastern bloc and support for the Arab world. Coming under increasing political pressure, he resigned as prime minister in 1984.

Ramon Perellos y Roccaful
Grand Master of the Order of St John 1697–1720

A member of the langue of Aragon, Catalonia and Navarre, Perellos y Roccaful was elected Grand Master by the chapter of the Order in 1697. A contemporary of Louis XIV, he was very much of the Baroque period. A man of great wealth, he marked his election as Grand Master by presenting 28 valuable Flemish tapestries on allegorical themes, some of them based on designs by Rubens and Poussin, to the conventual church. He also decorated the Grand Master's Palace with ten magnificent Gobelins tapestries depicting exotic landscapes woven in the royal manufactory in Paris on cartoons by Le Brun; refashioned the interior of the parish church of his langue, Our Lady of Victories, at his own expense; presented a picture of the Virgin of Mount Carmel to the pilgrimage church of St Gregory in Zejtun; and added a ward to the Hospital of the Order for the treatment of eye diseases and gynaecology. Part of his fortune also went to the strengthening of the Order's fleet and Malta's defences. Fort Ricasoli was given stronger walls and St Gregory's Bastion additional casemates, and a battery of cannon was established on the east coast of Comino.

Mattia Preti
Painter
(1613–99)

A native of Taverna in Calabria, Preti travelled round Europe in his study of painting. He was impressed by the work of Caravaggio in Naples and Rome, trained under Guercino in Bologna and was influenced by Correggio in Parma, Veronese and Tintoretto in Venice and Rubens in Antwerp. In 1642 Pope Urban VIII appointed him cavaliere dell'Ordine Gerusalemmitano di Malta. From 1656 he worked in Naples, and from 1661 he was employed on decorating the interior of the conventual church of the Order in Valletta, spending five years on oil paintings of scenes from the life of the Baptist on the stone vaulting of St John's Church. Thereafter he painted portraits of knights as well as altarpieces and figures of saints in churches all over Malta, where he lived until his death in 1699.

Roger I
Count of Sicily
(1031–1101)

After the conquest of Sicily between 1060 and 1090 Roger de Hauteville, a Norman knight, landed in Malta in 1091 and took the island without any great resistance. He restored Christianity to Malta after 220 years of Arab rule and exacted tribute from the Muslim governor and his subjects. On his initiative Mdina again became the see of a bishop and the dilapidated cathedral was rebuilt in Norman style. He established a council of nobles to govern Malta and granted the island his heraldic colours of white and red, which are still Malta's national colours. In many Maltese legends Roger is depicted as a wise and just ruler.

Antonio Sciortino
Sculptor
(1879–1947)

Under the influence of Rodin Sciortino created a series of works showing the influence of Naturalism and to some extent also that of Expressionism. His bronze group "Les Gavroches", in the Upper Barracca Gardens, is a masterly study of simple people. In Great Siege Square is his monument commemorating the siege, with allegorical figures of valour, freedom and faith, the virtues of the Knights of St John and by implication the Maltese people. Other notable works are a statue of Lord Strickland in the Upper Barracca Gardens and the statue of Christ the King at the gates of Valletta. In the Museum of Fine Arts is a plaster model for a dynamic group of horses with the title "Arab Horses" (1937).

Gerald Strickland, of Anglo-Maltese parentage, studied law at the University of Malta and at Cambridge. After being elected in 1887 to the

Council of Government, Malta's newly established organ of self-government, he rose quickly to become principal secretary to the British governor and worked for the interests of Malta while at the same time observing British ideas. After coming into conflict with the pro-Italian Catholic clergy in the field of language and education he was compelled in 1903 to leave Malta for a time and pursued a career in the British colonial service as governor of various Caribbean islands and in Australia.

In the new constitution of 1921 Strickland saw an opportunity for achieving democracy and self-government in Malta, and founded a Maltese-language newspaper and a new party, the Constitutionalist Party. Committing himself to work for an alliance between Britain and Malta, he became from 1927 to 1932 head of the Maltese government under British sovereignty. Again, however, he was frustrated by the rigid attitude of the Roman Catholic church, which did not approve of his policies and put him under interdict. In a strictly Catholic Malta this brought his career to an abrupt end. He has a place in Maltese history as a staunch liberal and protagonist of democracy in Malta.

Gerald Strickland, Conte della Catena and Lord Sizergh (1861–1940)

Jean de la Valette, a Provençal, joined the Order of St John at the age of 20. He fought for the Order on Rhodes until its withdrawal in 1522. His outstanding military capacity brought him the office of Admiral of the Order's fleet, a post traditionally held by a member of the Italian langue. Taken prisoner by the Turks, he spent a year as a galley slave before being ransomed. Elected Grand Master in 1557, at the age of 63, he was confronted with the growing threat of Turkish attack, and in 1565 a powerful Turkish fleet laid siege to Malta – a siege which the defenders successfully withstood for four months. His resolution, level-headedness and military experience, combined with the valour of the defenders, saved the day. Exhausted by the siege, the

Jean Parisot de la Valette Grand Master of the Order of St John (1494–1566)

Grand Master and the surviving knights considered abandoning Malta, but generous help from Europe encouraged them to stay. Within a few months new plans for the fortification of Malta were put forward by the Italian military engineer Francesco Laparelli, and on March 28th 1566 Jean de la Valette laid the foundation of the new stronghold which was to bear his name, Valletta. It was to have "sufficient ramparts, walls and towers to resist any attack and enable the Turkish enemy to be thrown back or at least to be withstood". Two years later de la Valette died and was buried in the conventual church in Birgu (now St Lawrence's Church in Vittoriosa), where his sword and helmet are still preserved. His remains were transferred in 1577 to the newly built church of St John in Valletta. His tomb bears a Latin inscription composed by his English secretary Sir Oliver Starkey commemorating "the scourge of Africa and Asia and the shield of Europe".

Alof de Wignacourt was a member of the French langue, which along with the langues of Provence and Auvergne formed a high proportion of the total strength of the Order: not surprisingly, therefore, the Grand Masters were frequently French. Wignacourt was Grand Master at a time when the Order was well supplied with money, thanks to lavish donations and the income from its possessions in Europe, and when the declining Ottoman Empire was no longer a serious threat. He was granted the rank of Prince of the Holy Roman Empire, with the style of Serene Highness, by the Emperor Ferdinand II – the first Grand Master to enjoy this honour. A great patron of art, in 1607 he summoned Caravaggio from Naples to Malta, where he painted a portrait of the

Alof de Wignacourt Grand Master of the Order of St John 1601–22

Grand Master and two works for St John's Church, "The Beheading of St John the Baptist" and "St Jerome". Other religious foundations by Wignacourt were the chapel of St Paul in St Paul's Bay and the monastic community in the Grotto of St Paul, Rabat. Between 1610 and 1615 he built an aqueduct to bring water to Valletta from the hills round Rabat, 15 km away, with a cistern for storing the water under the outlying district of Floriana. He also built a string of fortified signal towers round the coasts to give warning of any attack, for example the massive St Thomas's Tower (1614) at Marsaskala, St Lucian's Tower (1610) at Marsaxlokk and St Marija's Tower (1618) on Comino. After 21 years of a reign of great magnificence he died in 1622 and, like his predecessors, was buried in the crypt of St John's Church. Reminders of past splendour are his magnificent set of parade armour in the Order's collection of weapons, his portraits in the Grand Master's Palace and the Museum of Fine Art and his coach in Zabbar Museum.

Culture

History of Maltese Art

Strictly speaking, there can be no such thing as a history of Maltese art, since apart from the megalithic culture of the Neolithic period there are few distinctively Maltese achievements in architecture, sculpture or painting. It is more meaningful, therefore to talk of art in Malta rather than Maltese art, and thus to consider the artistic contribution of the various peoples who have left their mark on the Maltese islands over many thousands of years – Bronze Age settlers, Carthaginians and Romans, Byzantines and Arabs, Normans and Aragonese, the Knights of St John and Malta's British rulers of the colonial period. In some cases, however, particularly in architecture, these various foreigners inspired Maltese artists and craftsmen to produce original creations of their own.

Megalithic Culture (Neolithic Period)

After the original settlement of Malta by incomers from Sicily around 5200 BC there came into being on these isolated islands between about 4000 and 2500 BC a Neolithic culture unique in Europe which created a whole range of megalithic cult sites, from simple one-celled and later trefoil-shaped stone buildings to large double-kidney-shaped and multi-apsed stone temples and a large underground cult site on several levels, the Hypogeum of Hal Saflieni.

In establishing the chronology and method of construction of the first stone temples the sites excavated at Skorba and Xemxija, which can be assigned by modern dating methods to the period between 4500 and 3800 BC, were of prime importance. At Skorba the excavations yielded grey and red incrusted pottery of some quality and the oldest traces of human settlement on the island, the remains of a village of dwellings built of brick on stone foundations and roofed with a thatch of brushwood; previously the only dwellings had been caves. One structure interpreted by David Trump, who carried out important excavations on Malta, as a shrine consisted of an oval main chamber and a horseshoe-shaped subsidiary chamber surrounded by a double ring of stone foundation walls with a mass of rubble between them. No doubt this was a forerunner of the later stone temples.

Origins

The excavations at Xemxija brought to light kidney-shaped burial chambers, either single or double, some of them with a number of apse-like recesses and with slightly domed roofs – evidently also an early form of the megalithic temple. The underground rock tombs of subsequent centuries also seem to have begun as simple one-celled structures and developed later into multi-apsed stone structures.

Some 40 Neolithic temples are known in Malta, of which four are particularly worth a visit: on Gozo Ggantija (3600–3000 BC) and on Malta Mnajdra (3500–2800 BC), Hagar Qim (c. 3000 BC) and Tarxien, where the oldest temples date from 3800 BC and the later ones, which are well preserved, from 3000–2500 BC. Visitors with a particular interest in the subject should also see Ta Hagrat, Mgarr (3600–3500 BC) and Skorba (3600–3000 BC).

Temples

The underground cult and burial site of Hal Saflieni (3800–2500 BC), which in structure and layout shows numerous parallels with the temples built above ground, also gives very interesting insights into the megalithic culture of Malta.

Hagar Qim is one of the most impressive Neolithic temples on Malta. Built long before the pyramids in Egypt, they are one of the oldest large-stone structures in the world.

Layout and structure of temples

These temple complexes all consist of a number of individual temples which are adjacent to one another or linked together. Although built over a period of several hundred years, they are all constructed on the same structural principles. The walls are rounded rather than straight and the chambers are circular or oval and the façades slightly curved.

The older temples have a trefoil (clover-leaf) layout, with three rounded "apses" opening off a central passage. The central apse is the holy of holies. From around 3500 BC temples were built with two oval or kidney-shaped chambers linked by a passage, with the holy of holies, a smaller recess than the apses, opening off the end of the second oval chamber. In many temples there are oracular chambers opening off the first oval chamber. It is thought that the priestesses who delivered the oracles entered these chambers from outside and spoke through a hole in the wall to the worshippers who were waiting for the divinity's advice in the main chamber of the temple. Presumably only the outer chambers were open to worshippers, the rear chambers being reserved for the priesthood.

The sanctuary was surrounded by a massive

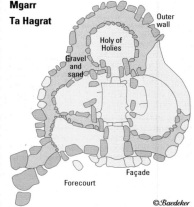

Mgarr
Ta Hagrat

Outer wall

Holy of Holies

Gravel and sand

Façade

Forecourt

©Baedeker

horseshoe-shaped outer wall. The lower part of this was constructed of orthostats (stone slabs standing on end) set alternately with their broad and narrow edges facing outward, and on top of these were laid one or more layers of horizontal slabs. It is difficult to imagine how Neolithic men, working with only the simplest of tools, could transport these huge blocks of roughly shaped stone, weighing up to 5 tons, to the site (probably on rounded stones acting as rollers), and set rhem on top of one another up to a height of 10 or 12 metres. The outer walls were constructed of slabs of coralline limestone, but for the inner walls the more easily worked globigerina limestone was used. The space between the outer and the inner walls was filled with gravel and sand.

From the votive offering of a miniature temple only 5 cm high found at Mgarr (now in the National Archaeological Museum in Valletta) it is known that the temples had roofs of intertwined branches smeared with clay and supported on wooden beams. The floor was either the native rock or constructed of stone slabs or torba, a compound of crushed limestone and mud.

The entrance to the temple was through a trilithon consisting of two orthostats topped by a horizontal slab on the curved (slightly concave) façade. Along the façade were bench altars for offerings. A threshold slab in front of the trilithon frequently still shows holes for tethering sacrificial animals. In front of the temple was a forecourt enclosed by a wall and floored with torba or stone slabs.

The interior of the temple was unlighted and cave-like. The inner walls were sometimes covered with reddish ochre paint, so that the temple had a mysterious aura of death and rebirth (the symbolic colour for which was red). Frequently the lateral apses were separated from the central chamber by orthostats, the passage between them being formed by trilithons or "window stones" (slabs pierced by rectangular openings). Sockets in the stone indicate that these openings could be closed by a wooden door or a leather curtain. Some of the orthostats and window stones had pecked decoration.

Interior of temple

In many of the temples there still remain a number of altars of various types on which animals were sacrificed as offerings to the Magna Mater, the Great Mother who was the principal goddess of the islands. The oldest and smallest type is the "threshold altar", which is only a little above ground level and often forms a threshold between one room and another. Bench altars are somewhat higher and are not, like the threshold altars, set into the ground. Trilithon and pillared altars developed at a later stage. Another late development is the double trilithon altar, with one trilithon on top of the other, which may be up to 2 m high. Many altars have cavities for offerings in the form of libations.

Altars

The altars of the later period in particular are finely decorated. One pillared altar from Hagar Qim has on each of its four sides a flowerless plant growing out of an earthenware vessel like a tree of life, probably associated with a fertility cult. Tendril, spiral and wave patterns occur frequently. Particularly fascinating are the spirals forming pairs of eyes on the high threshold barriers at Tarxien. Representations of animals are relatively rare. At Ggantija there is a relief carving of a snake on a 1 m high stele, again probably connected with a fertility rite. At Tarxien there are a remarkable representation of a sow with thirteen piglets and a relief of a sacrificial procession with a ram, a pig and male goats. A small altar from Bugibba has reliefs of fish. (The most important altars are now in the Archaeological Museum in Valletta and have been replaced by copies on the sites).

The earliest pottery (dishes and jars with rounded bottoms) comes from the oldest human settlement in Malta, Ghar Dalam, a cave which was occupied from 5200 BC onwards by incomers from Sicily. This impressed ware is very similar to the pottery found at Stentinello on Sicily. At

Pottery

Trilithon altars in Ggantija (Gozo)

Skorba was found locally made pottery dating from 4000 BC, spherical or carinated vessels with elaborate handles in grey and red incrusted ware. Beautifully shaped thin-walled sacred vessels with rich decoration, all fashioned by hand, were found at Tarxien, including a shallow dish with stylised representations of humpbacked cattle, a vessel with pecked decoration, a beautiful carinated jug with spiral ornament and other dishes with incised figures of animals.

Figural representations

The earliest human figure in Malta's Neolithic culture, probably dating from around 4000 BC – a fragment of a stele with crudely carved human features – was found in the rock tombs at Zebbug. Depicted more naturalistically are the numerous figures of the Magna Mater or of priestesses, frequently in standardised form. They are usually in a seated position, with interchangeable heads and disproportionately large lower parts. Two particularly striking examples are the "Venus of Malta", a realistically modelled female figure 50 cm high from Hagar Qim, and the lower half of

Tarxien: the lower half of a colossal statue of the Magna Mater

a colossal figure from Tarxien, almost 3 m high, with massive legs and a wide pleated skirt. There are also numerous female statuettes, including some showing symptoms of disease or represented in a sleeping position, mostly votive offerings found in the Hypogeum of Hal Saflieni – indicating the importance of that site, a place of healing by incubation (sleep), the home of an oracle and a place of burial, as the centre of a a fertility or mystery cult served by a female priesthood.

Around 2500 BC the megalithic culture of Malta came to an abrupt end. Possibly as the result of a devastating epidemic or a catastrophic drought the whole population (estimated at about 10,000) was wiped out, with not a single survivor. Thereafter the islands remained uninhabited for some 500 years.

End of the megalithic culture

Bronze Age

About 2000 BC Bronze Age settlers began to move into Malta from Sicily and southern Italy, bringing with them metal tools, weapons, gold and silver jewellery and painted pottery. They built fortified settlements (e.g. Borg in-Nadur) at strategic points and erected dolmens (tomb chambers formed from erect stone slabs roofed by a capstone).

The pottery of this period differs from that found at Tarxien, with its incrusted white lines: red ware with incised zigzag patterns from Borg in-Nadur, grey and black ware with incised meander ornament from Bahrija. Everyday objects found include bronze axes, spindle-whorls and anchor-shaped loom weights.

Of particular interest are the "disc idols" depicting a goddess, presumably a Magna Mater, in a squatting position, with an over-emphasised disc-shaped abdomen and a narrow, peg-like stump of a neck; except in one case the head of these idols is always missing. The bodies are richly decorated with incised geometric patterns.

Features which still puzzle archaeologists are the "cart ruts" (parallel grooves in the rock) which are found in many places on Malta (e.g. Clapham Junction) and Gozo, which are dated to the Bronze Age. Interpretations range from the tracks left by primitive carts to water channels for irrigating the fields or directing rainwater into cisterns. See Sights from A to Z, Clapham Junction.

Phoenician and Carthaginian Period

This period too, extending from around 1000 to 218 BC, is known to us mainly from finds in tombs. Depending on burial rite, they come either from shaft graves and passage graves or from funeral urns. In addition to domestic pottery and fragments of jewellery and ornaments made from precious metals, shells or stone the material includes tablets with inscriptions referring to sacrificial rites, offerings and temple precincts, as well as imported Attic vases of the 4th century BC. Items of particular importance are a ring of the 6th/5th century BC with a representation of a Phoenician galley, the figure of an unidentified mother goddess, an incense dish of around 600 BC and a famous cippus (prayer stele) with an inscription on the base, an invocation of Melkart, the patron god of Tyre and Carthage, in both Phoenician and Greek (all in the National Museum, Valletta). The scientific exploration and decoding of the Phoenician alphabets was only made possible through the discovery of this prayer stone in the middle of the 17th c.

Practically nothing remains of the temples of the Carthaginians. At Tas-Silg, near Marsaxlokk, however, partly excavated foundation walls have revealed the existence of a large temple dedicated to Astarte, goddess of fertility and war, dating from the late 6th century BC

Roman Period

At the outset of the second Punic War, in 218 BC, Roman forces occupied the Maltese islands. The temple of Astarte was dedicated to Juno, the principal Roman goddess, two large pillared courtyards were built round the central temple on its podium and the whole precinct was surrounded by a wall. Gozo also had a temple of Juno, on the site of the present-day citadel of Victoria, as fragments of columns found there (now in the Cathedral Museum) have shown.

The Roman Imperial period is represented by remains of Roman baths with mosaic floors at Ghajn Tuffieha and parts of a town villa in Rabat. The peristyle of the villa has a fine mosaic depicting doves, surrounded by meander and wave patterns There are also two charming actors' masks, worn in performances of comedies, as well as various fragments of statues and busts which testify to the provincial Roman taste in art.

The first evidence of Christianity in Malta dates from the 4th century. Remains of a baptistery of this period have been excavated on the site of the Tas-Silg temple of Juno – a typical example of the way in which Christian churches overlaid and displaced earlier pagan temples. Other impressive Christian remains are the catacombs of St Paul and St Agatha in Rabat, where between the 4th and 6th centuries large numbers of tombs, ranging from simple recesses (loculi) to large canopied and saddle-roofed tombs for the wealthier citizens, were hewn from the soft local limestone.

Arab Period

Almost all traces of the Islamic (North African and Arab) culture which prevailed in Malta from 870 to 1091 have disappeared. Mdina and Rabat have only their foundations and their names to recall that this was once the centre of Arab culture on the island. Only a girl's gravestone in Kufic script dating from the 12th century (Gozo Museum of Archaeology) remains to show that Malta's Islamic/Arab heritage continued into the period of Norman and Christian rule.

Maltese houses have inherited one feature from the Arabs, the wooden oriel window which was originally a latticed balcony from which Arab women could look out on the world.

Middle Ages

Architecture

Malta's most impressive medieval building, the 12th century Norman cathedral of Mdina, was totally destroyed, with the exception of the apse, in an earthquake in 1693. Only one feature, made outside Malta, has been preserved in good condition, a Romanesque wooden doorway of the 12th/13th century (now the doorway of the sacristy) made of Irish bog oak, with animal motifs in the Northern European tradition. The secular architecture of the High Middle Ages is represented in Malta's old capital of Mdina by a number of noble palaces in Norman-Sicilian style. The oldest is the Palazzo Falzon of 1095, known as the Norman House, which originally consisted only of the ground floor, with slit windows and narrow doorways. In the 15th century an additional storey was added and the façade was refashioned with wider doorways and double windows. Typically Norman is the strip of zigzag moulding on the façade. The ground floor of the Palazzo Santa Sophia, with beautiful Romanesque arches, dates from 1233; the upper floor is later.

Painting

Notable among religious paintings of the period are three 12th century frescoes in Sicilian/Byzantine style in the Catacombs of St Agatha – the Virgin, the Apostle Paul and a Virgin and Child. In the Chapel of the Blessed Sacrament in Mdina Cathedral (now Baroque) is another Virgin and Child, probably dating from the 12th/13th century, and in the Chapel of the Crucifix is a figure of St Paul, part of a 13th century Siculo-Catalan polyptych. In the Cathedral Museum in Mdina are some late medieval features from the destroyed Norman cathedral and a silver cross of the late 11th century which was carried into battle in the first Crusade and was brought back to Malta by the Knights in the 16th century.

Frescoes in the Catacombs of St Agatha in Rabat, attributed to Salvatore d'Antonio (1480)

Renaissance

When the Knights of St John came to Malta in 1530 there was a great burst of building activity, mainly for military purposes. To protect the Order's fleet in Birgu (now Vittoriosa) they renovated and strengthened the old fort at the tip of the peninsula, renaming it Fort St Angelo. Then, after a heavy Turkish attack in 1552, the adjoining promontory was fortified by the building of Fort St Michael; Fort St Elmo at the tip of the Sciberras peninsula, which had been largely destroyed, was enlarged and strengthened to protect the entrance to the Grand Harbour; and the fortifications of the old capital of Mdina were renovated and strengthened by the addition of two new bastions.

Military engineering

After the Great Siege of 1565 activity in the construction of fortifications was still further intensified in order to improve the defences of the Order's headquarters against a possible further attack. Antonio Laparelli, one of the leading military engineers of the day, was enlisted as planner and architect of a new fortified town, the future Valletta. In preparing his plans he was guided by the theoretical treatises of Leon Battista Alberti, Pietro Cataneo and others on the architecture of the Renaissance, his own practical knowledge, learned from his teachers Serbelloni and Michelangelo, and the specialised military experience and requirements of the Knights. Within a very short time, between 1566 and 1571, there came into being one of the most formidable strongholds in Europe, with an elaborate system of outworks, bastions, cavaliers (inner defence works) and curtains.

Although Valletta was built with purely military considerations in mind, it contains a whole range of interesting secular and religious buildings. The erection of these buildings, designed to meet the austere taste of the Knights, was entrusted to the Maltese architect Gerolamo Cassar,

Secular architecture

successor to Laparelli, who left Malta in 1569. Although the prevailing taste in Europe was for the ornate architecture of Mannerism, Cassar developed a conservative style of urban architecture composed of plain structural elements with the minimum of decoration. The Grand Master's Palace in the centre of Valletta – not at first sight a building designed for effect – was begun by Cassar in 1571 but completed, after much alteration, only in the 18th century. The long two-storey façade is not very satisfactorily articulated, even after the insertion of the Baroque doorways and in spite of the bold rustication at the corners. The auberges of the Order are better examples of the "Cassar style". The Auberge d'Italie (1574), another long building, was based on Italian models. It originally had only one main storey built round a square inner courtyard. An additional storey was added later, but the façade is nevertheless finely articulated, with a vigorously rusticated doorway (the cartouche is 18th century), windows framed by mouldings and finely chiselled cornerstones. The Auberge de Provence (now the National Museum), built between 1571 and 1576, is Cassar's maturest work. It has a charming symmetrical façade with a regular sequence of pilasters, in the centre of which is an antique temple motif with projecting columns bearing an entablature, flanked by windows with triangular and segmented pediments. The typical rusticated cornerstones are a borrowing from military architecture.

Religious architecture

Of Valletta's religious buildings only St John's Co-Cathedral, originally the conventual church, still bears the mark of Cassar's work: all his other churches have been so altered as to be unrecognisable. St John's was built between 1573 and 1577. Its broad twin-towered façade, austere and undecorated, is reminiscent of a fortress; articulated by flat pilasters, it is enlivened only by the columned portal and the triangular pediment on the upper storey. In contrast the aisleless interior, flanked by six chapels on each side for the various langues of the Order, is over-richly decorated (17th/18th c.). Stout arcades fronted by pilasters, on which are set the arches supporting the roof, break up the lateral walls and lead straight to the choir. The dome originally planned was not built, since it would have obstructed the free field of fire over the town.

Many village churches of the late medieval period, mostly simple aisleless structures, were altered in appearance in the late 16th century by the adoption of the classical forms and decoration of the Renaissance. In St Augustine's in Rabat (begun 1571) Cassar created the prototype of a Renaissance interior based on orders of pilasters, massive arcades with semi-columns and classical decoration, and coffered barrel vaulting. His son Vittorio designed St Philip's in Zebbug (begun 1591), a parish church on a Latin cross plan with a twin-towered façade and an imposing dome over the crossing borne on an octagonal drum.

The last great phase of Renaissance religious architecture in Malta was represented by the work of the Maltese architect Tommaso Dingli (1591–1661). Of his churches only the parish church of St Marija in Attard (1613) has survived the centuries unscathed. The façade, modelled on an ancient Roman temple, is rectangular, flanked by corner pilasters and surmounted by a triangular pediment, with six niches for statues. The interior is articulated by pilasters and bands of capitals along the walls. The nave and choir have coffered barrel-vaulted roofs, the transepts have low domes, and there is a shallow dome born on a high drum over the crossing.

Painting

A number of foreign painters were working in Malta in the late 16th century. Matteo Perez d'Aleccio (1547–c. 1629), according to eyewitness reports, painted twelve large frescoes in the Grand Master's Palace depicting scenes from the Great Siege. Intended to glorify the Knights' victory over the Turks, they are also important historical documents. An Italian painter, Palladini, decorated the great hall on the ground floor of the Verdala Palace (c. 1590) with scenes from the life of his patron,

St John's Cathedral in Valletta: the knights richly decorated their conventual church

Cardinal and Grand Master Hugues de Loubenx-Verdale. Caravaggio, who visited Malta in 1608 on the invitation of Grand Master Alof de Wignacourt, left two major works, "The Beheading of St John the Baptist" (St John's Cathedral, Valletta) and "St Jerome" (Cathedral Museum, Valletta). These two works, which can be classed as early Baroque, combine dramatic sense and realism with powerful use of colour and striking chiaroscuro effects. Caravaggio's work, however, had no influence on Maltese painting.

Renaissance sculpture is represented only by two important works in St John's Cathedral, the choir-stalls with their gilt carving and the lectern; both are Neapolitan work of the late 16th century.

Sculpture

Baroque

During the 17th century, under various Grand Masters, the fortifications of Malta were still further strengthened. Between 1632 and 1635 a beginning was made, to the design of the Italian military engineer Pietro Paolo Floriani, with the strengthening of Valletta's defences on the landward side through the construction of an outer ring of fortifications. Floriani's successor Vincenzo Masculano da Firenzuola (b. 1578) began in 1638 to construct the Margherita Lines round Cospicua. The still more monumental Cottonera Lines, 4.6 km long, protecting the "Three Cities" (Vittoriosa, Cospicua and Senglea) were built from 1670 onwards to the design of the Italian military engineer Antonio Maurizio Valperga. An inscription on the Zabbar Gate commemorates the munificence of Grand Master Nicola Cotoner in financing these fortifications. At the same time a string of watch-towers was constructed round the coasts to give early warning of enemy attack.

Military architecture

History of Maltese Art

Floriana

Between 1722 and 1736, under Grand Master Vilhena, the outlying district of Floriana was planned and developed. Laid out on a rectangular grid, it has numerous Baroque buildings, many of them with charming arcades, dominated by the parish church of St Publius (1733).

Baroque architects

The outstanding Baroque architects working in Malta were Lorenzo Gafà, Giovanni Barbara, Giuseppe Bonnici and Domenico Cachia, who built mainly religious buildings, as well as some secular ones. The numerous parish churches built during this period, which cannot be discussed in detail here, were also influenced by the work of these architects. Maltese architects developed their repertoire of forms and decoration mainly from the Baroque of Rome and southern Italy and Sicily, making much use of colossal orders, concave and convex façades with applied metal ornament and scrollwork, and centralised layouts with domes. In this way a sumptuous and showy style established itself in the territories of the Order.

Lorenzo Gafà

After studying the work of Borromini and other architects in Rome Lorenzo Gafà became the first architect to bring the Roman Baroque style to Malta. The parish church of St Nicholas in Siggiewi (1675) has a thoroughly Baroque feeling of space with its soaring dome, high barrel vaulting and small intersecting vaults, so arranged that ample windows can light the nave. The parish church of St Lawrence in Vittoriosa was built between 1681 and 1697. The parish church of St Catherine in Zejtun was begun by Gafà in 1692 but was not completed until 1778. After Mdina's Norman cathedral was destroyed in an earthquake in 1693 Gafà was commissioned in 1697 to rebuild it in Baroque style. The beautifully balanced two-storey façade, with twin towers, is designed to achieve an effect of breadth. Clustered pilasters with Corinthian capitals frame the central doorway and give emphasis to the

The Cathedral in Mdina is regarded as the finest achievement of the Baroque architect Lorenzo Gafà

ends of the façade. A simple triangular pediment forms a link between the pyramidal tops of the towers. The orders of pilasters are repeated in the interior of the church, and the barrel vaulting, the dome over the crossing, the semi-dome over the apse and the domeed side chapels offer constant variations on the dome structures of Baroque architecture. In Gozo Cathedral, also designed by Gafà, the vertical movement of the pilasters of the façade on its high stepped base is counterbalanced by the broad undecorated expanses of wall. Above a projecting cornice is an attic storey with a triangular pediment and inward-curving lateral pediments. The interior is very characteristic of Gafà's style, with a Latin cross plan, a barrel-vaulted nave, transepts, a semicircular apse and domed side chapels.

Giovanni Barbara was strongly influenced by Bernini's Roman Baroque style. The parish church of St Saviour in Lija (1694) is still relatively austere, with a tall façade, flanking towers and a modest dome. St James's Church in Valletta has a richly ornamented two-storeyed façade, with particular emphasis on the decoration of the door and window surrounds and a fine cartouche above the central window. Barbara's secular buildings show a highly decorative style. The Vilhena Palace in Mdina (1730), now the Natural History Museum, is entered through a grand courtyard, the portal of which has twin pilasters decorated with garlands and a magnificent cartouche with Vilhena's coat of arms. The façade is articulated by massive fluted pilasters, with richly decorated windows and luxuriant decoration on the doorway. The Seminary in Mdina (1733), now the Cathedral Museum, is another example of Barbara's florid Baroque style.

Giovanni Barbara

Giuseppe Bonnici designed St Barbara's Church (1739), the church of the langue of Provence, on an oval plan with an apsed choir and a harmonious street front. Among his secular buildings are the Custom House (1747), a massive building relieved by a light Venetian-style façade, and the Castellania, the courthouse of the Order (1748). The façade of the Castellania, with a strong emphasis on the central section, has a concave portal with figures of Justice and Truth by the Sicilian sculptor Maestro Gian.

Giuseppe Bonnici

Malta's last Baroque architect was Domenico Cachia. His parish church of St Helen in Birkirkara (1735–45) has a richly articulated, finely composed, façade on a broad stepped base, compartmented horizontally, vertically and diagonally by clustered pilasters. The side doorways and the open fronts of the towers mark the corner points of this vertical and diagonal symmetry, while the side doorways also combine with the central window on the second storey to form a triangular composition. The projecting central section of the façade has varying types of pediment. The interior is of typical rectangular type, articulated by a series of twin pilasters matching the double arches of the vaulting. Among Cachia's secular buildings is the Selmun Palace, which was probably inspired by the Verdala Palace. This charming summer palace with four corner towers (now part of a hotel) was a development of the old fortified castle. The battered lower floor supports the main floor, with richly decorated windows and a balcony running round the whole building. Cachia's master work is the Auberge de Léon et Castille in Valletta (1744), now the residence of the prime minister. Of harmonious effect in spite of its rich decoration, it consists of two storeys articulated by pilasters, with lavishly decorated windows; the lower storey is rusticated. The centre of the façade is given emphasis by a projecting portal approached by a broad flight of steps, flanked by twin columns and crowned by trophies, banners and weapons framing a bust of Grand Master Pinto, who ordered the construction of the building. A decorated pediment above the roof cornice reinforces the vertical movement of the central part of the façade, contrasting with the horizontal effect of the

Domenico Cachia

façade as a whole. The model for this building seems to have been the Prefettura in Lecce (Apulia), though the Auberge is very much an independent work of Cachia's.

Painting

Painting in Malta was much influenced by Italy: Italian artists came to Malta and Maltese artists followed Italian models. The outstanding figure in the 17th century was Mattia Preti (1613–99), a native of Calabria who settled in Malta in 1661 and painted many altarpieces for parish churches on the island. He also spent five years painting the vaulting of the conventual church of St John in Valletta with scenes from the life of John the Baptist. In the oratory of the church are three important works, the "Crowning with Thorns", "Ecce Homo" and "Crucifixion". Preti used Caravaggio's chiaroscuro technique combined with pronounced naturalism to produce large dramatic and sometimes also serene compositions with powerful light effects and strong, rich colours. There are other fine paintings by Preti in Mdina Cathedral and the Museum of Fine Arts in Valletta.

The Maltese painter Stefano Erardi (1650–1733) was a portraitist and also painted altarpieces, including an "Adoration of the Kings" for the chapel of the German langue in St John's Cathedral and "Paul casting a snake into the fire" for St Paul's Church in Rabat.

In the Museum of Fine Arts in Valletta there are a number of works by Baroque painters who were invited to Malta by knights of St John, among them Tintoretto, Guido Reni and Mathias Stomer. In the Grand Master's Palace are two works by the Spanish artist Ribera. A Sienese painter, Nicolo Nasini, decorated a corridor in the Palace with ceiling paintings (1724 onwards). The French painter Antoine de Favray (1706–92/93) spent many years in Malta, painting portraits and genre scenes. There are many of his works, mainly portraits of knights and Grand Masters, in the Museum of Fine Arts, and the Cathedral Museum in Mdina also has a number of his paintings, including a charming reredos of the Annunciation. Also in the Cathedral Museum are two views of the Grand Harbour by the German artist Anton Schranz (1769–1839).

Tapestries

Of particular interest are the fine Flemish and French tapestries of around 1700 to be seen in the Cathedral Museum and the Grand Master's Palace in Valletta. The 28 Flemish tapestries in the Cathedral Museum – vigorous Baroque compositions with brilliant colours – depict religious and allegorical scenes; some of them are after cartoons by Rubens and Poussin. The ten Gobelins tapestries in the Grand Master's Palace are based on cartoons by Le Brun after paintings by Frans Post and Albert Eckhout. The two Dutch painters had accompanied Johan Maurits van Nassau, gov-

Tapestry in the Grand Master's Palace

ernor of the Dutch Company of the West Indies, on his travels in Brazil and Africa and painted exotic subtropical landscapes in vivid colours.

Sculpture

In the field of sculpture there are few outstanding achievements to record, although many church interiors, notably St John's Co-Cathedral in Valletta, owe much of their sumptuous and sometimes overcharged effect to sculptural ornament. The most notable examples of this are the several hundred grave slabs of knights of the Order in St John's Cathedral, in colourful marble intarsia work. The tombs of the Grand Masters also have lavish sculptural decoration. The monument of Nicola Cotoner (d. 1680) has a massive base with an inscription on which are two Atlas figures bearing a portrait bust of the Grand Master flanked by trophies. The tomb of Grand Master Vilhena (c. 1729) is of black marble contrasting with heavy bronzework.

Many churches in Malta have fine marble altars. St John's Cathedral has a magnificent high altar of rare marbles and lapis lazuli with a gilt bronze relief of the Last Supper. The marble group of the Baptism of Christ in the apse of St John's (c. 1667) was a joint work by Melchiore Gafà and Giuseppe Mazzuoli. The choir screens in the Chapel of the Blessed Sacrament are magnificent silversmith's work. In the courtyard of the Grand Master's Palace is a fine astronomical clock of 1745 in which the hours are struck by bronze figures of Moors.

Modern Period (19th and 20th Centuries)

After the Knights of St John left Malta building activity during the period of British colonial rule was concentrated on the shipyards and port installations required for the development of Malta as a naval base.

Architecture

The Anglican Cathedral (St Paul's) of Valletta, in neo-classical style, was built from 1839 onwards. The Main Guard, a Doric portico built on to the former Chancery of the Order, is in the same style. The Royal Opera House in Valletta, a sumptuous neo-classical building, was opened in 1855, burned down in 1873, rebuilt and finally demolished after suffering heavy damage in the Second World War.

The largest building on Malta, though not necessarily the finest, is the huge domed church of St Mary's in Mosta. It was begun in 1833 to the design of Giorgio Grognet de Vassé, dedicated in 1868 to the Assumption of the Virgin and finally completed in 1871 with the help of voluntary work by the villagers. It shows a remarkable combination of a Roman rotunda (e.g. the Pantheon), a Greek portico and a Christian twin-towered façade. The interior is of overwhelming effect, both for its size and for its sumptuous decoration in white, blue and gold.

Painting

In painting the outstanding figure was Giuseppe Cali (1846–1930, who painted numerous landscapes, genre scenes and portraits under the influence of the French Romantic movement and later the Impressionists. In the early years of the 20th century he painted a large cycle of scenes from the life of Christ.

In conservative and Catholic Malta international and even contemporary painting is poorly represented.

Sculpture

The leading Maltese sculptor was Antonio Sciortino (1879–1947), who under the influence of Rodin created mainly lively and expressive groups of figures such as the "Arab Horses" in the Museum of Fine Arts and "Les Gavroches" in the Upper Barracca Gardens, Valletta.

Among works by Vincent Apap is the Triton Fountain outside Valletta's Main Gate. There are also various statues and monuments in streets and squares, mostly in naturalistic or social realist style. The contemporary international school of sculpture is almost completely absent.

Language and Literature

Language

Successive periods of foreign rule have left linguistic as well as cultural traces in Malta. The national language of the islands, Malti or Maltese, is descended from the Phoenician/Carthaginian language which was brought to Malta around 1000 BC from Lebanon and from 750 BC onwards from Carthage in North Africa. The Maltese language is mainly derived from Carthaginian, a late form of the Phoenician language. Malti is thus basically a Semitic language which has borrowed many words from the languages of its various rulers. Until the development of a literary and written language in the 18th and 19th centuries, however, it was merely an orally transmitted dialect spoken by the rural population: the Maltese ruling classes, of whatever nationality. continued to speak their own language.

In antiquity the Latin language extended its influence from 218 BC onwards, and after Malta was Christianised continued in use as the language of the church, although from AD 395 the islands belonged to the Byzantine Empire. The Arab conquest of Malta in 870 consolidated for 220 years the basic Arabic elements in the Maltese language, so that it is still possible for Maltese people to understand without great difficulty the North African dialects of Arabic.

Even after the Christian reconquest of Malta by the Norman prince Roger I in 1091 the Arabic linguistic tradition lived on, but was increasingly penetrated by Sicilian and Italian vocabulary and dialects, so that the basically Semitic features of the Maltese language were overlaid by Romance elements. Although during the medieval period the proceedings of Malta's organ of self-government, the Università, were conducted in Maltese the minutes were in Latin or in a hybrid Sicilian/Italian language.

When the Knights of St John came to Malta in 1530 they made Italian the official language and imposed it on the native Maltese. For centuries, therefore, Italian was the only language of administration, education and the ruling classes. After Malta was occupied by Britain in 1800 the inhabitants of this poor country had to speak English if they wanted employment in the colonial administration or the armed services.

Towards the end of the 19th century there was a long conflict between supporters of the Italian and the English languages. Against this background the Maltese language became a unifying force in the struggle for self-government and independence and gained increased importance as the language of educated people.

Official languages

The language problem was finally settled only in 1934, when Italian, hitherto the language of administration and the courts, was replaced by English and Malti as official languages and at the same time a standardised orthography was introduced for the Malti written language. It is now the only Semitic language to use the Latin alphabet (see Practical Information, Language).

Since Malta achieved independence in 1964 Malti has been the first official language and English the second. In view of Malta's increasing international involvement in economic and political affairs English, as a world language which is learnt from an early age in school, is still playing the principal role. Newspapers, books and television all contribute to the wider use of English, and literature written in Malti can reach a wider public only in an English translation.

Beginnings of an independent Maltese literature

Maltese written literature appeared only in the 17th century. Previously there had been only an oral tradition which preserved the memory of folk tales, legends and folk songs from generation to generation while Malta was under foreign rule. One of the first poems in the Malti language was written by C. F. Bonamico (1639–80) for Nicola Cotoner, Grand Master of the Order of St John. During the 18th century there were a number of songs both religious and secular, writings in prose and dictionaries of the Malti language. In 1750 Agius de Soldanis (1712–70), writing in Italian, published his Maltese grammar, "Nuova scuola di grammatica per apprendere la lingua maltese". He also produced a complete dictionary in four manuscript volumes, "Damma Tal-kilem Kartaginiz". He was followed by the Maltese lexicographer Mikiel Anton Vasalli (1764–1829), who published a Latin grammar of Maltese in 1791 and his "Lexicon Melitense Latino-Italiano" in 1796.

The first Maltese author to make a name for himself was G. A. Vassallo (1817–67), a historian and professor of Italian at the University of Malta. In addition to poems he wrote a short epic, "Il-gifen tork" ("The Turkish Galley"). The most important writer after Vassallo was G. Muscat-Azzopardi (1853–1927), a great lover of the Italian language. He also wrote poems and prose in Maltese and helped to establish it as a literary language. Anton Manuel Caruana also made a contribution to this in the field of the novel with his "Inez Farrug" (1889), the story of a Maltese family, which turns on conflicts between Maltese and foreigners.

19th and 20th centuries

Among later writers are Carmelo Psaila (1871–1961), Anastasio Cuschieri and N. Cremona, whose main contribution was to the development of Italian and Maltese lyric poetry. Psaila decided in 1912 to write only in the Maltese language and, under his pen name of Dun Karm, became Malta's national poet. In his poems, particularly in the sonnets, he combines national, existential and religious themes with a rhythmic and musical style, giving the Maltese language an expressive force which it had never previously achieved.

A concern with social reform is given expression in the prose work of Guzé Aquilina, whose "Under Three Reigns" (1938), a criticism of social conditions in Malta, attracted much attention. Other writers such as J. J. Camilleri, Lino Spiteri (b. 1938) and Frans Sammut have produced similar works of social criticism. In lyric poetry, however, Anton Buttigieg (b. 1912) writes in a Romantic style, while Mario Azzopardi is individualistic and eccentric. Azzopardi is also a successful dramatist of the modern school.

Francis Ebejer (b. 1924) writes novels in both English and Maltese, and as a result is perhaps the Maltese writer who is best known outside Malta. His novels "The Evil of King Cockroach" and "The Wreath for the Innocents", published in the 1950s, take as their theme the contradictions of Maltese society between tradition and progress. His "Requiem for a Malta Fascist" (1983) tackles a problematic chapter of Maltese history in the 1920s and 30s, when Italophile groups in Maltese society were drawn to Mussolini's Fascist ideology. Ebejer has also made a name for himself as a dramatist with plays written in the everyday language of the people.

The most recent author to gain a wide reputation is Oliver Friggieri (b. 1947), who works in Malta as a university teacher, translator and literary critic. His important novel "L'istramb" ("The Turn of the Wheel") depicts a young intellectual from a Catholic background whose desperate quest for identity is frustrated by the rigid social traditions of Malta.

Malta has a rich heritage of orally transmitted rhymes, proverbs and riddles, only a few of which can be given here:
"A sleeper catches no fish"
"Spit into the sky and it will fall back on to your face"
"If you are born round you won't die square"
"Not everyone who beats his breast is a saint"
"Don't foul the stream: you may be glad to drink at it one day" – an indication of the importance of water on the barren rocky island of Malta.

Proverbs

Music, Festivals and Customs

Folk music

Maltese folk music reflects in its songs and tunes the many foreign influences to which the island has been subjected over the centuries. Alongside simple traditional native instruments such as tambourines, kettledrums, snare drums and bagpipes, the Spanish guitar has long been a popular instrument. Spanish influence is also detectable in folksongs and ballads. Maltese folk tunes are influenced also by the Sicilian tarantella and Arab and Oriental melodies. Folk singers are still popular in the villages, often competing with one another but always striving to preserve the traditional repertoire of folksong against the encroachment of modern light music.

Choral singing

Choral singing has been practised in Malta for many centuries: long an important element in church music, it is now increasingly popular on the concert platform. Famed for their excellent singing are the Malta Choral Society and the choir of St Julian's Church. Two of the few well-known Maltese composers are Nicoló Isouard (1775–1818) and Robert Samut (1870–1934) who composed Malta's national anthem.

Folk dancing

Two folk dances are still popular – Il-parata, a sword dance, and Il-Maltija, a peasant dance incorporating figures from 18th century courtly dances.

Costumes

The wearing of traditional dress is now wholly out of fashion. Only rarely can women be seen wearing the black faldetta or ghonnella, a voluminous silk hood, originally worn by fine ladies in the 18th century, which developed out of the traditional practice of peasant women, who protected themselves against sun, wind and rain by throwing their long petticoat over their head.

Il-Festa

Throughout the year towns and villages all over Malta celebrate festivals in honour of their local patron saint. These annually recurring events, known simply as Il-Festa, are the expression of a strong feeling of religious and social community. In the absence of any other local authorities the parish community headed by the village priest has from time immemorial been the basic form of social organisation. In recent decades political attitudes and elements of social criticism have increasingly found expression in these local festivals, calling in question the traditional social structure. Hence alongside the usual festivals in honour of the local saint there are now festivals honouring other saints, such as the festival of St Joseph, which are in effect demonstrations by the socially disadvantaged members of the community. Thus there are now also "festival contests" giving expression to differing political views and drawing attention to social differences within the local community (see Baedeker Special).

On high church and public holidays there are other ceremonies. At Christmas marvellous "mangers" (Nativity scenes) are set up in churches and Nativity figures are displayed in houses. During Holy Week there are numerous processions in which local people in costumes of Christ's day re-enact his Passion. Heavy wooden crosses and figures of the Man of Sorrows are carried through the streets, and in the churches there are models of the Holy Sepulchre and the Last Supper. On Maundy Thursday it is an old traditional custom that families should visit seven churches and pray in them, or alternatively offer seven prayers in the same church – a reference to the Seven Sorrows of the Virgin and the traditional visit to the seven principal churches of Rome. On Easter Day there are processions in many villages carrying a figure of the Risen Christ.

Carnival

Malta's Carnival tradition reaches back to the 16th century. Every town and village has its Carnival club which organises parades and other

Good Friday procession in Valletta

celebrations. The chief centre of Carnival activity, however, is Valletta. During the Carnival season thousands of people flock to the capital to see the gaily decorated floats, the grotesque masks, the bands in traditional costume and the dancing competitions. The celebrations are a mixture of the contemporary and the historical. In the traditional Il-parata dance (see p. 66) the fighting between the Turks and the Knights of St John in 1565 is re-enacted, to the great delight of children, while disco music and dance bands provide for the entertainment of dancers at the masked ball.

In June the old folk festival of Mnarja (the "festival of lights") is celebrated in Mdina and Rabat. It begins on June 28th with illuminations in the Buskett Gardens, where the celebrations, with music, singing and dancing, continue throughout the night.

Mnarja

On June 29th, the festival of SS. Peter and Paul, a solemn mass is celebrated in Mdina Cathedral and there is a procession principally devoted to the Apostle Paul, Malta's patron saint.

The Mnarja festival, probably derived from pagan fertility rites at the summer solstice (June 21st) and Christian celebrations of St John's day (June 24th), was already being held before the coming of the Knights and since then has still further increased in popularity. Since the Apostle Paul is believed to have brought Christianity to Malta, the festival was linked at an early stage with the celebration of St Paul's feast-day on June 29th.

The donkey and horse races held on that day in Rabat are celebrations of a more secular character – unless they are to be seen as demonstrations of strength and endurance in the spirit of ancient fertility rites.

Until the beginning of the 20th century the Mnarja festival was a traditional marriage market to which the local peasants brought their marriageable daughters and negotiated marriage contracts.

Quotations

Report by the
Commission of
the Knights of St
John in the year
1524

"The island of Malta is nothing but a rock of soft sandstone called tuff"
– in reality it was limestone – "approximately six or seven miles long
and three or four miles wide; the rocky ground is covered by hardly
three or four foot of topsoil, and even this is stony and extremely
unsuited for growing cereals. It does, however, yield plentiful figs,
melons and other fruits. The island's trade consists largely of honey,
cotton and cumin seeds which the inhabitants exchange for cereals.
Apart from a few springs in the island's interior, there is no running
water, nor any wells, so that the inhabitants have to make do with cisterns in which they collect the rain water. Timber is so sparse that it is
sold by the pound and, in order to cook their food, the inhabitants have
to burn dried cow dung or thistles ..."

"The capital, Città Notabile, lies on a hill in the interior of the island.
Most of its houses stand empty ..."

"Malta has a population of about twelve thousand inhabitants who,
for the most part, live in poverty and misery due to the infertility of the
ground and frequent attacks by the Corsairs who, without any com-
punction, abduct all those Maltese unlucky enough to fall into their
hands. In a word, a stay on Malta seems extremely unpleasant, nay even
unbearable, especially in the summer ..."

"On the western coast, there are neither smaller nor larger bays, and
the beach is extremely rocky. On the eastern coast, however, there are
numerous promontories, smaller as well as larger bays and two particularly beautiful large harbours, sufficiently large to accommodate
fleets of any size."

Théophile Gautier

And I shall settle,
For age makes me somewhat weary,
On Malta's white terraces
Between blue sky and blue sea.

From a translation of Eckart Peterich. Munich 1963. The French poet
Théophile Gautier (1811–1872) wrote poems and novels as well as travel
reports.

Dun Karm

My Malta (Lil Malta)

For no other land do I love as
much as you, my Malta,
For you alone are my mother, you alone
gave me a name,
Your bones support me, your blood
runs in me.
No other land is as large as you, even though your
outline may be small,
You are large in mind and in body,
Many a mighty country
Envies you for your beauty.

Dun Karm (1871–1961) who has been writing only in Maltese since 1912
is the national poet of Malta. His sensitive and expressive poetry bears
witness to a great artistic achievement.

Dashiell Hammett

What do you know, sir, about the Order of the Hospital of St. John of
Jerusalem, later called the Knights of Rhodes and other things?'

Spade waved his cigar. 'Not much – only what I remember from history in school – Crusaders or something.'

'Very good. Now you don't remember that Suleiman the Magnificent chased them out of Rhodes in 1523?'

'No.'

'Well, sir, he did, and they settled in Crete. And they stayed there for seven years, until 1530 when they persuaded the Emperor Charles V to give to them' – Gutman held up threee puffy fingers and counted them – 'Malta, Gozo, and Tripoli.'

'Yes?'

'Yes, sir, but with these conditions: they were to pay the emperor each year the tribute of one' – he held up a finger – 'falcon in acknowledgement that Malta was still under Spain, and if they ever left the island it was to revert to Spain. Understand?

'Well, now, the Emperor Charles has given them Malta, and all the rent he asks is one insignificant bird per annum, just as a matter of form. What could be more natural than for these immeasurably wealthy knights to look around for some way of expressing their gratitude? Well, sir, that's exactly what they did, and they hit on the happy thought of sending Charles for the first year's tribute, not an insignificant live bird, but a glorious golden falcon encrusted from head to foot with the finest jewels in their coffers. And remember, sir – they had fine ones, the finest out of Asia.'

"The Maltese Falcon", 1930.

Lookouts on the eastern hills of the island reported 472 sailing boats, including 15 frigates, led by Napoleon's flagship, L'Orient. The secret service, not given to exaggerations, had spoken of 40,000 men on board this fearsome fleet. **Nicholas Monsarrat**

A French dinghy advanced towards the coast and the Grand Harbour. It delivered a letter from Napoleon to the Grand Master in which in unmistakable terms he requested permission to dock in the harbour and to fill up with water. Hompesch did a heroic deed: he called a meeting.

One eye on the hostile fleet, the other on the unmanned fortifications, a surprisingly mild-mannered response was drafted which, as the Grand Master emphasised, could not have been worded any other way. "With the deepest regret" the French request was rejected in consideration of Malta's neutrality. Daringly, Napoleon was even reminded of the Peace Treaty of Utrecht in which Malta had been declared a neutral harbour and that the statutes of the Order did not permit the admission into the harbour of more than four war vessels at a time.

Napoleon reacted with a temper tantrum of the type that dictators tend to resort to if their wishes are not immediately granted. "They will not give me water", he shouted like a child dying of thirst in the desert, "barbarians! This is war!"

"It was war, but nobody could say that Napoleon had not been prepared for it. The same night, his troops landed on four different, well planned points: in Marsa Scirocco in the south, in St Julian on the eastern coast, in Mellieha Bay in the north and in Ramla Bay on the north-eastern coast of Gozo.

Without clear command and mostly without soldiers, there was practically no resistance. By eight o'clock in the morning, the entire coastline was occupied, and by midday the old capital of Mdina had fallen into enemy hands. Gozo resisted a little longer, until Fort Chambray was bombarded by a service ship. In front of the Cottonera walls there was a brief manly defence, and some of the Knights, suspected of treason, were mown down by these resolute men.

But after twenty-four hours the Grand Master sent a delegation to the flagship L'Orient and asked for a ceasefire. Around lunchtime – it was 11th June – Napoleon's Aide, General Junot, rode up to Valletta to dictate to Hompesch his terms for the handover.

"The Chaplain of Malta", 1975.

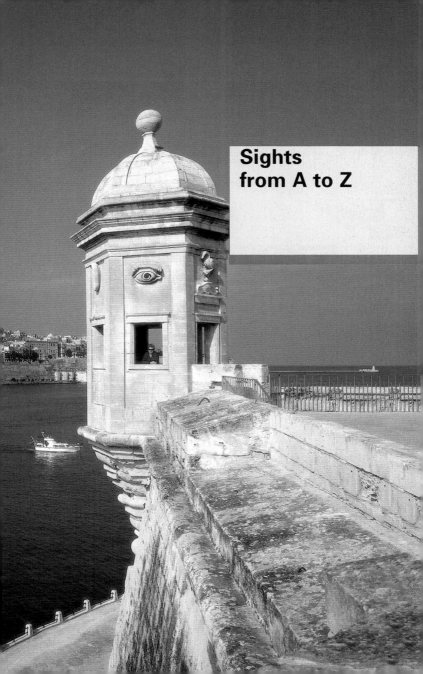

Sights
from A to Z

Suggested Routes

The routes suggested in this section take in the principal sights and scenic beauties on Malta. Since the description of Gozo in the Sights from A to Z part of this guide takes the form of a tour of the island Gozo is not included in this section.

The rubrics in the margin indicate the course of each route. The names of places which are the subject of a separate entry in the A to Z part of the guide are given in bold type. Descriptions of other places can be found by reference to the Index.

Tours on Malta

———	Route 1
———	Route 2
———	Route 3

Route 1: Northern Malta

This 80 km tour covers the northern parts of the main island of Malta, which are relatively sparsely populated and have fewer sights of historical or artistic interest. Time should be allowed for a walk at Ghajn Tuffieha and on the Marfa Ridge and/or for bathing on one of the beautiful beaches on the route.

◀ *One of the famous views, from the Vedette in Senglea across the Grand Harbour towards Valletta*

Evening at the Marfa Ridge: there are magnificent views to be enjoyed from the north-western tip of Malta to the south as far as Anchor Bay

The route runs south-west from ★★**Valletta**, passing through the outer districts of **Floriana**, Pietà and **Msida**, now joined up with **Birkirkara**, to the west. The main attraction of Birkirkara, apart from its old houses with their attractive oriel windows, is the parish church of St Helen. Then on through **Balzan** and **Lija**, which still have a village-like air.

Valletta

The next town is **Mosta** with ★Rotunda, its huge domed church, claimed by the people of Mosta to be the third largest in Europe. From Mosta the route continues west for a short distance and then takes a road on the right signposted to Zebbieh. In a few hundred metres it leaves the main road and follows a narrow country road on the left which runs through the Victoria Lines, a range of hills along which the British authorities built a series of forts in the late 19th century. On this road there is only the occasional peasant's house to be seen; it is not much frequented by tourists, and the signposting is poor, but it does offer beautiful views of this lonely landscape. In 5 km the route takes a road on the right and continues via Bingemma to **Zebbieh**, where visitors with a particular interest in the megalithic culture of Malta can visit the Skorba temples.

Mosta

Zebbieh

Beyond Zebbieh the road climbs gently, running through a very fertile region. Soon a signpost points to the Roman Baths lying below the road on the left, with scanty remains of walls and some notable mosaics. A few hundred metres farther on a road goes off on the left and ends abruptly above the coast. From here can be seen Golden Bay, with a sandy beach and a group of hotels, forming the hamlet of **Ghajn Tuffieha**. To the south is ★Ghajn Tuffieha Bay, another beautiful beach, still with little in the way of tourist facilities. Along Ghajn Tuffieha Bay and on the higher ground above the bay there are pleasant walks.

Ghajn Tuffieha

Now back to the main road, which turns east through the very fertile Pwales Valley. At Xemxija it reaches the coast. From here the road runs north, skirting the sea, passes the hotel complex of Mistra Village on the

71

left and climbs rapidly. The landscape is much eroded by karstic action and vegetation is sparse. Once up on the plateau a road goes off on the right to Selmun Palace, now part of a hotel.

Mellieha

The main road now comes to **Mellieha**, the largest place in the north of the island. A prominent landmark is its neo-Baroque parish church, built over the cave church of St Marija. Soon after Mellieha the road begins to lose height. At Ghadira (hotels) a road goes off on the left to Anchor Bay. Near here is Popeye Village, once the set for a film of that name and now a popular attraction for children.

The route continues north along Mellieha Bay, with a long sandy beach, and comes to the ★**Marfa Ridge**, at the northern tip of Malta, where side roads go off to east and west. Taking first the road to the right, we run east along the ridge road, with beautiful views of Mellieha Bay and over the sea to Comino and Gozo. Side roads go off on the left to small coves with bathing beaches. The road ends at a statue of the Madonna. Returning along the same road, we rejoin the main road and turn right off this into a road running north to Cirkewwa and Marfa Point, from which ferries and, in summer, smaller boats run a shuttle service to Comino. There is good bathing in Paradise Bay, to the south of Cirkewwa.

Xemxija
St Paul's Bay

Then back to Xemxija on the same road. The route then continues east on the dual-carriageway coast road, above **St Paul's Bay** and Bugibba. The villages around St Paul's Bay rank after Sliema and St Julian's as Malta's second largest tourist centre. There are no sights of particular interest. The road then runs round Salina Bay, where salt is still won from seawater and continues close to the sea, though in this rather inhospitable part of the island there are no sandy beaches. If you feel like going for a walk along the beach promenade or having a snack in one of

St Julian's

the terrace restaurants along the coast, turn off towards] ★**St Julian's**.

Valletta

The coast road continues through **Sliema** and returns to Valetta via **Gzira** and **Msida**.

Route 2: Central Malta

This 50 km tour of central Malta takes in the island's tourist highlights. Those who are pressed for time should concentrate on Malta's old capital of Mdina with its fine Baroque buildings, the striking scenery of the cliff-fringed south coast and the impressive Neolithic sites. Those who have more time at their disposal are recommended to get a first general impression by following this route, reserving some of the sights for a later visit. Mdina and Rabat merit a separate excursion.

Valletta

Beyond the outer district of **Floriana** is **Hamrun**, in which there are many small craft workshops. The road then runs by way of **Santa Venera**, passing the Wignacourt Aqueduct, to **Attard**, where the principal sight is the ★San Anton Palace with its gardens. The main road to Mdina and Rabat passes a side road leading to the Ta'Qali Crafts Village, where visitors can see (and buy) an extensive range of Maltese arts and crafts and can watch craftsmen at work.

Attard

Mdina/Rabat

Soon after this the road comes to Malta's old capital of ★★**Mdina**. It is best to park your car near the green belt between Mdina and Rabat. The City Gate leads into the car-free old town of Mdina, where time seems to have stood still. The modern town of ★**Rabat**, to the south, also has many features of interest, including St Paul's and St Agatha's Catacombs and the Roman Villa.

Buskett Gardens

From Rabat the road runs south and follows the signposts to the ★**Buskett Gardens**. To the left of the road can be seen the Verdala Palace (cannot be visited). Below the palace are the Buskett Gardens; there is

Coastal landscape near Mnajdra, in the south of Malta

parking at the south end of the little patch of woodland, which offers pleasant walking. From the car park it is a few minutes' walk to ★**Clapham Junction**, with the "cart ruts" which still puzzle archaeologists.

From here it is a short walk (or drive by car) south to the ★★**Dingli Cliffs**. This is also good walking country.

Dingli Cliffs

Here a road to the left runs through attractive scenery in the direction of Siggiewi. A side road on the right leads to the Inquisitor's Palace, the Inquisitor's summer residence, which can be seen only from the outside. A little way away to the east, the Laferla Cross, on one of the highest hills on the island can be seen.

Skirting **Siggiewi** on the bypass to the south, we come to a road on the right which runs south by way of the hamlet of Tal Providenza to the Neolithic temples of ★★**Hagar Qim** and ★★Mnajdra. These two Neolithic temples excavations are only 300 m apart from each other and form a temple park in a particularly beautiful setting near the cliff-fringed south coast. From Hagar Qim a good road runs south-east to the Wied iz-Zurrieq, a narrow fjord on Malta's south coast. From here a fishing boat can be taken to the ★**Blue Grotto**, which owes its name to the play of colours on the surface of the water.

Siggiewi

The return route is by way of **Zurrieq**, which, like Mqabba immediately to the north, is noted for its quarries of globigerina limestone. The quarrying can be seen even from the road that links Mqabba and Tas Salvatur. The road then past Malta's international airport to the little town of **Luqa**.

Zurrieq

Luqa

The road then continues by way of **Qormi**, with enticing smells from its many bakeries, and **Hamrun** to Valletta.

Qormi
Valletta

Route 3: Eastern Malta

Although scenically this is the least attractive part of Malta, this 50 km tour contains numerous major sights, so that it holds particular attractions for visitors interested in the history and culture of Malta. It also passes through the romantic fishing village of Marsaxlokk and the less well known but equally charming village of Marsaskala, beautifully situated at the head of a broad inlet with numbers of colourful boats lying at anchor.

Valletta
Paola

From Valletta the route runs south to **Paola**, on the southern edge of the built-up area which surrounds the capital. It has one of the most important sights in the Maltese islands, the ★★Hypogeum of Hal Saflieni, an underground labyrinth of caves which was a place of worship and of burial (currently not open to visitors). A few hundred metres away in the district of ★★**Tarxien** is another Neolithic temple complex. The Tarxien temples are the best preserved megalithic remains on Malta, particularly notable for the rich relief decoration on the altars found here.

Tarxien

Cospicua

From Paola the road runs north to **Cospicua**, one of the "Three Cities", the others being nearby **Senglea** and ★**Vittoriosa**. The most interesting of the three is Vittoriosa, which has many buildings dating from the time when this was the headquarters of the Knights of St John. Immediately south-east of Cospicua, reached through the Zabbar Gate, is **Zabbar**, which has an impressive Baroque parish church, with an adjoining museum containing votive offerings and other items dating from the time of the Knights. Very different is the fishing village of **Marsaskala**, 3 km east, which is gradually being taken over by the tourist trade. The road now runs along the south side of Marsaskala Bay, passing Fort St Thomas, at the east end of the peninsula between Marsaskala Bay and St Thomas Bay, which has a short sandy bay and a longer one of shingle and rock. The coast road ends in St Thomas Bay, and the route now follows a road which runs inland to the little town of **Zejtun**, which has two interesting churches. Visitors prepared to give them a miss can take a road which goes off on the left before reaching the town and runs south by way of Misrah Strejnu to ★**Marsaxlokk**. There is hardly a book or a tourist brochure about Malta that does not include a view of this fishing village with its brightly coloured fishing boats (luzzi). The market held daily on the harbour and the village's restaurants may tempt visitors to linger here. From Marsaxlokk an excursion can be made to the Delimara peninsula, which has a series of beautiful bathing beaches on the east side facing the open sea. The stretch of coast between here and St Thomas Bay is almost unspoiled by tourism and offers pleasant walks with magnificent views of the coast.

Zabbar

Marsaskala

Zejtun

Marsaxlokk

From Marsaxlokk the route continues south along the coast to **Borg in-Nadur**, with scanty remains of a Neolithic temple and a Bronze Age settlement. Only 1 km north is **Ghar Dalam**, geologically the most interesting site in Malta. The route now returns to the coast and continues to **Birzebbuga**, on Pretty Bay, which is no longer so pretty as it was. From here a road runs south between port and industrial installations to **Ghar Hassan**. Even those who do not want to visit the Ghar Hassan Cave (not yet equipped with tourist facilities) will find the trip worth while for the sake of the impressive views of Malta's steep south-east coast.

Birzebbuga

From Ghar Hassan we return to the main road coming from Kalafrana and follow it to the west. Soon after the former British military airfield of Hal Far a road goes off on the right to Gudja, on the northern outskirts of which, on the road to **Luqa**, is a chapel dedicated to the Virgin, one of the oldest churches on the island. Return to Valetta by way of Paola or Qormi.

Gudja
Qormi
Valletta

Sights from A to Z

Attard
G 6

Attard (pop. 9000) lies in the centre of Malta, roughly half way between Valletta and Mdina/Rabat. It is one of the "Three Villages" (the others being Lija and Balzan: see entries) – a parallel group to the "Three Cities" of Vittoriosa, Senglea and Cospicua. The three villages have now almost joined up to form a single agglomeration. They are among the oldest settlements in Malta, and all three have a similar village-like air. The surrounding country is highly fertile: at one time the principal crop here was oranges.

Attard, founded in 1575, took its name from a local family. A 17th century Grand Master of the Order of St John built a summer residence here, and it was soon followed by other splendid country houses. It is still a village of handsome villas set in gardens.

The parish church of St Marija is one of the finest Renaissance buildings in Malta. On a Latin cross plan, it was designed by Tommaso Dingli (1591–1661; see History of Maltese Art, p. 58). | **St Mary's Church**

Alongside the road from Attard to Santa Venera runs the Wignacourt (see Santa Venera). | **Aqueduct**

Between Attard and Balzan, surrounded by villas and other houses, is the San Anton Palace, set in extensive gardens (opening times: daily 7am–7pm). It was built between 1623 and 1626 for Grand Master Antoine de Paule as a country residence. During the period of British rule it was the residence of the governor; it is now the private residence of the President of Malta. It is therefore not open to the public, though the gardens are (admission free). The gardens contain numerous exotic trees between borders of beautiful flowers. Children will enjoy the animal enclosure, with sheep, monkeys and even a dromedary. | **★San Anton Palace**

Balzan
G 6

Like Attard and Lija (see entries), Balzan (pop. 3500) is one of the "Three Villages". It lies in the centre of Malta, only 7 km south-west of Valletta. On the east it is now joined up with Birkirkara (see entry), on the south with Attard and on the east with Lija. Originally part of Birkirkara, it became an independent township in 1655.

The centre of Balzan has still very much the feeling of a village, with narrow, winding streets. The outer districts are very different, with fine broad streets lined with modern houses and villas.

In the centre of Balzan is the parish church of the Annunciation (1669–95), in a style which shows clear Spanish influence. Close by, in Three Churches Street, are three other churches: the former parish church of St Marija Assunta from the 17th century, St Leonard's and the chapel of St Roch, built by the villagers in 1593 in thanksgiving for being spared during an outbreak of plague in the previous year.

Birkirkara
G/H 6

Birkirkara is the south-western outpost of the built-up area which has developed round Valletta and Sliema. With a population of some 20,000, it is one of Malta's larger towns, with numerous craftsmen's workshops and small industrial firms.

The main streets of Birkirkara, through which pours a never-ending stream of traffic, are lined with typical Maltese houses with oriel windows. The narrow streets in the town centre, however, are relatively quiet.

★St Helen's

In a spacious square is the parish church of St Helen, built by Domenico Cachia between 1735 and 1745. The Knights were so impressed by this handsome Baroque building that he was entrusted with the task of building the Auberge de Castille in Valletta. The church has a Latin cross plan, with three chapels on each side of the nave. The interior has fine carving and wall paintings (see also History of Maltese Art, p. 49).

Old Railway
Station Garden

The park area surrounding the former station building with its aviaries and children's playground is another attraction in the centre of Birkirkara. A restored railway coach commemorates the brief history of railways on Malta – a 13 km-long stretch connected Valletta and Mdina/Rabat between 1883 and 1931. Despite the short distance it covered, the railway was a popular means of transport at the turn of the last century. More than 1 million passengers made the journey in 1904/1905. When, by 1931, passenger numbers had slumped to less than half, the line was suspended.

Birzebbuga   J 8

The little town of Birzebbuga (pop. 7200) lies on a small peninsula on the east coast of Malta. To the south it is now joined up with Kalafrana. Since 1988 it has a new container port with deep-water wharves. The predominantly level country inland from Birzebbuga is eminently suitable for the laying out of an airport. North-west of the town is the end of the runway of Malta's international airport (see Luqa), and to the south-west is the former British military airfield of Hal Far, used as a base in the Second World War, now an industrial estate.

This unpretentious little town does little to cater for tourists, and has few cafés and restaurants. Pretty Bay, to the south of the town, has a long sandy beach but otherwise does not live up to its name. Here cranes and industrial installations are increasingly taking over the scene.

At the north end of the town, beside the little chapel of St George, a road (signposted) goes off to the Neolithic temple and Bronze Age settlement of Borg in-Nadur (see entry). Below the chapel are Bronze Age "cart ruts" running down the rocky beach to the sea.

★Blue Grotto   G 8

South-west of Zurrieq (see entry) is the Wied iz-Zurrieq, a narrow fjord on the south coast of Malta, from which, sea conditions permitting, boats take visitors to the Blue Grotto. At the end of the road is a large car park (with a few souvenir shops, bars and restaurants. The attractively laid out terrace and promenade along the sea-front and excellent views of the coastal scenery and across the sea to the rocky island Filfla also invite the visitor to linger.

★Scenery

The brightly coloured fishing boats skirt the cliff-fringed coast and visit a number of sea-caves; the trip takes 20–25 minutes. The largest of the caves was named the Blue Grotto by the British: the Maltese call it Taht il-Hnejja ("under the arch"), after the monumental rock arch at the entrance to the cave. In this cave, and also in the smaller ones, there is

Borg in-Nadur: only sparse remains of the Neolithic temple complex have stood the test of time

a marvellous play of colour. Thanks to the blue algae that grow here the water has taken on a light blue colouring. The effect is at its finest in certain light conditions: the best time to visit the cave, therefore, is late morning. Sometimes flashes of bright orange can be seen below the surface: this touch of colour is also due to a particular species of alga – and not coral, as the local guides like to say.

Borg in-Nadur   J 8

On the east coast of Malta, 1 km south of the much visited cave of Ghar Dalam (see entry), are the remains of a Neolithic temple and a Bronze Age settlement known as Borg in-Nadur ("heap of stones on the hill"). The site, which is accessible at any time, is reached on a signposted field track which takes off at the simple chapel of St George, standing directly on the sea on the northern outskirts of Birzebbuga (see entry).

The track climbs on to the plateau and in 100 m passes on the left the remains of a Neolithic temple dating from about 3000 BC. There are only scanty remnants of megalithic walls and a few orthostats. The temple, with two kidney-shaped chambers, stands on the west side of an oval courtyard.

Neolithic temple

150 m from the temple, on the highest point of the ridge, are remains of Bronze Age structures. There is no road or track to the site: the best plan is to walk along the edge of the escarpment and then bear left, crossing a number of field walls, to reach the remains of a semicircular defensive wall which is believed to date from around 1200 BC. It is built of irregularly shaped stones fitted together without mortar. The strategic situation of the settlement and the strength of the walls indicate that the occupants feared attack by enemies. Within this bulwark the

Bronze Age structures

remains of two stone huts with traces of hearths were discovered in 1959.

Bugibba

See St Paul's Bay

Bur Marrad   F 5

Bur Marrad is a small village in northern Malta, on the road from St Paul's Bay to Mosta. The houses of the village, which was established only in the 19th century, are widely scattered.

In the main street is the Farmer's Wine cooperative (open Mon.–Fri. 9am–4pm), where visitors can taste and buy Maltese wines.

St Pawl Milqi

On a hill to the west of the village is the little chapel of St Pawl Milqi (1616–22), on the spot where the Apostle Paul, after his shipwreck, is said to have met the Roman governor, Publius (see Baedeker Special). Under the foundations of the chapel were found remains of a Roman villa (open Oct.–Jun. 15th: Mon.–Sat. 8.15am–5pm, Sun. 8.15am–4.15pm; Jun. 16th–Sep.: daily 7.45am–2pm).

★Buskett Gardens   F 7

Scenery 2 km south of Rabat, below the Verdala Palace, are the Buskett or Boschetto Gardens. They are not so much gardens as an area of woodland – an unusual feature on this almost treeless island. A small part of the Buskett Gardens belongs to the Verdala Palace and is normally not open to the public, but the rest of the area is a very popular resort of the Maltese, who come here to picnic at weekends, and there is a popular restaurant at the entrance ot the gardens. Visitors too will find it well worth to come here, perhaps taking in the "cart ruts" at Clapham Junction (see entry) on the same excursion. Here they can stroll on shady paths under pine-trees, passing plantations of lemons and oranges, or seek out a pleasant spot to relax and enjoy the scenery.

The Buskett Gardens were laid out by the Knights in 1570 as a hunting preserve. It still attracts Maltese sportsmen, although shooting in this area was officially prohibited in 1980. Numerous native species of birds nest in the trees.

★Verdala Palace

Prominently situated on a hill above the Buskett Gardens is the Verdala Palace, built in 1586 as a summer residence for Grand Master Verdale (1581–1595). A fortress-like structure, almost square in plan, with four corner towers, surrounded by a moat, it was designed by Gerolamo Cassar. Beside the main front of the palace is a small 16th century chapel, probably also designed by Cassar. After renovation in 1858 the palace was also used as a summer residence by the British governors. No doubt the French officers who were detained here as prisoners of war in the early years of the 19th century found it a less agreeable residence than the Grand Masters and governors.

More recently the palace was occasionally used to accommodate guests of the government and at other times was open to the public on conducted visits. In 1994 the newly elected President of Malta, Ugo Mifsud Bonnici, made it his summer residence, and it is no longer open to the public.

Cart ruts – like these in Clapham Junction – can be found in many places on Malta and Gozo. Until today no satisfactory explanation of their origins has been found

★Clapham Junction F 7

Clapham Junction is the name given – evidently by an English visitor familiar with the junction of that name in London – to the largest assemblage of Malta's unique and mysterious "cart ruts", a system of parallel grooves cut or worn in the rock, with intersections and crossings, which resembles the tracks at a busy railway junction.

The site, above the Dingli Cliffs on the south coast of Malta, is best reached by way of Mdina/Rabat, from which a road runs south, passing the Verdala Palace and the Buskett Gardens. At the south end of the gardens, opposite the Buskett Forest Aparthotel, is a small car park. From the end of the car park signposts on the left point the way to the site. The path runs alongside a wall for some 200 m, then turns right on a wide field track and right again by a small house. To the right of the path the cart ruts can be seen running over the rock in parallel lines. The site is not enclosed.

★Cart ruts

The cart ruts found at Clapham Junction and many other places in Malta show uniform characteristics. The parallel grooves are between 1.32 and 1.47 metres apart. The grooves, V-shaped and slightly rounded at the base, are up to 75 cm deep and usually 25–30 cm across at the top. At many points the tracks run parallel, cross and intersect.

Dating It is now established that the cart ruts were made and used in the Bronze Age, between 2000 and 1000 BC. They are found mainly near Bronze Age settlements, which, unlike the Neolithic temples, were usually sited in defensive positions on hills and not directly on the coast. Since shaft graves of the Phoenician/Carthaginian period are cut through the tracks, they appear to have been no longer in use after 1000 BC.

The **purpose** of the cart ruts is still a puzzle. The most probable explanation is that they were part of a system for the transport of goods (mainly agricultural produce). The vehicles used may have been slide-cars consisting of two strips of wood joined by cross-bars and supporting a woven net. Since the distance between the grooves varies, the nets were probably also variable in width. On the under side of the strips of wood were attached (probably with leather straps) stone runners. These structures – of a type found elsewhere in Europe and Asia – were drawn either by animals or by men. The grooves, originally shallow, would become steadily deeper in the course of time. Since the local limestone was relatively soft until exposed to the air (and the rock in those days probably still had a covering of soil), it is not surprising that the ruts can be up to 75 cm deep. It is possible that, as soon as the ruts became too deep, new ones were made right next to them. This would explain why so may cart-ruts are now found. Remarkably, no traces of humans or animals have been found in the vicinity. Even bare-footed men pushing the slide-cars would in course of time wear down the rock between the grooves and leave signs of their passage.

Some scholars, therefore have doubted this interpretation of the cart ruts as a transport system, and have suggested that they formed part of a water supply system. But this explanation too comes up against diffi-culties. Why are the grooves always in pairs, why do they sometimes run down to the sea (a fact explained by the "transport" theory as con-nected with the transport of fish and salt), and why are they so uniformly hewn out of the rock?

Ghar il-Kbir

Beyond Clapham Junction is the "Great Cave" (Ghar il-Kbir), in reality several cave-like chambers hewn out of the rock under a rocky precipe which has now collapsed. The cave complex was inhabited by humans until the 19th century, at times by up to 100 people. The caves were cleared by the British authorities in 1835 for hygienic and political reasons – the cave-dwellers refused to pay taxes.

Comino   D/E 2/3

Area: 2.75 sq. km
Population: c. 20

Comino, the third of the main islands in the Maltese archipelago, lies in the channel known as Il Fliegu between Malta and Gozo. It is 2.4 km long by 2 km across and rises to a height of 75 m. For administrative pur-poses it belongs to Gozo. The name Comino is the Italian version of its Maltese name Kemmuna, which means caraway, a herb which was grown here in the Middle Ages.

Comino now has only a sparse scrub vegetation covering its rocky surface. The inhabitants grow fruit and vegetables for their own con-sumption. Pigs have also been reared here since the early eighties, when disease wiped out almost the whole stock of the Maltese archipel-ago.

Although Comino has only small sandy beaches, tourism plays a major part in its economy. There are two jointly-run hotels with a total of some 300 beds in summer. The island is a paradise for holidaymakers seeking peace and relaxation, with facilities for a variety of water sports and the entertainments put on by the hotels in the evening to provide variety.

Most visitors come to Comino, however, on a cruise round the Maltese islands. The excursion ships usually anchor for a midday break

The Blue Lagoon between Comino and Cominotto shimmers in various shades of blue and green

in the Blue Lagoon between Comino and the tiny offshore islet of Cominotto. It is also possible to take a day trip to Comino on your own: there are daily boat services in summer from Cirkewwa on Malta and Mgarr on Gozo to the landing-stage near the Comino hotels (see Practical Information, Ferries and Shipping Services). It should be borne in mind, however, that the facilities of the hotels, including the restaurants, are for residents only. A day tripper, therefore, will be unable to get anything to drink anywhere on Comino, and may have difficulty in finding a place to sit in the shade!

There is evidence of human settlement on Comino reaching back to the Bronze Age. Four Carthaginian or Phoenician tombs have been found on the west coast of the island, and there is a small necropolis of the Roman period in Santa Maria Bay. During the Middle Ages the island had at times a population of over 200, and until the 17th century it was mainly a pirates' lair. This changed in 1618, when Grand Master Alof de Wignacourt built a watch-tower on Comino. Apart from its strategic situation, Comino served during the time of the Knights – and later under British rule – as a quarantine station.

History

Comino's principal tourist attraction is the Blue Lagoon, which is only a few minutes' walk from the landing-stage (beyond the hotels bear right). This strip of water between Comino and the rocky islet of Cominotto, only some 125 m across and 1–3 m deep, shimmers in a variety of bluish and greenish tones. The water is crystal-clear. There is only one tiny beach on the Blue Lagoon, but during the summer months the rocky coast is frequently overcrowded with bathers and sunbathers, with visiting yachts and excursion boats adding to the numbers.

★**Blue Lagoon**

Apart from a lonely cemetery and a tiny church the only other feature of interest on Comino is the Santa Maria Tower (or Fort St Mary) on the west coast. This watch-tower was built by Vittorio Cassar in 1618, in the time of Grand Master Alof de Wignacourt. With 18 cannon and a garrison of 130 men, it was designed as a bulwark against the Turkish threat (not open to the public).

Cominotto ("little caraway seed"), separated from Comino by the Blue Lagoon, is an uninhabited bare rocky islet with an area of only 0.25 sq. km. On the east side is a flight of steps hewn from the rock leading up to the remains of a building. The remains are possibly Roman, but it has not been possible to establish an exact dating.

Cospicua   J 6

Cospicua (pop. 10,000), in Maltese Bormla, is one of the "Three Cities" (the others being Vittoriosa and Senglea: see entries) which existed on the east side of the Grand Harbour before the foundation of Valletta. The last of the three cities to be founded, Cospicua immediately adjoins Senglea and Vittoriosa, both built on promontories reaching out into the harbour. After the foundation of Valletta the three cities became suburbs of the capital in which the poorer members of the population lived.

Cospicua is surrounded by two massive rings of walls. The inner ring, known as the Margherita Lines, was begun in 1638, the outer ring, the Cottonera Lines, in 1670. Otherwise Cospicua, which was almost completely destroyed during the Second World War, possesses no notable buildings except the richly decorated Baroque parish church of the Immaculate Conception.

★★Dingli Cliffs   E/F 7/8

The Dingli Cliffs, on the south coast of Malta, are one of the most impressive natural features on the island. The cliffs, and the nearby village of Dingli, take their name from an English knight, Sir Thomas Dingley, who settled here in 1540.

Dingli is the highest village in Malta. The surrounding plateau rises to a height of 250 m and falls sheer down to the sea in the famous light-coloured cliffs.

On the edge of the cliffs is the St Magdalen Church (closed), and several stone benches invite the visitor to rest. In this section, the Dingli Cliffs drop to the ocean in two stages, with a terrace used for agricultural purposes between them. The views are even more impressive if you follow the road parallel to the coastline in a south-easterly direction: here the cliffs ive almost vertically down to the sea.

There are cart ruts at many points in the rocky terrain of this area, particularly at Clapham Junction (see entry).

Off the coast is the tiny rocky islet of Filfla, the nesting-place of rare species of birds and the home of an endemic species of lizard, Lacerta filfolensis. It was declared a nature reserve in 1988.

◀ *The Dingli Cliffs on Malta's southern coast are magnificent in the evening sun*

Floriana   H/J 6

Lying outside the fortifications of Valletta (see entry), Floriana (pop. 2700) shares the Sciberras peninsula, between Marsamxett Harbour and the Grand Harbour, almost equally with the island's capital. The town has no outstanding tourist sights, but it offers opportunities for getting away from the crowds of tourists in its parks and gardens.

History In order to protect the landward side of Valletta Grand Master Antoine de Paule commissioned the Italian architect Pietro Paolo Floriani, from whom the town takes its name, to build a series of bastions across the neck of the Sciberras peninsula. The work was carried out between 1636 and 1640. The area within these fortifications was not at first built up, but remained empty until the time of Grand Master Vilhena, who ordered the building of the town on a regular rectangular plan in 1724.

Town There is an extensive green belt between the fortifications of Valletta and the houses of Floriana. In front of the City Gate of Valletta, but still within the territory of Floriana, is the central bus station, surrounding the Triton Fountain. Here too, amid shady trees, is the old-established luxury hotel Phoenicia. In this area are a number of large guarded car parks (though there is never enough parking space in Floriana and Valletta!).

In this area are a number of large guarded car parks (though there is never enough parking space in Floriana and Valletta!).

Between the green belt and the fortifications at the head of the peninsula is the regular street grid of Floriana. The main street is St Anne Street with its busy four lanes of traffic. It is lined by tall arcaded buildings erected since the Second World War.

Kalkara Gardens

The Kalkara Gardens are laid out on a terrace on the south side of the Triton Fountain. They offer fine views of the Grand Harbour and Senglea on the far side of the harbour.

St Publius

The most striking feature in central Floriana is the church of St Publius, built in 1733 but much altered thereafter. It was the last major church built by the Knights. Almost completely destroyed during the Second World War, it was rebuilt after the war on the basis of the original plans. According to legend St Publius was appointed by the Apostle Paul in AD 60 to be the first bishop of Malta.

Granaries

In the large square in front of the church can be seen a series of regularly arranged circular stone slabs. These cover the underground granaries constructed in the mid-17th century on the orders of Grand Master Martin de Redin. The Knights always maintained large stores of grain in order to ensure food supplies in the event of a siege; Sicilian hard wheat was preferred because of its keeping qualities.

Maglio Gardens

To the west of St Publius Square, between the Mall and Sarria Street, are the Maglio Gardens. The name comes from a ball game, pallamaglio, played here by young knights. The narrow strip of gardens was laid out in 1805.

At the north entrance to the gardens is the Indipendenza monument erected in 1989 to commemorate the 25th anniversary of Malta's independence (September 21st 1964). In the park itself there are a number of monuments to distinguished Maltese figures.

Sarria Church

At the south end of the Maglio Gardens, on the left, is the little Sarria Church, on a circular plan. It is named after Fra Martino de Sarria, who initiated the building of an earlier church in 1585. This was completely rebuilt by Lorenzo Gafà in 1678. The church contains a number of paint-

In Floriana, in front of Valletta's town gates, the central bus station surrounds the Triton Fountain. In the background the church of St Publius.

ings by Mattia Preti, including a figure of St Roch, the saint invoked against plague.

Opposite is the Wignacourt Tower, built in 1615. This water tower, named after the grand master of the same name on whose orders it was built, is the end point of the Wignacourt aqueduct. Wignacourt's coat of arms is clearly visible on the tower.

Wignacourt Tower

The Argotti Botanic Gardens, originally laid out in 1774 on the bastions of Floriana as the botanical garden of the University of Malta, make for a restful place in bustling Floriana. Among its attractions is a large collection of cactuses. Open daily 7am–sunset; admission free.

Argotti Botanic Gardens

The Porte des Bombes, built in 1721, is the entrance to Floriana from the southern side. Originally it had a single arch; the second arch was added by the British in the second half of the 19th century to cope with the increasing traffic.

Porte des Bombes

Ghajn Tuffieha   E 5

Ghajn Tuffieha, on the north-west coast of Malta, consists only of two hotels and a number of subsidiary buildings. Visitors come here for the sake of the sandy beaches to the west and south-west, the finest in Malta. This is also a good district for walkers: they can stroll along the beaches or, more strenuously, wander up hill and down dale on the plateau above the coast to the south, enjoying incomparable views.

This area has a long history of human occupation, as evidenced by remains of Bronze Age settlements on the small peninsula to the south

Ghajn Tuffieha

of Ghajn Tuffieha Bay and a few megalithic blocks on the Pellegrin peninsula, a short distance farther south. There are also remains of Roman baths (see below) 1 km south-east of Ghajn Tuffieha. In those days the area must have been well provided with water, and the country round Ghajn Tuffieha is still a thriving agricultural area.

Golden Bay

Immediately in front of the Golden Sands Hotel at Ghajn Tuffieha is Golden Bay, with a beautiful long sandy beach on which sun umbrellas, recliners, pedalos and other equipment can be hired. There are also snack bars. During the main season, however, you must book your "place in the sun" in plenty of time.

★Ghajn Tuffieha Bay

The road from St Paul's Bay to Ghajn Tuffieha ends immediately above the north-west coast. To the left is a flight of steps leading down to Ghajn Tuffieha Bay. Although equipment for various water sports can be hired here too, this beautiful bay has preserved more of its natural character than Golden Bay.

Gnejna Bay

Beyond the little peninsula at the south end of Ghajn Tuffieha is Gnejna Bay (which can be reached direct by car from Mgarr). This bay has been less affected by tourism than the other two, but it lacks something of their scenic beauty. It has a beach of reddish sand around 100 m long. The many boat-sheds in the southern part of the bay belong to fishing enthusiasts.

Roman Baths

A few hundred metres from Ghajn Tuffieha on the road to Zebbieh the Roman Baths are signposted on the right. Times of opening are irregular, but the site is usually open in the late morning and in the afternoon; a tip is expected.

The baths were excavated in 1929 and restored at the expense of

Malta's best beaches: Golden Bay and, in the foreground, Ghajn Tuffieha Bay, still completely undeveloped

UNESCO in 1961, when some of the mosaics were given protective roofs. Although the baths have all the features normally found in Roman baths the remains are not particularly impressive.

Just after entering the site the remains of the piscina (swimming pool) can be seen on the right. To the north of this is a corridor paved with rhomboid tiles, on one side of which can be seen the stone channels of the water supply system. The small rooms between the corridor and the piscina were probably changing rooms. To the north of the corridor are remains of the walls of the tepidarium (warm bath), which was roofed. On the floor is a circular feather mosaic. On the east side of the tepidarium is the frigidarium (cold bath).

To the west of the tepidarium is the caldarium (hot bath), recognisable by its hypocausts and apse-like recess; the floor over the hypocausts is missing. To the north of this, at the north-west corner of the enclosure, are the remains of a communal latrine.

★★Ghar Dalam   J 8

Importance On the east coast of Malta, on the road between Paola and Birzebbuga is Ghar Dalam ("Cave of Darkness"), a site of outstanding geological interest. It is entered through the museum, from which steps lead down into the cave Wied Dalam ("Valley of Darkness"; open in summer daily 7.45am–2pm, in winter 8.15am–5pm). From the main cave, 140 m long, shorter side passages branch off. The first 80 m of the cave are easy of access, with artificial lighting. In this section the cave is between 8 and 10 m wide and between 5 and 8 m high. There are remains of stalactites and stalagmites and occasional animal bones sticking out of the ground.

Tertiary river-bed The central passage of the cave cuts across the Wied Dalam at right angles. It is the bed of a river of the Tertiary era which continued beyond Ghar Dalam.

Excavations The German-Italian palaeontologist Arturo Issel came to Malta in 1865 to look for fossils in its caves, and in the course of his excavations in Ghar Dalam discovered fragments of pottery and the bones of a hippopotamus and a wild sheep. Thereafter there were further excavations, particularly in the early years of the 20th century; the last major excavations were those of Joseph Baldacchino between 1933 and 1938.

Finds The excavations recovered large numbers of red deer bones and also the bones of brown bears, wolves, foxes, giant swans and, particularly at the lower levels, hippopotamuses and elephants. The finds show that Malta was not always an island. All the animal bones belonged to species found in the rest of Europe, indicating that in the Pleistocene era, 2 million years ago, there must have been a land bridge between Europe and Malta. Many of the bones found, for example of elephants and hippopotamuses, belonged to dwarf forms: it is still not known whether these smaller species were an adaptation to changed living conditions (increasing aridity and consequent reduction in vegetation and water supply) or were the result of forced inbreeding. At the deeper levels remains of dwarf elephants and also of larger species were found.

It is astonishing that such large numbers of bones of different species were found in Ghar Dalam. The current theory is that the skeletons accumulated in the bed of the Wied Dalam, which flows at right angles to the cave; erosion gradually opened up a link between the river and the cave; and these openings exerted a strong suction effect, so that huge quantities of bones were deposited on the floor of the cave. This process came to an end in the Upper Pleistocene (300,000 years ago), when the Wied Dalam had completely cut through the cave.

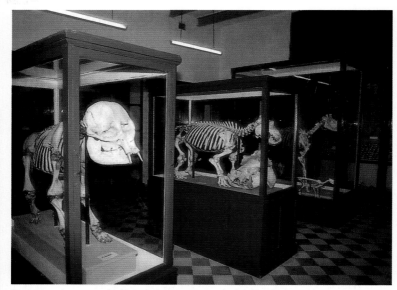

Skeletons of a young elephant and rhinocerosses in the Ghar Dalam

In addition to animal bones the excavators found in the upper levels of the cave pottery dating from around 5200 BC – the earliest traces of human settlement in Malta. Finds of implements and human bones showed that the cave was occupied during the whole of the Neolithic period and the Bronze Age.

Gharghur   G 5

Gharghur (pop. 2000), 10 km west of Valletta, is one of the oldest villages on the island.

St Bartholomew

In the centre of this modest village is the 17th century parish church dedicated to St Bartholomew, its patron saint. It has a curious figure of the saint, shaped from plaster over a human skeleton, which can be seen through holes in the surface.

Ghar Hassan   J 8

The cave of Ghar Hassan, 3 km south of Birzebbuga on Malta's south-east coast, is dramatically situated in the cliffs immediately above the sea. From the car park steps lead down to its entrance, 80 m above the sea. Legend has it that the cave, which, like Ghar Dalam (see entry), was originally the bed of an underground river, was once the home of a Saracen named Hassan. During the Second World War it served as an air raid shelter for several hundred people.

Ghar Hassan is always open but it has no facilities for tourists. If you want to venture into the interior of the cave a torch is essential, and there will usually be one of the local inhabitants available to lend you one in return for a small voluntary payment.

At many points in the cave the ground is wet and slippery and the roof extremely low; but those who are not put off by these difficulties will be rewarded by a fine view of the sea from a second entrance to the cave.

★★Gozo · A–D 1–3

Area: 67 sq. km
Population: 29,000
Chief town: Victoria

The 6 km crossing from Cirkewwa at the northern tip of Malta to Mgarr on Gozo takes the ferry (see Practical Information, Ferries and Shipping Services) about half an hour; the helicopter that flies a regular service from Malta's Luqa airport to the heliport on Gozo, takes about 15 minutes to reach the smaller island – barely enough to allow visitors to adjust to an entirely new world. For Gozo is not a mere appendage to the main island of Malta but an island with characteristics of its own. Most visitors to Gozo come on a day trip from Malta, and certainly the main sights on the island can be seen without difficulty in one day; but this will not allow them to discover the real beauty of Gozo. That will only be revealed to those who have time for long walks through the green and well cultivated landscape of the island. If you are looking for a restful holiday, if bathing and other water sports and the beauties of nature mean more to you than evenings out in a town, you will find it well worth while to spend your holiday on Gozo and see the tourist highlights of Malta on two or three sightseeing trips.

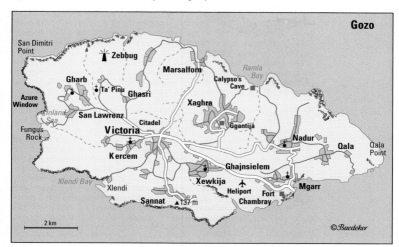

Gozo (in Maltese Ghaudex, pronounced "owdesh") is only 14 km long by 7 km across: an island that you can really get to know. It is an island of low flat-topped hills and fertile valleys, with its highest point only 176 m above sea level. Much of the coast is lined by cliffs falling sheer down to the sea, but there are also, particularly on the north-east coast, some small sandy bays, the most beautiful of which by far is Ramla Bay.

★★Topography

89

Gozo

Fertile farming country on Gozo

Population

The island has a population of 29,000 and a population density of 432 to the sq. kilometre. The main concentration of population is in the chief town, Victoria, situated in the centre of the island. The other thirteen villages all have a markedly rural character; many of them have a population of only 1000 or 2000.

The relatively high population density and the lack of employment opportunities have led and are still leading many Gozitans to emigrate, particularly to Australia, the United States and Canada. Many have also moved to Malta or commute to work there.

Economy

Agriculture is still the predominant branch of the economy. More than 900 people earn their living from agriculture, and for 2500 others it is a part-time occupation. The main crops are potatoes, onions, melons, peaches, nectarines, apples, citrus fruits and wine, which are produced in sufficient quantity to meet local needs and leave a comfortable margin for exports. Some 60 per cent of the agricultural produce of the Maltese archipelago, indeed, comes from Gozo. This is all the more surprising because much of Gozo's agriculture is uneconomic. Machinery cannot be used on the many small terraced fields, and only a fraction of Gozo's 1890 hectares of arable land is irrigated. Fishing and stock-farming also make contributions to the economy. Gozo has 2000 cows, but these are rarely seen: they are kept in stables, since land is too valuable to be used for grazing. A traditional branch of the economy is winning salt from the sea, particularly in the salt-pans at Qbaijar, on the north coast of the island – though the sun is strong enough to produce satisfactory yields only in the summer months.

A characteristic feature of Gozo is the globigerina limestone which is quarried on the island, particularly in the western part. Almost all the houses on the island are built of this yellowish stone. The soft limestone is sawn from the quarries in large blocks and must then be left to dry out for at least two years until it is hard enough to use.

Industry plays only a small part in the economy of the island, employing no more than 800 workers. The main products of the small industrial zone at Xewkija are clothing, shoes and windscreen wiper motors.

Tourism is a growing branch of the economy. Some 300,000 day trippers come to Gozo every year, and efforts are being made to increase the number of visitors who make a longer stay.
 Gozo has at present rather more than 1000 beds for visitors in some ten hotels (including two luxury hotels) and a number of guest-houses and apartment houses. An attractive alternative is offered by the numerous old cottages which have been converted into holiday homes. The island's hotels, restaurants and other tourist facilities are concentrated at Marsalforn on the north coast and the smaller resort of Xlendi on the south coast.

Tourism

Archaeology has yielded evidence of human occupation in the 5th millennium BC. In the middle of the 4th millennium one of the earliest Neolithic temple complexes in the Maltese archipelago was built at Ggantija. In subsequent millennia the history of Gozo – known to the Phoenicians as Gîl and to the Greeks and Romans as Gaulus, and first referred to as Gozo by 14th century Italian chroniclers – was closely bound up with that of the larger neighbouring island. In 1551 a Turkish raid led by Sinan Pasha left Gozo almost depopulated: the stronger inhabitants were sold into slavery and almost all the others were killed. This led the Knights of St John to build fortifications on the island, but in spite of this Gozo was subsequently the target of another Turkish attack and numerous raids by pirates. During the 19th and 20th centuries the island was overshadowed by its larger neighbour. The people of Gozo are determined to change this, and have already had some success. Since 1987 Gozo has been represented in the Maltese Cabinet by its own minister and has had its own budget.

History

Victoria · Rabat

All roads on Gozo lead to its chief town, Victoria, situated in the centre of the island. Although it was given the name of Victoria in 1897 on the occasion of Queen Victoria's Diamond Jubilee the Gozitans still use its old Arabic name of Rabat. With a population of 6500, Victoria is the largest town on the island and its economic and cultural centre.
 The town consists of its Citadel, prominently situated on a hill, and the outer districts which have grown up round it since the 17th century.
 The origins of the Citadel go back to Carthaginian and Roman times. The Arabs also took advantage of this strategically situated site and built new fortifications from 870 onwards. The Citadel was totally destroyed by the Turks in 1551. In the late 16th and early 17th century the Knights rebuilt it in stages. A law which was in force until 1637 required all the inhabitants of Gozo to sleep within the Citadel at night, and no houses could be built within its walls. After this law was repealed the local people only moved into the Citadel in an emergency, preferring to live in the new town which was gradually growing up below the Citadel.
 The best starting-point for a tour of Victoria is the Main Square (It-Tokk), from which it is a few minutes' walk up to the Citadel. After seeing the Citadel, if time permits, it is worth while strolling round the busy little shopping streets surrounding the Main Square. There are no features of particular interest in this part of the town.

The masonry of the Citadel dates mainly from the 16th to 18th centuries. Few houses were built within its walls from the 17th century onwards, and much of the area consists of ruins. In spite of this a visit to the Citadel is still very rewarding. The original street network was brought

★★Citadel

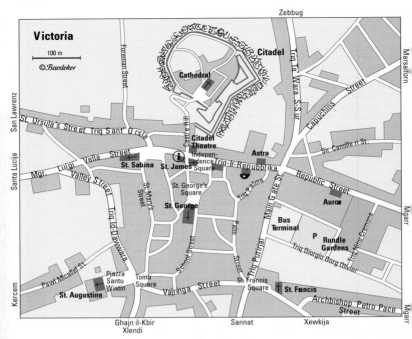

View from the Citadel to Victoria's suburbs

Victoria • Rabat
Citadel

1 Bishop's Palace
2 Chapel of St. Barbara
3 Old Prison
  (Craft Centre)
4 St. John's Cavalier
5 Cathedral Museum
6 Archway
7 Chapel of St. Joseph
8 Governor's Palace
9 Courts of Justice
10 Old Clock Tower
11 St. Martin's Cavalier
12 Armoury

to light in the 1960s and various houses were rebuilt, some of them now occupied by interesting museums. A walk round the walls of the Citadel offers marvellous views over the whole of Gozo.

The main gate of the Citadel leads into Cathedral Square, dominated by the Cathedral, which is approached by a broad flight of steps. On the north side of the square are the Courts of Justice, originally built in the 17th century and altered in the 19th, which are now occupied by government offices. On the south side is the late 19th century Bishop's Palace.

The Cathedral of the Assumption (open Mon.–Sat. 9am–1pm and 1.45–5pm; Sun. only during mass) was built by Lorenzo Gafà between 1697 and 1711, on a site once occupied by a Roman temple and later by a medieval church. It is a plain Baroque building on a Latin cross plan. The architect dispensed with a large dome on grounds of cost, but the architectural balance of the church was restored by the later addition of a bell-tower at the north-east end. It was given cathedral status in 1864, after Gozo became a separate episcopal seat.   ★Cathedral

The floor of the Cathedral is decorated with inlay work. On the walls are altarpieces by local artists, including the patronal altarpiece of the Assumption (1791), and other paintings, including works by Francesco Zahra (1710–73), of the Neapolitan school. The position of the absent dome is occupied by a trompe-l'oeil ceiling painting of a dome by Antonio Manuele (1739). The paintings on the barrel vaulting are modern. The sumptuous high altar dates from 1855, the alabaster font from 1742.

The Cathedral Museum (open Mon.–Sat. 10am–1pm and 1.30–4.30pm) was installed in the former sacristy in 1979. It displays in three rooms a small collection of pictures, liturgical utensils, richly embroidered bishop's robes and documents on the history of the Cathedral.

The Gozo Museum of Archaeology (open Mon.–Sat. 8.30am–4.30pm, in summer to 5pm, Sun. 8.30am–3pm; joint admission ticket covering the Folklore and Natural History Museums as well) has been housed since   Gozo Museum of Archaeology

1960 in the Casa Bondi, a restored 16th century palace. In eight small rooms it displays archaeological finds dating from the Neolithic period to the Middle Ages, including some items only recently discovered.

A special room on the ground floor is devoted to material from the Ggantija temple, including a pillar with a carving of a 107 cm long snake which probably played a part in a fertility cult. There is also a model of the temple. The main room on the upper floor contains material of the Carthaginian and Roman periods, including fragments of statues, inscriptions, jewellery, a skeleton of the Carthaginian period which was buried under an amphora and a Roman glass amphora (1st/2nd c. AD) used as a funerary urn. There is a fine collection of coins ranging in date

Victoria, Cathedral

from the 5th century BC to the end of the Roman Empire. An important relic of Arab culture is the Majmuna marble gravestone of 1174, with an inscription in Kufic script commemorating a girl who died young (on the upper floor, in a small room to the right of the staircase).

Old Prison/Craft Centre

The building at the end of Prison Street dates from 1614. At the end of the 19th century it was enlarged and thereafter served as a prison until 1964. It now houses a collection of Maltese arts and crafts.

★Folklore Museum

The most impressive museum in Victoria is the Folklore Museum (open Mon.–Sat. 8.30am–4.30pm, in summer to 5pm, Sun. 8.30am–3pm), which was installed in 1983 in three houses dating from around 1500. The double windows separated by elegant columns, the arched doorways and the fine carving are characteristic of Sicilian-Norman architecture.

The collection includes domestic objects and agricultural implements, craft products, sacred articles and traditional costumes. There are also demonstrations of certain crafts. Apart from the interest of the exhibits themselves, it is fascinating to walk through the old houses with their numerous small rooms extending from the cellars to the upper floor and get an impression of the life of the nobility on Gozo in the late medieval period.

Armoury

In a building near the western boundary of the Citadel is the Armoury (open Mon.–Sat. 8.30am–3pm). The building, which dates in its present form from 1776, was originally a granary. In the 19th century and during the Second World War the British used it as a barracks. Since 1984 it has housed a collection of arms and armour of the period of the Knights.

Opposite the Armoury is the Natural Science Museum (open Mon.–Sat. 8.30am–4.30pm, in summer to 5pm, Sun. 8.30am–3pm), which has an interesting collection of material on the geology, flora and fauna of the Maltese islands.

Natural Science Museum

The hub of Victoria's life is the Independence Square (It-Tokk) below the Citadel. A market is held here every morning. On the west side of the square is the Banca Giuratale, a semicircular Baroque building erected in 1733.

Independence Square

The Citadel Theatre at the corner of Independence Square and Castle Hill has a half-hourly multi-media show (Mon.–Sat. 10.30am–3.30pm, Sun. 10.30am–1.30pm; duration about 25 minutes) called "Island of Joy" about Gozo's past and present.

Citadel Theatre (Island of Joy)

A little way south of Independence Square is St George's Square, with St George's Church. Built in 1672–78, it was badly damaged by an earthquake in 1693. The west front was rebuilt in 1818, and in 1935–45 the transept and lateral aisles were added. The ceiling paintings in the interior were the work of the Roman artist Gian Battista Conti. There are a number of 17th century altarpieces, including one dedicated to the church's patron St George, by Mattia Preti and Francesco Zahra. There is also a richly painted figure of St George (1841).

St George's Church

Victoria has two opera houses within a few hundred metres of each other in Republic Street, the Astra and the Aurora, each with over 1000 seats. They belong to Gozo's two competing Philharmonic Societies. Once or twice a year they put on operas performed by foreign companies, with the people of Gozo supplying the choir, ballet and part of the orchestra; but they are mainly used as cinemas and lecture halls. The bars of the two opera houses are friendly meeting-places for local people and visitors, and at weekends the young people of Gozo dance to hot rhythms.

Astra, Aurora

Farther east along Republic Street are the Rundle Gardens (open daily until dusk), a well cared for park, with both native and exotic flowers and trees, laid out in 1914–15 on the initiative of Governor Leslie Rundle. There are a number of aviaries.

Rundle Gardens

South of the town centre, to right and left of the road to Xlendi, are two public wash-houses (Ghajn il-Kbir and Ghajn Bendu). They were constructed in the late 17th century in two natural caves, with washing troughs hewn from the rock. Women can still be seen doing their washing here.

Ghajn il-Kbir and Ghajn Bendu

Other Sights on Gozo

The main sights of historical or artistic interest and natural beauties of Gozo can be seen without difficulty in a single day. They are described here in the form of a tour starting from Mgarr.

With its brightly painted fishing boats and the neo-Gothic church of Our Lady of Lourdes (19th c.) prominently situated on a hill above the town, Mgarr is a pleasant and attractive little place. From time immemorial its harbour has been Gozo's only link with the outside world, and there is a regular ferry service to and from Malta, running roughly every hour. Round the harbour are a number of modest restaurants and cafés, a bank, post office and other service facilities as well as a tourist information office.

★Mgarr

Gozo

Fort Chambray

Fort Chambray, above Mgarr harbour, was built in the mid-18th century by a French knight named Jacques de Chambray. In the early 19th century it was used by the British authorities as a barracks, and later it became a mental hospital. In the mid-1990s it was planned to develop it as a tourist centre, but work has come to a halt as investors withdrew.

Gozo Heritage

On the main road from Mgarr to Victoria is Gozo Heritage (open Mon.–Sat. 9am—5.15pm). This show of "history as a living experience" is designed to give visitors a quick overview of Gozo's history. It consists of a series of rooms which, at first completely dark, light up to reveal a series of tableaux illustrating events in the island's long history, with a recorded commentary accompanied by music. The last room leads into a showroom offering arts and crafts for sale. The admission charge for this 15-minute spectacle, with debatable historical value, is high.

Xewkija

3 km beyond Mgarr is the straggling village of Xewkija (pronounced "shevkiya"): the name, from Arabic, means "place where thorns grow". It has one of the largest domed churches in Europe: the dome has an external width of 86 m and is just under 75 m high. The church, dedicated to John the Baptist, was built between 1952 and 1973 round the old parish church, in which services continued to be held until it was demolished in 1972.

Mgarr ix-Xini

3 km south-east of Xewkija is Mgarr ix-Xini, a long fjord-like inlet at the mouth of which is a watch-tower built in the 17th century to ward off pirate raids. The glass-clear waters invite swimmers, the rocks and stone plateaux sunbathers.

★Ta'Cenc

One of the most beautiful parts of Gozo is the Ta'Cenc plateau, which extends westward from Mgarr ix-Xini to Sannat; it is best reached by car from Sannat. It is pleasant walking country, with the prospect of coming across Bronze Age "cart ruts" and dolmens.

At the south-east end of Sannat is the Ta'Cenc luxury hotel. Built of local stone, it fits beautifully into the landscape.

Victoria

Now back to Xewkija, from which it is a short distance to the island's chief town, Victoria.

Xlendi

3 km south of Victoria is the former fishing village of Xlendi (pronounced "shlendi"), now one of the island's two main tourist centres. Round the narrow inlet of Xlendi Bay are a number of modest hotels and apartment houses, restaurants, cafés and shops. During the main holiday season the resort tends to be overcrowded.

A narrow paved path runs west round the inlet, ending at a small cave. The seafront promenade runs east, passing one or two rocky bathing beaches, and then turns south to reach a watch-tower built by the Knights in the second half of the 17th century.

Ta'Dbiegi

From Xlendi back to Victoria through the fertile Xlendi valley. From there the route continues west. Just before the village of San Lawrenz, on the left of the road, is the Ta'Dbiegi craft centre, where woollen and leather goods, jewellery, pottery and other craft products are offered for sale. The chances of finding anything of real value here are slight: the goods on display are mainly mass-produced articles aimed at the tourist market.

★Azure Window

From here a road runs west to end at a large car park immediately above the sea, from which it is a short walk to the Azure Window, a rock arch rising out of the water. The top of the arch

Xlendi is Gozo's second tourist centre. Smaller hotels line the narrow bay, and the small promenade is a popular meeting point during the day and at night.

is steadily being eroded and is likely to collapse in the not too distant future. Collapsed 08/03/17 9-40am ☹

From the car park a track runs down to the Inland Sea, as the Dwejra Lake is known. Tall cliffs separate this little lake from the open sea, but a natural opening in the rock allows seawater to flow into the lake. Some of the local fishermen have built boat-sheds round the lake and run boat trips to nearby Fungus Rock. A small bar and a short shingle beach may tempt visitors to linger. **Dwejra Lake**

A few hundred metres south of the car park is Dwejra Bay. Here, just offshore, is Fungus Rock, a 20 m high crag covered with a plant known as the Maltese sponge (Cynomorium coccineum). This dark brown plant growing to a height of around 20 cm, found in Europe only on Fungus Rock, was used by the Knights for the treatment of injuries and wounds because of its haemostatic properties. A dark-red extract from the plant, which was also sold to European princely houses at a high price, was a jealously guarded monopoly of the Knights. Fungus Rock could be reached only in a large basket which was pulled along ropes slung between the rock and the mainland of Gozo. To ensure that no unauthorised person could steal the precious plants a guard was permanently stationed on the rock and a watch-tower was built on the coast nearby. **Fungus Rock**

Dwejra Bay is lined by imposing cliffs. On the north side of the bay a flight of steps below the watch-tower leads down to the sea (though if the sea is rough bathing here is extremely dangerous). There are a number of rocky promontories on which both local people and visitors like to sunbathe and enjoy the beautiful scenery.

Gozo looks like a giant rocky lump that grows straight out of the sea. The main scenic attractions on its western coast are the Azure Window, an archway carved into the rock by erosion, and Fungus Rock, an offshore rock, about 20 m high.

Gozo

Gharb

Returning on the same route to San Lawrenz and then continuing in a northerly direction you get to Gharb (pronounced "arb"). This village with less than 1000 inhabitants has an atmospheric main square, dominated by a mighty baroque church. Construction was begun at the end of the 17th century but it was not completed until 1732. Only a few steps from the church is the Gharb Folklore Museum (open Mon.–Sat. 9.30am–4pm, Sun. 9am–1pm) which is also worth a visit. Based in a beautifully restored 18th-century building in Gharb's main square, its 28 rooms tell of the crafts traditions and peasant life on Gozo in past centuries.

The pilgrimage church of Ta'Pinu

Ta'Pinu

The next place of interest on the route is the pilgrimage church of Ta'Pinu (open daily 6.45am–12.30pm and 1–6.30pm, in summer to 7.30pm), 1 km east of Gharb. From Gharb it is reached on extremely narrow field tracks, you're better off returning via San Lawrenz to the road to Victoria and taking a side road on the left to the prominently situated church, the most celebrated Marian shrine in the Maltese archipelago. There was a 16th century chapel here in which a peasant woman called Carmela Grima claimed that on June 22nd 1883 the Virgin had spoken to her. Thereafter people flocked to the chapel, and miraculous healings were said to have occurred. It was then resolved to replace the modest country chapel by a large church. Work began in 1920 and the church was dedicated in 1931. A year later Pope Pius XI granted it the status of a basilica. The church, in neo-Romanesque style and on a Latin cross plan, is built of pinkish-yellow globigerina limestone. Carmela Grima's tomb is in a small chapel to the left of the altar.

San Dimitri

There is pleasant walking on field paths north and west of Ta'Pinu. One attractive walk is to the chapel of San Dimitri, 2 km north-west of the village of Gharb (signposted from there); the chapel can also be reached by car. Originally built in the 15th century, it was considerably enlarged in 1736. The altarpiece depicts St Demetrius flanked by a praying woman and a man wearing fetters.

From here a stretch of lonely country reaches down to the coast, from which there are superb views of the cliffs falling steeply down to the sea.

Zebbug

The route continues by way of the villages of Ghammar and Ghasri to Zebbug ("olive-tree"), the largest village in north-western Gozo. The Baroque village church (1739) has two clock-towers; one of the clocks shows the time but the other does not work – in order, it is said, to mislead the Devil.

From Zebbug a road runs north to the coast and then turns right. Here, extending along the coast, are the salt-pans of Qbaijar, which are still in use. Seawater is collected in shallow ponds only a few centimetres deep and evaporates within a week or so, leaving a crust of salt which is raked into heaps and left to dry. The sun is strong enough for the purpose only in summer.

Qbaijar

1 km east of Qbaijar on the coast road is Marsalforn, a former fishing village which is now one of Gozo's two leading tourist centres. It is a resort suited for holidaymakers for whom beautiful scenery and relaxation are more important than variety of entertainment. Round the bay are modest houses, recently built hotels and apartment blocks and unpretentious restaurants and cafés. Outside the main holiday season life in Marsalforn follows its own quiet way, livening up only at weekends, when people come over from Malta for a quick break. Bathing is possible on the tiny sandy beach in the village or on the shelving rocks round the bay. More attractive for bathers, however, is Ramla Bay (see subentry), which is just under an hour's walk from Marsalforn.

Marsalforn

From Marsalforn a road runs inland to Xaghra (pronounced "shahra"), one of the largest villages on Gozo, with a population of 3600. In the village are signposts pointing the way to Ninu's Cave and Xerri's Grotto, two stalactitic caves which were discovered by accident during the construction of cisterns for water storage at the end of the 19th century. The entrance to both caves is through private houses (open daily 9am–6pm).

Xaghra

On the eastern outskirts is a restored windmill, originally built in 1724 by Grand Master Manoel de Vilhena. It now houses a small windmill museum (open Mon.–Sat. 8.30am–4.30pm, in summer to 5pm, Sun. 8.30am–3pm). Another sign in the centre of the village points to the Pomskizillious Museum of Toys (open mid-Oct.–Mar. Sat. 10am–1pm; April Thu., Fri. Sat. 11am–1pm; May–mid-Oct. Mon.–Sat. 10am–12pm and 3–6pm). This private collection boasts many lovingly handmade toys, including some very beautiful dolls' houses.

On the south-eastern outskirts of Xaghra is Gozo's most important tourist sight, the megalithic temple of Ggantija (pronounced "jgantiyâ"; open Mon.–Sat. 8.30am–4.30pm, in summer to 5pm, Sun. 8.30am–3pm).

★★Ggantija

Built in the middle of the 4th millennium BC, the complex was covered in the course of time with a layer of earth and sand, from which only a few of the tallest stones projected. From time immemorial it was regarded by the local people as a sacred place and believed to be the work of a legendary giantess: hence its name. Excavation of the site began in 1827 on the orders of the British commandant of the island, Otto Bayer, but the work was not carried out in a systematic way: no written records of the excavations were kept, and after the completion of the work the site was simply abandoned. Not surprisingly, therefore, many of the finds were lost. Evidence of this was provided by the watercolours and descriptions of the German painter H. von Brockdorff, who was present during the excavations. Systematic investigation of the temple complex began only in 1933, after the National Museum in Valletta had acquired the site. Further excavations were carried out in 1953 and 1960–63.

The Ggantija complex consists of two adjoining temples. The South Temple is larger and older than the North Temple; the cloverleaf rear chamber is dated to 3600 BC, the double-apsed front chamber to 3200 BC, while the North Temple was built around 3000 BC. The two temples are surrounded by a common outer wall, built of huge stones which are laid alternately vertically and horizontally. The largest of the stones measures 5.70 m by 3.80 m and weighs 57 tons. The wall still stands to a height of 8 m and is estimated to have originally been 16 m high. The stones were brought from a quarry 5 km away on stone rollers and hoisted into position with the help of earth ramps. The space between the outer wall and the temples was filled in with gravel and earth.

Ggantija

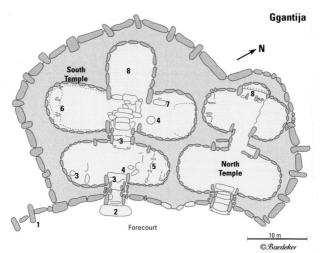

1 Remains of forecourt wall
2 Threshold stone
3 Libation holes
4 Hearth
5 Spiral patterns
6 Double trilithon altar
7 Bench altar with fragment
  of window stone
8 Holy of holies

While the megaliths in the outer wall are mostly undressed, the stones in the walls of the temples were carefully smoothed and sometimes elaborately decorated – a considerable achievement when it is remembered that the builders had only the simplest of stone tools. It was possible only because the softer yellowish globigerina limestone was used for the massive orthostats in the walls of the temples, the doorways and the altar and sacrificial stones rather than the coralline limestone of which the outer wall was built. The stones were then covered with a coat of reddish stucco of which only scanty remains have survived. The floors of the temples are of globigerina limestone or torba, a cement-like mixture of crushed limestone and water. The temples are thought to have had a timber roof. On an artificially built up terrace in front of the temples was an oval forecourt 40 m long surrounded by a high wall of which only fragments remain. The façades of the temples looking on to the forecourt originally met at an obtuse angle (some stones are now missing). To the left of the entrance to the South Temple the façade is still standing to a height of 6 m, and on a bench altar in front of this wall are a number of stone balls, thought to be remains of the rollers used to transport the huge stones.

In front of the South Temple is a massive threshold stone with a raised rim and traces of burning which indicate that it was an offering table. A passage flanked by orthostats leads into the temple. Immediately beyond the entrance is a square stone with a shallow cavity on top, evidently for libations. There is a similar libation dish hollowed out of a floor slab at the end of the corridor. On two stone blocks in the first apse on the right are spiral patterns in relief (in this room too there stood the orthostat with a carving of a snake which is now in the Archaeological Museum in Victoria: see sub-entry), and to the left is a well preserved torba floor. In the floor slabs of the short, slightly rising passage between the front and rear chambers of the temple are more libation

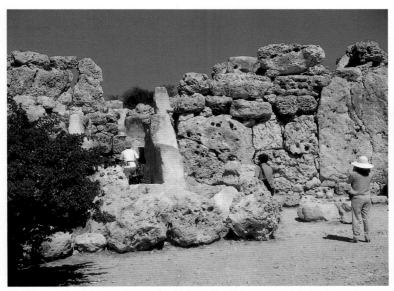

The outer walls of the temple complex of Ggnatija still just up to a height of 8 m. At one point they were probably 16 m high.

dishes. The cloverleaf rear chamber is 23 m wide. In the right-hand apse are a hearth, a bench altar and, to the rear, the remains of a window stone. In the left-hand apse is a two-storey trilithon altar, the top slab of which is missing. The uppermost course of the wall above the altar projects, as if it were the beginning of a dome. The builders of the temple did not possess the technical skills to construct a stone roof by this method, and the projecting stones were probably mountings for a roof of plaited branches smeared with clay and borne on timber beams. Unlike later temples, this temple has a central apse, probably the holy of holies to which only priests were admitted. In the floor in front of the threshold of this apse is an inscription in Phoenician characters.

Although the North Temple is smaller than the South Temple the oval front chamber is considerably larger than that of the South Temple. The central apse of the rear chamber is reduced to a shallow recess containing a reconstructed trilithon altar. Otherwise the temple is largely empty. In this temple too the orthostats are finely worked; some of them have holes for the insertion of cross slabs.

From Xaghra a road (signposted) runs north to Calypso's Cave, in a rocky bluff above the coast. Here, according to legend, the nymph Calypso detained Odysseus for seven years. After his ship was destroyed by lightning Odysseus drifted for nine days on a raft before landing on the fertile island of Ogygia, which the Gozitans at any rate are sure was Gozo. Finally Calypso was commanded by the gods to release him and he was able to return to Ithaca.   **Calypso's Cave**

The cave itself is not particularly impressive, and it is accessible only to experienced rock-climbers. There is, however, a marvellous view from the platform above the cave, extending over the fertile Ramla valley and Ramla Bay's beaches of fine sand. If the sea is sufficiently calm it is possible to see, some 30 m out to sea, the line of a wall running parallel to

From the rocky promontory near Calypso's Cave there are great views of Gozo's best beach, in Ramla Bay

the coast. The wall was built by the Knights about 1730 to keep pirates' ships at a distance. On either side of the bay were cavities in the rock filled with gunpowder and stones. When pirates appeared the powder was ignited and a hail of stones poured down on the unwelcome visitors.

★Ramla Bay

From Calypso's Cave there is a path down to Ramla Bay (by car, return along the road to Xaghra and take a side road signposted to Ramla Bay). This bay, 500 m long by 50 m wide, has by far the finest sandy beach on the island, if not in the whole of the Maltese archipelago. It tends to be crowded during the summer months, but in May and September you will have no difficulty in finding a quiet little corner of your own. During the main holiday season there are two modest restaurants and sun umbrellas can be hired.

Nadur

From Ramla Bay a road runs south-east to Nadur (pop. 3800), the second largest place on the island. It owes its name, derived from the Arabic word nadar ("viewpoint"), to its situation on one of Gozo's highest hills (160 m). From time immemorial Nadur has been the wealthiest place on Gozo, and accordingly the inhabitants are called by other Gozitans the Maltese of Nadur – which says something about the relationship between the people of Gozo and the inhabitants of the larger neighbouring island.

Nadur's parish church was built in the 18th century and much altered in the 20th.

San Blas Bay

To reach San Blas Bay, which has a good sandy beach, take the road which runs north from the town centre and park your car at the last houses in the town. From here a path runs down through fertile fruit orchards to San Blas Bay; the last section is quite steep. The beach is shorter and narrower than the beach in Ramla Bay and, unlike that beach, has no tourist facilities.

The bay of Dahiet Qorrot, 1 km farther east, is very different. Here fishing dominates the scene. There are quays and boat-sheds, and also a tiny and not particularly inviting beach. **Dahiet Qorrot**

The return to Mgarr can be by way of Qala, where there is a well preserved windmill dating from the second half of the 19th century. From the road which runs south-east from Qala to the sea there are fine views of Comino and Malta. It ends at Hondoq Bay which has a short artificial sand beach (with toilets, kiosk). **Qala**

Gzira   H 6

Gzira (pop. 7700) is part of the conurbation that has grown up round Valletta. To the north it runs into Sliema, to the south into Msida (see entries).
    The coast round Gzira has now been taken over by tourism. A broad promenade runs along the seafront, where many excursion ships anchor. The lower floors of many houses are used as retail outlets. The streets are lined with travel agencies, bars and shops. Gzira owes its name ("island") to little Manoel Island, which lies just offshore, linked with the mainland by a bridge.

Manoel Island is named after Grand Master Manoel de Vilhena, who in 1723 built Fort Manoel, at the eastern tip of the island, to protect the harbour area. Part of the **fort** is now occupied by Valletta Yacht Club, with a restaurant. **Manoel Island**
    Another attraction on Manoel Island is the **Phoenician Glassblowers** establishment, where visitors can watch the glassblowers at work and can buy their coloured glassware (open Mon.–Fri. 8am–4.30pm, Sat. 9am–12.30pm).
    The Knights used Manoel Island as a quarantine station, and in 1643 built a **hospital** on the side of the island facing Lazzaretto Creek. It was used until the middle of the 20th century but has now fallen into a state of dilapidation.
    Lazzaretto Creek, on the south-west side of the island, is a yachting harbour. Here too is a boatyard belonging to Malta Dockyards which builds yachts.

★★Hagar Qim · ★★Mnajdra   G 8

Hagar Qim ("stones of prayer"; pronounced "hajjar im") and Mnajdra ("view"; pronounced "imnai-dra") are two of the finest Neolithic temple complexes in the Maltese archipelago. The sites lie about 4 km south of the village of Siggiewi in a tract of almost entirely unspoiled country above Malta's rocky south coast. From Hagar Qim a footpath runs down for some 300 m to the equally impressive Neolithic site of Mnajdra. Open Oct.–Jun. 15th Mon.–Sat. 8.15am–5pm, Sun. 8.15am–4.15pm; Jun. 16th–Sep. daily 7.45am–2pm. The ticket gives admission to both sites.

The ★★Temple Complex of Hagar Qim

The first excavations were carried out in 1838 on the initiative of the

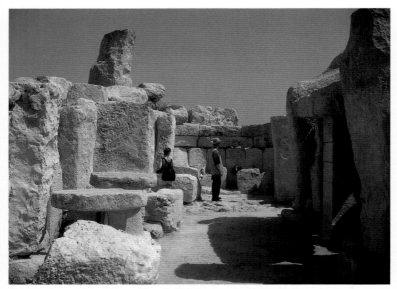

The temple complex of Hagar Qim – built to honour the Magna Mater

British governor, but the site was not completely excavated to display the temple complex as we see it today until 1909–10. The remains were restored and thoroughly surveyed in the 1950s.

The complex consists of three separate temples. Only the central temple is well preserved; the scanty remains of the other two lie close to it on the north and east.

The ground-plan of the Hagar Qim temples, which date from around 3000 BC, is markedly different from that of other Neolithic temples in Malta. Here a massive outer wall encloses a temple consisting of six oval chambers, with various subsidiary chambers and recesses. The outer wall is estimated to have had an original height of 8 m and several entrances, of which only one survives along with the façade of the complex.

The temple complex was built of soft globigerina limestone which has been much weathered, particularly on the seaward side.

The slightly curved façade of the temple complex faces south-east. It consists of a trilithon doorway flanked on either side by three huge and carefully dressed megalithic slabs. The slabs at the corners stand 3.50 m high and have notches near the top into which horizontal slabs fit exactly. Along the façade are bench altars, which probably extended originally round the whole of the outer wall. Even more massive than the stones on the façade is a monolith, set horizontally, on the east side of the complex. 6 m long, 3 m wide and 60 cm high, it is the largest block of stone found in any Neolithic temple. It is difficult to understand how the builders of the temple contrived to move this 60-ton monster with only the primitive means available to them.

Passing through the trilithon doorway (immediately in front of which is a threshold slab with holes for tethering sacrificial animals),

Hagar Qim

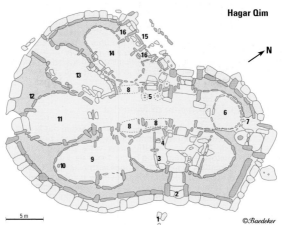

↗ N

1 Stone slab with holes
   for tethering animals
2 Trilithon doorway
3 Window stone
4 Altar with plant reliefs
5 Mushroom altar

6 Oracle chamber
7 Oracle hole
8 Trilithon altar
9 Chamber with torba floor
10 Limestone column
11 Circular chamber

12 Part of Magna Mater
   relief
13 First oval chamber
14 Second oval chamber
15 Threshold
16 Trilithon recess

©Baedeker

we enter a passage constructed of three pairs of orthostats. This leads into an oval chamber with intermediate walls separating the central part of the chamber from the rounded ends, which are entered through "window stones" (large slabs with a rectangular opening). In the window stones are holes for fixing a leather curtain or a wooden door. In the central part of the chamber are several small altars with narrow cavities and a reproduction of the famous altar from Hagar Qim, decorated with plant reliefs, which is now in the Archaeological Museum in Valletta. Behind the altar were found many figures of the Magna Mater, including the celebrated "Venus of Malta".

Three pairs of orthostats lead into the next large chamber, on the far side of which was the holy of holies (now a passage leading out of the temple complex). To the left are a number of "mushroom" altars with raised rims to prevent the blood of sacrificial animals from flowing on to the ground. Beside and opposite these altars, built into the walls, are tall trilithon altars. In the rounded right-hand end of the chamber the lower part of the wall is constructed of 18 orthostats about 1.50 m high, on top of which are two or three courses of horizontal slabs projecting slightly inward. In front of the wall is a circular arrangement of low stone slabs. In one of the stones in the wall is an oval hole opening into a small chamber, generally interpreted as an oracle hole. It is supposed that a priestess in this chamber communicated the oracular pronouncement through the hole to the worshippers assembled within the ring of low stones. At the south end of the large chamber modern steps lead into another chamber, also roughly oval, whose irregular plan is probably the result of later additions

Altar with plant reliefs

to the structure. The torba floor of the chamber is well preserved. On the south wall is a limestone column of unknown function.

Adjoining this chamber is another, on a roughly circular plan. This chamber and two other oval chambers could be entered only from outside. The stones lying on the floor probably came from the façade. On the outer wall of the circular chamber is a figure of the Magna Mater in low relief, now difficult to distinguish. The rear oval chamber is entered over a 65 cm high threshold flanked by two trilithon recesses.

The ★★Temples of Mnajdra

The first excavations at Mnajdra were carried out in 1840; but they were incompetently directed and the finds were not properly studied or catalogued. Thorough investigations were carried out in the 1920s by Themistocles Zammit and in the 1950s by J. D. Evans. Unfortunately, in 1996, vandals defaced the stones with black paint. Despite great efforts it has not been possible to remove the paint completely.

The Mnajdra complex consists of three adjoining temples unconnected with each other. Each temple had originally its own surrounding wall. In front of them was a common forecourt floored with stone slabs.

The oldest of the three is the East Temple, which is believed to date from around 3500 BC. After that came the West Temple, followed soon afterwards by the Central Temple, which is dated to 3000–2800 BC.

Mnajdra

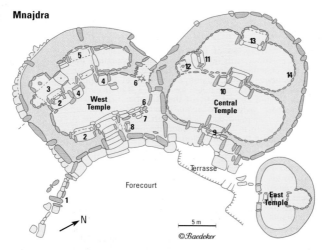

1 Remains of forecourt wall
2 Trilithon recesses
3 Chamber with three double trilithon altars
4 Slab altars
5 Central recess with trilithon altar
6 Oracle holes
7 Window stone
8 Window stone framed by trilithon, with pillared altar
9 Window stone entrance
10 Slab altar and orthostat with representation of temple front
11 Window stone
12 Chamber with pillared altar
13 Trilithon altar
14 Oracle hole

East Temple

The East Temple is the smallest and least well preserved of the temples. It consists of a single oval chamber with a central recess. The only original parts found in situ were one or two megaliths at the entrance and the central recess; other parts of the walls have been reconstructed.

Spectacular views over Malta's south coast from the Temples of Mnajdra – in the background the islet of Filfla

The Central Temple stands some 1.50 m above the level of the forecourt, with a terrace in front of it. The temple is entered through a large window stone. (Although window stones are found in most Neolithic temples, this is the only case in which a window stone serves as the entrance to a temple). The first, kidney-shaped chamber of the temple, walled by orthostats 1 m high, is empty apart from two recesses, one on either side of the entrance to the second chamber, containing slab altars 30 cm high. On an orthostat in the left-hand recess is an incised representation of a temple front.

Central Temple

   The torba floor of the second chamber is well preserved. Other features of this chamber are the trilithon altar in the central recess, an oracle hole in the right-hand apse and a finely dressed window stone in the left-hand apse leading into a small chamber with a pillared altar.

Unlike the Central Temple, the semicircular façade of the West Temple, with bench altars running along in front of it, is relatively well preserved. It has a trilithon entrance leading into the main chamber, 14 m long by 7 m across. In the right-hand apse the walls are preserved to a height of 4.30 m. The walls are built of orthostats supporting horizontal slabs which project inwards over one another, forming a support for some kind of roof structure. In the walls are two oracle holes. One of these, along with a window stone, leads into a chamber of some size between the main chamber and the outer wall containing a carefully dressed altar recess. Here a window stone is framed by a trilithon, with a pillared altar to the rear.

West Temple

   In the left-hand apse of the main chamber are three trilithon recesses, the one to the rear being dressed with particular care. Here too a window stone is closely fitted into a trilithon. To right and left are orthostats, which, like the window stone and the trilithon, are covered with pecked holes. The window stone leads into a chamber with three double trilithon altars. The one to the right abuts the end of the kidney-shaped rear chamber of the temple.

The rear chamber is also entered from the main chamber through a trilithon, on either side of which is a slab altar covered with pecked ornament. The central recess containing a trilithon altar is shallow compared with the two lateral apses.

Hal Saflieni (Hypogeum)

See Paola

Hamrun   H 6

The town of Hamrun (pop. 11 000), immediately south of Floriana, is part of the conurbation that has grown up round Valletta. It is the seat of Malta's College of Technology.

Hamrun has little to offer visitors. Its main street is lined by houses (many of them with the characteristic Maltese wooden oriel windows), small shops and craftsmen's workshops. There is a never-ending stream of traffic through the town. A prominent landmark is the early 20th century parish church of St Cajetan.

Kalkara   J 6

Kalkara (pop. 2800) lies on the most northerly of the promontories reaching out into the Grand Harbour. This former fishing village, almost completely destroyed during the Second World War, is still a haven and shipyard for luzzus (Maltese plural luzzi), the brightly painted Maltese fishing boats, and dghajsas, the rather larger boats used for coastal traffic.

Bighi Hospital

Kalkara is dominated by the former Royal Navy Hospital, a neo-classical building on Bighi Hill at the end of the promontory. A 17th century palace which originally stood here was converted into a naval hospital by Nelson in 1805. After various alterations and extensions the side wings were added about 1840. During the Second World War it still served as a hospital; it is now occupied by government offices.

Fort Ricasoli

On a promontory opposite Fort St Elmo is Fort Ricasoli, built by the Knights in 1670 to guard the entrance to the harbour. It is now largely ruined.

Fort Rinella

A few hundred yards further to the south-east is Fort Rinella, a fortification built in the second half of the 19th century. It has been restored and can be visited (open Oct.–mid-Jun. daily 10am–4pm; mid-Jun.–Sep. daily 9.30am–1pm). The main attraction in the fort is the supposedly largest cannon in the world: the 100-tons monster, however, never had to prove its worth.

Rinella Movie Park

The Rinella Movie Park surrounding Fort St Rocco was opened in 1998 and offers entertainment for the whole family (open Wed.–Sun. 10am–10pm). Everything here revolves around film, as the name indicates. Beyond the entrance gates, different films are shown in several exhibition halls, while in the park itself other performances take place, for example a simulated sinking of the Titanic in a specially constructed

The Rinella Movie Park: several times a day the show "That's Entertainment" is being performed on this reproduction of Columbus' ship

building. Of course there are also restaurants and bars for refreshments, and the admission ticket includes a visit to the adjoining sets of the Mediterranean Film Studios (FS). A little train takes you there and en route you will be informed on the various important films that have been shot here in the 35 years of the studios' existence, including "Midnight Express" and "Christophorus Columbus". A speciality of the studios is the large water basin where scenes at sea – with the ocean in the background – are easily filmed. From Valletta you can reach the film studios on bus No. 4 which leaves from the bus station; there are also bus shuttle services from some of the hotels in Bugibba and Sliema.

Laferla Cross

See Siggiewi

Lija   G 6

Lija (pop. 2500) is part of the built-up area a few kilometres west of Valletta known as the "Three Villages" (the other villages being Balzan and Attard: see entries).

Lija has long been a favoured residential area. It has preserved a number of handsome 18th century country villas. In the main square is the parish church of St Saviour (1694), an early work by Giovanni Barbara in a plain Baroque style.

Luqa

Our Lady of
Miracles

In the Tal-Mirakli district to the west of the town centre, at the geographical centre of the island, is the church of Our Lady of Miracles (Tal-Mirakli), which dates in its present form from the mid-17th century. The altarpiece, painted by Mattia Preti for Grand Master Nicola Cotoner, depicts the Virgin and Child with St Nicholas and St Peter, the patron saints of the Grand Master and his brother Raphael.

Luqa   H 7

Luqa (pop. 6000) lies in the centre of Malta, 6 km west of Valletta. It is known mainly for its international airport, whose runways are immediately south of the town.

Luqa is named after Luke the Evangelist, who is said to have been shipwrecked on Malta along with St Paul in AD 60 and to have preached the Gospel in this area.

St Mary's Church

On the road from Luqa to Gudja, shortly before Gudja, is the little 15th century Gothic church of St Mary (St Marija ta'Bir Miftuh), which has early 17th century wall paintings.

Marfa Ridge   D/E 3/4

★Scenery

The Marfa Ridge is a low range of hills running from east to west at the north-western tip of Malta. There are no remains of Malta's past in this area, but instead it offers landscapes, sparsely covered by vegetation though they are, of unspoiled natural beauty. A narrow road runs along the 5 km long ridge, with charming views at many points. A number of side roads on the north side run down to various small coves.

Paradise Bay

Although Paradise Bay does not quite live up to its name, its 100 m long sandy beach is, by Maltese standards, a very attractive place to bathe. From the car park above Paradise Bay steps lead down to the beach at the foot of the cliffs. There is a small restaurant.

Cirkewwa
Marfa Point

Cirkewwa (Marfa Point) is the departure point of the ferry to Gozo (see Practical Information, Ferries and Shipping Services). Smaller boats take passengers to bathe in the Blue Lagoon on Comino (see entry).

Ramla Bay

Little Ramla Bay is mainly used by residents in Ramla Bay Hotel, but it is a public beach open to all (pedalos, wind-surfing school).

Armier Bay

Armier Bay, with a 100 m long sandy beach, also offers good bathing. There are restaurants and changing cabins.

White Tower Bay

The containers and wooden shacks in White Tower Bay make this a less attractive beach for bathers. The tower from which it takes its name is private property.

Marsa   H 6

At the south end of the Grand Harbour is the town of Marsa (pop. 5300). The history of the town began in 1860, when the British authorities declared French Creek a closed area and to replace it as a commercial harbour dredged out Marsa Creek (the name Marsa means "harbour"). Soon industrial firms began to establish themselves in the area, and Marsa is still one of the most important industrial zones in Malta.

On the south-western outskirts of the town is the Marsa Sports Club, with a golf course, a racecourse, a football pitch, tennis courts and other sports facilities.

Marsaskala   K 7

On the north-east coast of Malta, at the head of Marsaskala Bay, a fjord-like inlet, is the fishing town of Marsaskala (pop. 4700), which in recent years has increasingly been taken over by the tourist trade. The best bathing here is in St Thomas Bay, to the south of the town (shelving rock).

The houses of Marsaskala reach along the shores of Marsaskala Bay and are now extending on to the peninsula to the south. There are still only a few large hotels and apartment blocks, and Marsaskala retains much of its character as a Maltese fishing village, with its brightly painted boats at anchor in the sheltered bay. Although it does not come up to the standard of Marsaxlokk (see entry), it has the advantage of being quieter. It is planned to develop the town as a tourist centre; the first evidence of this is the promenade running round Marsaskala Bay.

At the tip of the peninsula between Marsaskala Bay and St Thomas Bay is Fort St Thomas, built after the Turkish raid of 1614 when Zejtun (see entry) was looted. It now houses a restaurant.

Fort St Thomas

Marsaxlokk   J 7/8

Marsaxlokk (pronounced "marsashlock"; pop. 2800) is a very picturesque little fishing town in a bay on the east coast of Malta which attracts large numbers of day trippers, both local people and foreign visitors. For their benefit a market is held every day in the morning and early afternoon on the seafront promenade, selling mainly clothing, household linen, leather goods and souvenirs.

Marsaxlokk ("harbour of the warm wind") has on more than one occasion played a prominent role in Maltese history. Here Turkish forces landed in 1565, and here too French troops came ashore on June 10th 1798. More recently Marsaxlokk was the scene of a summit meeting between US President Bush and Soviet President Gorbachev in December 1989.

With its small, typically Maltese houses, Marsaxlokk has preserved much of its original character. There are no large hotels, and the scene is still dominated by the many brightly painted fishing boats (luzzi) in the spacious harbour. An eye is almost always painted on the bow of the boats to protect the fishermen from the evil eye of the Devil – a tradition which goes back to Phoenician times. In the background of the picturesque scene round the harbour is the parish church of Our Lady of Pompeii.

Town

Marsaxlokk Bay is bounded on the north-east by the Delimara peninsula. A new power station on the west side of the peninsula adds little to the scenery. The west side is scenically more attractive: here you can bathe in the crystal-clear water or sunbathe on the shelving rock. Particularly attractive is Peter's Pool. At the southern tip of the peninsula is Fort Delimara, which was built during the period of British rule; it is not open to the public.

Delimara Point

North-east of Marsaxlokk, on both sides of the road from Zejtun to Delimara, is the excavation site of Tas-Silg, hidden behind walls; it is

Tas-Silg

113

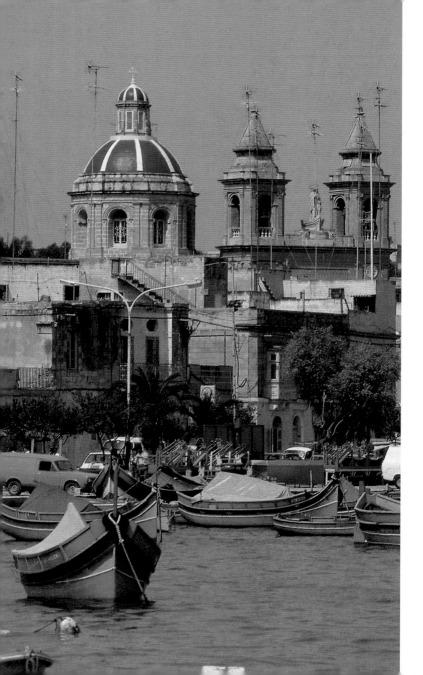

usually not open to the public. Here the excavators discovered remains of a Neolithic temple with two kidney-shaped chambers. On its foundations was built during the Phoenician and Carthaginian period a temple dedicated to the fertility goddess Astarte, which in turn gave place in Roman times to a temple of Juno. Remains of a baptistery with its font were dated to the 4th century AD.

At the tip of the peninsula which projects into Marsaxlokk Bay to the south of the town is St Lucian's Fort, built by Grand Master Alof de Wignacourt in 1611. It now houses a research institute and is not open to the public.

St Lucian's Fort

Mdina   F 6

Mdina, Malta's former capital, situated in the centre of the island, is one of its most rewarding sights. With its palaces, churches and religious houses the town, which has a population of only 360, has still a medieval air. This impression is reinforced by the almost total absence of motor traffic and the small number of shops, cafés and restaurants. The names applied to the town in earlier centuries – Città Notabile, the Noble City, and Città Vecchia, the Old City – are still entirely appropriate. Mdina is prominently situated at an altitude of 185 m on an outcrop of the Dingli plateau. On the east, north and north-east are steeply scarped slopes which in the past provided protection against unwelcome visitors; on the south and south-west sides it is separated from the newer neighbouring town of Rabat (see entry) by a beautifully laid out green belt with flowerbeds, benches and a café.

The strategic importance of the site was recognised from the earliest times. There are traces of human settlement as far back as the Bronze Age. Around 1000 BC the Phoenicians are thought to have fortified the town, which they called Malet ("place of refuge"). This became Melita under the Romans, who surrounded the town and the neighbouring town of Rabat with massive walls. In those days the town was three times its present size. The name Mdina ("walled town") was given by the Arabs, who captured Malta in 870. To improve the town's defensive strength they reduced it to about its present size. Outside the walls of Mdina there continued to exist the more or less independent settlement to which they gave the name of Rabat. During the period of Norman rule (1090–1194) the walls were rebuilt and strengthened. In 1422 they withstood an attack by a force of 18,000 Turks: whereupon Alfonso of Aragon granted Mdina the style of Città Notabile. After the Knights of St John took control of Malta the importance of Mdina declined: after a brief period (1530–32) during which the Knights ruled the island from Mdina the headquarters of the Order were moved to Birgu. During the Great Siege of 1565 the town again played an important role: a number of successful sorties against the Turks were mounted from here, and communications with Sicily were maintained through Mdina. Thereafter, although Malta's noble families continued to live in Mdina and the town remained the seat of the Università, the self-governing institution of the nobility, the population steadily declined as the new capital, Valletta, began to flourish in the late 16th century. To the Knights Mdina was Città Vecchia, the Old City. In a severe earthquake which devastated Sicily and Malta in 1693 most of the buildings in the town were destroyed. The town was rebuilt by Grand Master Manoel de Vilhena. In June 1798 Mdina surrendered to the French without a fight but rebelled against the occupying forces when they continued to loot churches and religious

History

◀ *The picturesque harbour of Marsaxlokk, with its colourful Luzzi, the traditional Maltese fishing boats*

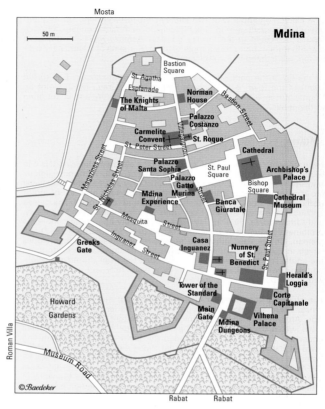

Mdina

houses and thus started the resistance against the French occupiers. It lost all political importance in 1814, when the British authorities dissolved the Università, whose rights had already been curtailed. Thereafter there were practically no alterations to the old buildings of Mdina, and life increasingly moved to neighbouring Rabat.

Town

Even from a distance Mdina, with its massive walls rising high above the plain, is an imposing sight; and this first impression is confirmed on a closer acquaintance with this little Baroque city with its palaces, churches and religious houses of yellowish limestone and its narrow lanes, in which time seems to stand still. Visitors will be struck not only by the magnificence of the buildings themselves but also by a host of details (door-knockers, ornament of windows, etc.).

There are three entrances into the town, which is ringed by massive bastions. Two of them, the Greeks' Gate and the Main Gate, date in their present form from the time of Grand Master Vilhena; the third was broken through the west wall at the end of the 19th century to give direct access to the railway station. The best starting-point for a tour of Mdina is the Main Gate, which is approached over a bridge. The distances are short, and the sights can all be seen on foot without any difficulty – and

Mdina: massive walls enclose the old capital. Here a view of the cathedral.

there are always horse-drawn carriages waiting outside the gate whose drivers are very ready to offer their services.

The Main Gate, in the form of a triumphal arch, was built by Grand Master Manoel de Vilhena in 1724, replacing an older gate approached by a drawbridge of which traces can be seen near the present gate. Above the gateway is Grand Master Vilhena's coat of arms. On the inner side are the arms of the Inguanez family, one of the town's oldest and most influential noble families, and statues of the Apostle Paul, St Publius and St Agatha. When a new Grand Master was appointed he was received at the Main Gate by representatives of the Università's, who, after receiving confirmation of the Università's rights and privileges from him, symbolically offered him the keys of the city.

Main Gate

Inside the gate is a small square, on the left-hand side of which is the 16th century Tower of the Standard. Once a watch- and signal-tower, it now houses the police station.

Tower of the Standard

Immediately to the right of the gate steps lead down to the entrance of the Mdina Dungeons. In the medieval prison, the torture methods used in past centuries are represented by tableaux in a surprisingly realistic manner (open daily 10am–6pm, in summer till 7pm) – not for the feeble-hearted!

Mdina Dungeons

A gate leads into the grand courtyard of the Vilhena Palace, a richly decorated Baroque town palace built for Grand Master Vilhena about 1730 by Giovanni Barbara. Round the grand courtyard are the three wings of the palace, with decorated plaster façades. In 1908 the British authorities converted the palace into a hospital, which continued in operation until 1956. Then in 1973 it became the Natural History Museum (open Jun. 16th–Sep. Daily 7.45am–2pm; Oct.–Jun. 15th Mon.–Sat. 8.15am–5pm,

Vilhena Palace/Natural History Museum

Sun. 8.15am–4.15pm), with numerous rooms displaying insects, birds, shellfish, fish and mammals found in and around the Maltese islands. There are also extensive collections of material on Maltese geology and mineralogy.

Nunnery of St Benedict

To the north of the Vilhena Palace is the Nunnery of St Benedict, founded in 1418. This is a fully enclosed order: the nuns may never leave the convent. Until 1974 this rule applied even after their death, and the nuns were buried in the convent.

St Agatha's Chapel

St Agatha's Chapel in Villegaignon Street (named after a French knight who organised the defence of the town against the Turks in 1551) is incorporated in the same building as the Benedictine nunnery. Originally dating from 1417, the chapel was rebuilt by Lorenzo Gafà in 1694.

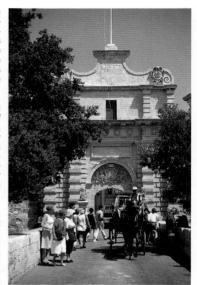

The Main Gate in Mdina

St Benedict's Chapel

Immediate beyond St Agatha's Chapel is the chapel of St Benedict, a plain building which has an altarpiece of the Virgin with saints by Mattia Preti.

Casa Inguanez

Opposite St Benedict's Chapel is the Casa Inguanez. The coat of arms of this ancient noble family, now extinct, is on the Main Gate. The palace was built about 1370 but much altered in later centuries. King Alfonso V of Aragon stayed in the palace in 1432, as did King Alfonso XIII of Spain in 1927.

Mdina Experience

Mesquita Street, on the left, leads to Mesquita Square, in which, at No. 7, is the Mdina Experience (open Mon.–Fri. 10.30am–4pm, Sat. 10.30am–2pm), an audio-visual show which brings to life the history of Mdina from its origins to the present day.

Banca Giuratale

Now return to Villegaignon Street. Farther along this street, on the right, is the Banca Giuratale. Formerly the seat of the Università, it was built by Manoel de Vilhena about 1730.

Palazzo Gatto Murina/Tales of the Silent City

An exhibition in the Palazzo Gatto Murina opposite, dating back to the 14th century, also tells of Mdina's history (Tales of the Silent City; open daily 9.30am–4.30pm).

★Cathedral

Beyond the Banca Giuratale is St Paul's Square, on the east side of which is the Cathedral, dedicated to St Paul (open Mon.–Sat. 9.30–11.45am and 2–5pm; Sun. 3–4.30pm). It is the master work of Lorenzo Gafà, who was commissioned to build it in 1697. Its 12th century predecessor, in Sicilian/Norman style, had been destroyed in the 1693 earthquake apart from the sacristy and the choir. The restrained Baroque façade with its twin towers is articulated by Corinthian pilasters and its two-storey structure. The central section is topped by a triangular pediment. Above the main doorway is the town's coat of arms, flanked by the arms of Grand Master Perellos y Roccaful (1697–1720) and Bishop Cocco-Palmieri (1687–1713), who consecrated the Cathedral in 1702.

The Cathedral, on a Latin cross plan with lateral aisles flanking the nave, is entered through the side door on the right. The order of pilasters on the façade is continued as a decorative system in the interior. The barrel vaulting, dome over the crossing, semi-dome of the apse and domed side chapels exemplify the Baroque liking for domed structures. The floor of the Cathedral is covered with the richly decorated grave slabs of the spiritual and secular aristocracy of Mdina in coloured marble inlay work. The vaulting has paintings by the Sicilian artists Vincenzo and Antonio Manno depicting scenes from the lives of St Peter and St Paul. The painting in the dome, the work of a Turin artist, dates only from 1955.

The sacristy door, of Irish bog oak carved with animal motifs in the Nordic tradition, came from the main doorway of the original Norman cathedral and dates from the 12th/13th century. The high altar is inlaid with lapis lazuli and marble. The fresco in the apse of "St Paul Shipwrecked", by Mattia Preti, came from the original cathedral; the altarpiece depicting the conversion of St Paul is also by Preti. The choir-stalls are 18th century, with 19th century inlay work. In the Chapel of the Blessed Sacrament are a Byzantine icon of the Virgin and a silver tabernacle by the 16th century Florentine sculptor and goldsmith Benvenuto Cellini (1500–1571).

Adjoining the south front of the Cathedral is the Archbishop's Palace (1722).

Archbishop's Palace

Bird's eye view of Mdina

Mdina

Cathedral Museum

Opposite the side entrance to the Cathedral is the Cathedral Museum (open Mon.–Fri. 9am–4.30pm, Sat. 9am–2pm; admission charge includes admission to St John's Co-Cathedral Museum in Valletta), housed in a Baroque building (by Giovanni Barbara, between 1733 and 1740) which was originally a seminary. The nucleus of the Museum, founded at the end of the 19th century, was the art collection of Count Saverio Marchese (1757–1833), but it also includes paintings by Maltese, Italian and Flemish artists of the 14th–19th centuries, a collection of coins, liturgical books and old documents. Unexpectedly, the Museum also has many engravings and woodcuts by Dürer, including a complete set of the 22 engravings of his "Life of the Virgin" (1511) and 37 wood-cuts of the "Little Passion" (1509–11; six are 16th century copies), as well as graphic work by pupils of Dürer (including Hans Schäufelein and Hans Baldung Grien).

Palazzo Santa Sophia

Diagonally across Villegaignon Street from the Cathedral is the Palazzo Santa Sophia, believed to be the oldest building in Mdina. The ground floor, in Sicilian/Norman style with beautiful Romanesque arches, dates from the 13th century (the date 1233 on the façade, a later addition, may not be correct), the upper floor only from 1938.

Carmelite Church and Convent

Farther along Villegaignon Street, on the left, is the Carmelite convent, built between 1630 and 1690. This was the starting-point of the rebellion against the French in 1798 when French troops tried to seize the church treasury.

Chapel of St Roque

Opposite the Carmelite convent is the little chapel of St Roque (Roch), dedicated to the saint invoked to protect against the pest and other epidemics, which dates in its present form from 1728.

Palazzo Costanzo/ Medieval Times

On the ground floor of the Palazzo Costanzo, also in Villegaignon Street, is a restaurant with a shady inner courtyard. On the upper floor is the Medieval Times exhibition, with 15 scenes of medieval life (open Mon.–Sat. 9.30am–9.30pm, Sun. 9.30am–8pm).

★Norman House

The Norman House (Palazzo Falzon), at the north end of Villegaignon Street, is the best preserved medieval building in Mdina. While the upper floor with its double windows dates only from the end of the 15th century, parts of the ground floor are much earlier (1095); the zigzag moulding on the façade is a Norman feature. The building, now run by a trust, has been thoroughly renovated and is open to the public (open Mon.–Fri. 9am–1pm and 4–5.30pm; if door is not open, ring). The house is completely furnished in the styles of the 16th–18th centuries, with furniture, paintings, glass, china and weapons. There is a very picturesque inner courtyard dating from the late 16th century.

Bastion Square

Villegaignon Street ends in Bastion Square, with trees, benches and magnificent views of the surrounding country which may tempt visitors to linger after their sightseeing.

The Knights of Malta

The exhibition "The Knights of Malta" is housed in the former powder stores which are incorporated into the fortification walls, not far south-west of Bastion Square (open Mon.–Fri. 10.30am–4pm, Sat. 10.30am–3pm). Around 120 life-sized figures illustrate the history of the Knights.

From here the tour continues along Bastion Street, which runs along the walls on the east side of the town. A short distance along the street are the Fontanella Tea Gardens, with a terrace on the walls of a bastion from which there are fine views of the north and east of the island. Beyond the Cathedral we come into St Paul Street.

Herald's Loggia

St Paul Street runs into a small square, on the east side of which is the

Herald's Loggia. From the balcony of this building the decrees of the Università were announced.

On the south side of the square is part of the Vilhena Palace (see sub-entry) which served as a courthouse, the Corte Capitanale. The two figures above the doorway symbolise Mercy and Justice; above them is the motto "Legibus et armis" ("By laws and by arms").

Corte Capitanale

Mellieha   E 4

With a population of around 6000, Mellieha is the largest town in north-western Malta. The town centre is well supplied with restaurants and shops. There was a settlement here in the 15th century but it was abandoned in the 16th century because of repeated raids by pirates. The town was re-established only in the mid-19th century.
   The old town of Mellieha, situated on a hill which falls steeply down to Mellieha Bay, has preserved its authentic character; in recent years, however, many new hotels and apartment blocks have been built in the outer districts, particularly along Mellieha Bay. In the centre of the town is the neo-Baroque parish church, a prominent landmark which was built only in 1948. From the terrace beside the church there are fine views of the surrounding country.

Under the church is the rock church of St Marija, a popular place of pilgrimage with an image of the Virgin painted directly on the rock which according to local tradition was created in the 4th century but which probably dates in fact from the 11th or 12th century. Even before the Knights came to Malta this was a place of pilgrimage. The chancel is still in its original form, but the walls of the nave were faced with marble in 1644. In the sacristy, which is hewn from the rock, are large numbers of votive offerings.

St Marija

Not far north of Mellieha is the wide reach of Mellieha Bay, which has one of the longest and finest sandy beaches on the island. The only trouble is that the main road runs directly above the beach.
   On the other side of the road is the Ghadira bird sanctuary, an area of wetland which offers ideal nesting conditions for rare species of birds (not open to the public).

Mellieha Bay

Popeye Village – perhaps the most interesting sight for children in the whole of Malta – lies in Anchor Bay, 3 km north-west of Mellieha (opening times daily 9am–7pm, in winter to 5pm)
   This little village of brightly painted wooden houses was built in 1979 as the set for Robert Altman's film "Popeye", starring Robin Williams and Shelley Duvall, the timber required being shipped in directly from Canada. After shooting finished in June 1980 it was decided to turn the set into a tourist attraction. Most of the houses cannot be entered, but children will delight in climbing on to the verandas or the lookouts on the roofs of some of the houses. Those who want only to take a photograph of a romantic little fishing village do not need to pay the fairly high admission charge: the best view of the village, free of charge, is from the south end of Anchor Bay.

Popeye Village

Above Mellieha to the east, in a bare and rocky landscape, is Selmun Palace. Now part of a hotel, it was built in the 18th century for the Knights of St John by Domenico Cachia, who, taking the Verdala Palace as his model, created a fortress-like building with corner towers and a battered substructure. The state apartments are on the upper floor, round which runs a balcony. Originally designed as a summer residence, it was never used as such by the Knights but was leased out, with the surrounding country, as a hunting lodge.

Selmun Palace

Popeye Village in Anchor Bay, once used as a film set, is a favourite children's attraction.

Mgarr   E 5

Mgarr (pronounced "mjarr") is a village of 2700 inhabitants in north-western Malta. In the centre of the village is the modern domed parish church, which was financed by contributions from the parishioners. Visitors usually make only a brief stop in Mgarr to see the (not particularly well preserved) temple of Ta Hagrat.

Ta Hagrat

The Neolithic temple complex of Ta Hagrat ("the stones") is reached by turning off the road from Zebbieh at the entrance to the village, just beyond the school, into a road on the left. The site is fenced in and is normally not open to the public; the key can be obtained at the Archaeological Museum in Valletta. For most visitors, however, a glance through the gate is sufficient.

Excavations in 1923 and 1925 brought to light two adjoining temples which were dated to around 3600/3500 BC, ranking them among the oldest monuments of the megalithic culture in Malta. For the ground plan, see History of Maltese Art. The irregularly shaped lateral "apses" of the smaller and older temple are reminiscent of the rock-hewn tombs of the Neolithic period; the larger temple is more like other Neolithic temples. From a forecourt steps lead up to the trilithon doorway, which gives access to the rectangular central chamber, floored with a single stone slab. Off this chamber, entered through a doorway formed by two orthostats, are three apse-like chambers of different sizes. Immediately left of the entrance is another chamber, probably a later addition.

Mnajdra

See Hagar Qim · Mnajdra

"The Maltese Falcon. . ."

. . .and "The Falcon's Maltese" – confusing, isn't it? The solution to this riddle: both are the titles of crime thrillers (one also exists in a filmed version), in which fearless detectives search for an item of great value.

The novel "The Maltese Falcon", written in 1930 by Dashiell Hammett, tells of the search for a golden falcon, richly bedecked with precious gemstones. The falcon was supposed to have been a gift from the Knights to Emperor Charles V, in gratitude for his generous presentation of the perpetual fiefs of Malta and Tripoli (North Africa) to the homeless Knights, subject only to the condition that, every year on All

better as their feudal duty than an unassuming falcon. Instead, so it is said, they sent him a valuable bird sculpture. However, this precious treasure never arrived at the Spanish court. For a long time, the falcon statuette was regarded as lost. It did not appear again until the 1920s in the USA, where a gangster boss, a shady loner and a young, beautiful woman attempted to seize it, not shying away from murder in its pursuit. Sam Spade, a small private detective, accidentally becomes entangled in the chase while pursuing a routine case. He finally succeeds in obtaining the falcon – only to find that he has acquired a copy made from lead.

Scene from "The Maltese Falcon" with Humphrey Bogart, Peter Lorre, Mary Astor and Sidney Greenstreet

Director John Huston filmed the story in 1941, and as in the original novel, he placed the emphasis on the pessimism, disillusion, cynicism and unscrupulousness that determine the battle for existence, and for big money. His film debut made him famous overnight, and he is credited with starting the American "film noir".

Saints Day, the Spanish court be honoured with the symbolic donation of a Maltese falcon. When the Knights had accumulated great wealth in their plundering raids against the Saracens, they decided to send Emperor Charles something

In the year 1986, Anthony Horowitz published his book "The Falcon's Malteser" – this book, however, is a parody of the "black series" and "film noir" with actors such as Humphrey Bogart, James Cagney and others.

Mosta   F/G 5/6

Mosta, 15 km south-west of Valletta, is a busy little town of some 17,000 inhabitants. Since it is an important road junction its streets are crowded with endless columns of cars at peak times.

Mosta has retained much of its original character. Most of its shops are round the large square in front of the church and along Constitution Street (Triq-il-Kostituzzoni), and the main bus station and car parking facilities are also in the square.

★Rotunda · Santa Marija Assunta

The people of Mosta proudly claim that they have the third largest domed church in Europe; and certainly the dome of their church of the Assumption, usually known simply as the Rotunda, is of impressive dimensions, with a height of 60 m and a diameter of 52 m. The church was built between 1833 and 1871 to the design of the Maltese architect Grognet de Vassé, who took as his model the Pantheon in Rome. The portico of six paired Ionic columns is flanked (as the Pantheon still was in the 19th century) by two tall bell-towers. The church was financed by contributions from the people of Mosta, who also contributed their labour. For the sake of economy the whole church, including the dome, was built without the use of scaffolding.

The interior of the church (open daily 9am–noon and 3–5pm), which can accommodate a congregation of 12,000 is decorated in blue, white and gold. The paintings by Giuseppe Cali (early 20th c.) depict scenes from the life of Christ, from the Nativity to the Ascension.

In the sacristy is preserved a German bomb from the Second World War, commemorating what was regarded as a miracle. In 1942 three bombs hit the church during a service. One of them pierced the dome but did not explode, and not one of the congregation of 300 was injured.

Victoria Lines

At the northern town exit, along the road to St Paul's Bay, a section of the Victoria Lines was restored and incorporated into the green belt around the Salvatore Dimech Crafts & Artisan School. The Victoria Lines are fortification lines running across the entire island. In order to be able to defend the northern tip of the island with its many bays, the British built a fortification belt on the ridge of a mountain range, which stretched from Fomm ir-Rih Bay in the north-west to the north-eastern coast near Madliena, in around 1880. Several forts and trenches secured the fortifications.

Fort Mosta

Fort Mosta, only a few hundred yards east of the art academy, is one of the forts built in the 19th century along the Victoria Lines. Today the fort is used as a barracks and as the base for the police dogs. The fort can be visited with guided tours (daily 9.30, 10.30 and 11.30am). Admission includes a visit to a small tomb from early Christian times and a storage silo dating back to the Bronze Age.

Msida   H 6

Msida (pop. 6800) lies on Msida Creek, at the south-western tip of Marsamxett Harbour. It is now a residential district occupied by workers in the local industries as well as the seat of the University of Malta, founded in 1769 and now installed in new premises on the hill of Tal-Qroqq.

A building of gigantic proportions: the Rotunda in Mosta

The most attractive part of Msida is round the harbour, where numbers of luxurious yachts are moored, with the 19th century parish church of St Joseph in the background. In Birkirkara Road is an 18th century wash-house built by a German knight called Guttenberg out of sympathy with the women who had to do their washing in all weathers at the fountain of Ghajn tal-Hasselin.

There is a very select residential area on the Ta'Xbiex (pronounced "ta shbiesh") peninsula, on the borders of Msida and Gzira (see entry). A walk through its quiet streets, many of them tree-lined, will reveal some sumptuous villas, often now the residences of foreign ambassadors.

Between Msida and Floriana is the district of Pietà. In Pietà Creek is the landing-stage used by the Gozo ferry, and to the south of this is the little chapel of Our Lady of Sorrows, which dates from the late 16th century.

Pietà

Naxxar   G 5

Naxxar (pop. 9700) lies in the centre of Malta, 10 km south-west of Valletta. This little agricultural town is increasingly becoming a sought-after residential area for families who find the rents in Sliema and other coastal towns too high.

The first two weeks of July are a time of great activity in Naxxar, when Malta's International Trade Fair is held here.

Naxxar

Our Lady of Victories

The parish church of Our Lady of Victories in the centre of the village, originally a small. plain church (built 1616), was enlarged in the early 20th century by the addition of two lateral aisles and an outsize façade. Palazzo Parisio

Palazzo Parisio

Another prominent feature in the village is the Palazzo Parisio, opposite the church, built in the first half of the 18th century for Grand Master Vilhena. There are guided tours to the privately owned palace (Tue., Thur., Fri. 9am–1pm).

San Pawl Tat-Targa

In the district of San Pawl Tat-Targa, north of the town centre, are a 17th century chapel and a statue of 1770 – reminders that the Apostle Paul is believed to have preached the Gospel here (see Baedeker Special). He was said to have preached so loudly that his words could be heard on Gozo. Near here are two watch-towers erected by the Knights, Gauci's Tower and the Captain's Tower (both are privately owned and cannot be visited).

Carts ruts

At the far end of San Pawl Tat-Targa, on the left of the road to Bugibba, are well preserved Bronze Age "cart ruts".

Paola   H/J 6/7

Paola (pop. 9300), 5 km south-east of Valletta, takes its name from Grand Master Antoine de Paule, who founded the town in the 17th century. Its great tourist attraction, in the Hal Saflieni district, is the labyrinth of caves known as the Hypogeum. Only a few minutes' walk away is the Neolithic temple complex of Tarxien (see entry), with which Paola is now joined in a single built-up area.

★★Hypogeum of Hal Saflieni

At present closed The entrance to the Hypogeum of Hal Saflieni is in Burial Street. These underground cult chambers are considered to be one of Malta's most important sights, and in 1980, they were declared a World Cultural Heritage Sigth by UNESCO. In recent years the climate in the underground caves of the Hypogeum has seriously deteriorated as a result of the hordes of visitors, and high humidity has caused the growth of lichens on the walls. Restoration work has been in progress now for many years, and the re-opening of the Hypogeum has been announced for the new millennium.

In the entrance hall to the Hypogeum is a small museum, with a model of the complex and objects (mainly copies) recovered by excavation.

To explore the Hypogeum properly it is essential to have stout footwear and a pocket torch.

The Hypogeum is a labyrinth of caves on three different levels with a total area of 500 sq. m. Its 33 chambers and recesses, hewn with primitive tools from the soft globigerina limestone, reach down to a depth of 11 m.

The caves on the uppermost level were constructed first, the walls of the simple burial chambers being only roughly dressed. The "main floor" seems to have been the second level with its more carefully constructed cult chambers. A flight of irregular steps leads down to the third level. It is notable that all the chambers in the Hypogeum are either oval or almost circular: there are no straight lines, and even the roofs of the caves are slightly vaulted. Most of the chambers painted a reddish ochre colour; some also had various signs and ornaments, mostly in red – a colour inter-

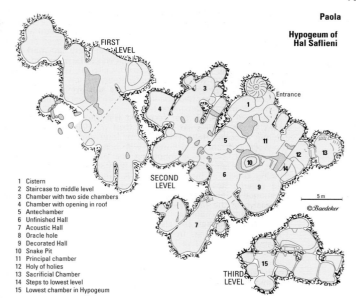

FIRST LEVEL

SECOND LEVEL

Entrance

THIRD LEVEL

5 m

©Baedeker

1 Cistern
2 Staircase to middle level
3 Chamber with two side chambers
4 Chamber with opening in roof
5 Antechamber
6 Unfinished Hall
7 Acoustic Hall
8 Oracle hole
9 Decorated Hall
10 Snake Pit
11 Principal chamber
12 Holy of holies
13 Sacrificial Chamber
14 Steps to lowest level
15 Lowest chamber in Hypogeum

preted as a symbol of rebirth. Traces of paint can still be seen at some points.

All the evidence – the structure of the Hypogeum and the objects found in it – suggests that this underground complex belonged to the same culture as the megalithic monuments on the surface. The earliest caves are believed to have been constructed about 3800 BC, and the Hypogeum remained in use until the end of Malta's megalithic culture about 2500 BC.

History

In the Hypogeum were found the remains of over 7000 individuals, and the many separate bones found suggest that more than 30,000 people may have been buried here. A striking feature is that among all the skeletons only one has been certainly identified as that of a man. It may be, therefore, that this was the burial-place of a particular caste, the priestesses of the various temples.

The Hypogeum was not, however, merely a place of burial. The larger rooms, highly finished, on the middle level served cult purposes. The divinity worshipped may have been the Magna Mater, the creator of all life, who here received the dead back into her bosom.

The Hypogeum was discovered by accident in 1902 during digging for the construction of a cistern. Systematic excavations were carried out between 1903 and 1911.

Excavations

In addition to human remains the excavators found pottery, jewellery, amulets and other objects – burial objects and votive offerings.

One of the most celebrated finds is the figure of a sleeping woman, now in the Archaeological Museum in Valletta. This little red-painted terracotta figure probably represents a priestess lying on a couch in a temple to receive the commands of the divine power in her sleep – a rite still practised in antiquity.

A modern spiral staircase leads down to the middle level of the Hypogeum; the upper level is not open to the public. From here a passage leads to an antechamber and then the Unfinished Hall.

Only some of the walls of the **Unfinished Hall** have been dressed. On the other walls holes have been bored and there are marks left by pointed implements: presumably the hall was to be extended.

The **Main Hall**, which is almost exactly circular, is entered from the Unfinished Hall, in which is a representation in low relief of a temple façade with a trilithon entrance. On one side wall are two rows of recesses, on the other two openings with imitations of trilithons, one of which leads into the Decorated Hall.

Instead of entering the Decorated Hall, however, it is better to return to the Unfinished Hall and then go down a flight of steps into the **Acoustic Hall**, which is 8 m long and up to 2.40 m high. The walls and roof are decorated with ochre-coloured spiral and tendril patterns, perhaps symbolising the eternal cycle of birth and death. In the left-hand wall of the hall, 1.35 m from the floor, is an opening known as the oracle hole. A deep voice speaking into this hole reverberates throughout the whole of the Hypogeum. It is questionable, however, whether this effect, which is particularly impressive in the Main Hall, really justifies the conclusion that this was an oracular chamber.

The **Decorated Hall** can also be entered from the Unfinished Hall. The coloured drawings from which it takes its name are now barely distinguishable. The hall is almost exactly circular, with a diameter of 5.50 m. On the north side of the hall pilasters with pecked ornament mark the entrance to the so-called Snake Pit, a small chamber which tapers towards the top. Although in all early cultures snakes featured in fertility rites, it is not certain that snakes were in fact kept here.

From the Decorated Hall a corridor leads to the **Holy of Holies**, in which a concave temple façade with a trilithon entrance flanked by two recesses, the whole thing topped by a massive projecting slab, has been carved from the rock. In front of the façade, just as in the temples above ground, are holes in the floor for the tethering of sacrificial animals or the reception of libations. At the time of their discovery the holes were plugged with goats' horns.

The trilithon entrance in the mock temple façade leads into the kidney-shaped **Sacrificial Chamber**. The recess opposite the entrance was probably used as an altar. In its upper part is a hole to which presumably the animals to be sacrificed were tethered.

From the Holy of Holies a flight of irregular steps leads down to the **lowest level** of the Hypogeum. Before the construction of a modern gangway the steps ended abruptly above a 2 m deep cavity into which an unwelcome visitors would inevitably have fallen. Those who knew their way about could turn immediately right to the next burial chamber.

On this level are a number of rooms separated by 2 m high walls, also painted red. No skeletons were found in these rooms; it has been suggested, therefore, that the lowest level may have been used for the storage of grain. Other scholars believe, on the evidence of the wall painting, that the third level was intended to be used for further burials.

Popeye Village

See Mellieha

Qawra

See St Paul's Bay

Qormi   G/H 6

Qormi (pop. 18,000) lies on the south-western edge of the built-up area round Valletta. In the late Middle Ages the town stood directly on the Grand Harbour, the edge of which later silted up and finally was drained. The Knights called Qormi Casal Fornaro (from Italian forno, "oven"), because almost all the bakers on the island had their establishments here. The tradition has been maintained, and Qormi is now the main centre on Malta for the production of bread and pasta.

In Qormi's maze of narrow lanes are many houses with attractively decorated stone balconies, mostly dating from the 19th century. The Palazzo Stagno, also with fine carved decoration, was built in 1589.

The parish church, dedicated to St George, was built in 1456 and enlarged in 1584. The façade is articulated by Doric pilasters. The nave has a fine coffered ceiling,

Qrendi   G 7/8

Qrendi is a village of 2300 inhabitants in the south of Malta, near the Neolithic temples of Hagar Qim and Mnajdra (see entry). Along with the neighbouring village of Mqabba it is a centre for the quarrying of globigerina limestone – the stone of which most of Malta's buildings are built – which is soft and easily workable until it comes in contact with the air, when it rapidly hardens. It is worth while looking into one of the quarries, which are usually rectangular in shape, to see the stone being quarried and sawn into blocks.

The main road runs through Qrendi, which still preserves a very rural air, from north to south. To the west of the road is the Gwarena Tower or Cavalier Tower, built in the time of Grand Master Martin de Redin (1657–60); it is the only octagonal tower in Malta. Of Qrendi's three churches the finest is St Catherine Tat-Torba, in Mqabba Road, with a magnificent Baroque façade built on to the older nave in 1625.

At a small chapel at the far end of the village, on the road to the Blue Grotto (see entry), a side road goes off on the left to Il-Maqluba, a large hole in the ground, some 50 m deep and 100 m across, caused by the collapse of the roof of an underground cavern.

Il-Maqluba

Rabat   F 6

Rabat (pop. 13,000), on Malta's south-western plateau, immediately adjoins the island's old capital, Mdina (see entry). It cannot compare in magnificence with its neighbour, but it has a number of interesting sights and has a feeling of pulsating life that its neighbour lacks.

History

In Roman times Mdina and part of present-day Rabat lay within the same town walls, outside which both Jews and Christians buried their dead. The Arabs separated the two towns in 870, and thereafter the walls fell into ruin. In the 14th and 15th centuries many religious orders built convents in the Rabat area, and Dominican, Augustinian and Franciscan houses have been in part preserved.

Town

The contrast between Mdina and Rabat could hardly be greater. Rabat is a modern town with numerous shops and craftsmen's workshops and busy markets. It has long outgrown its ancient boundaries, and its Early Christian catacombs are now hidden under residential districts.

Roman Villa

On Museum Esplanade, on the edge of the gardens separating Mdina and Rabat, is the Roman Villa (open Oct.–mid-Jun. Mon.–Sat. 8.15am–5pm, Sun. 8.15am–4.15pm; mid-Jun.–Sep. daily 7.45am–2pm). In neo-classical style, it is in fact a museum, built in 1925 on the foundations of a Roman house. The remains of this Roman town house were discovered in 1881 and excavated between 1920 and 1924.

On the ground floor of the museum are displays of pottery and glass, architectural fragments, gravestones and an olive-press. Stairs lead down to the basement, in which the foundations of the Roman villa can be seen. It was built round an open courtyard surrounded by a colonnade (peristyle). The mosaic floor of the atrium is well preserved; the central scene, two pigeons perched on the rim of a bowl, is surrounded by trompe-l'oeil geometric patterns. There are also remains of mosaics

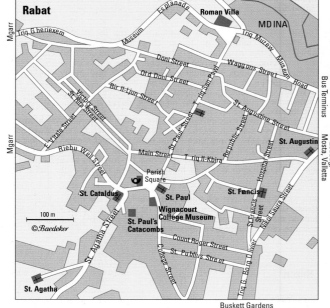

Buskett Gardens

in the adjoining vestibulum (reception room) and triclinium (dining room).

In another room in the basement is a collection of gravestones from an Arab cemetery which was later established over the Roman villa.

From the Roman Villa St Paul's Street runs south to St Paul's Church, built by Lorenzo Gafà in the late 17th century over the remains of an earlier church and much altered in later centuries; the 18th century façade is ascribed to Francesco Buonamici. Gafà incorporated in his church the little chapel of St Publius built in 1617 by Giovanni Renegues, who lived here as a hermit (entered from the right-hand side entrance to the church). The altarpiece in the chapel of St Publius is by Mattia Preti. In a recess to the left of the high altar, protected by a grille, is a golden arm, said to contain a relic of St Paul.

St Paul's Church/St Paul's Grotto

From the chapel steps lead down to the crypt and St Paul's Grotto. The local guides describe with great eloquence how the Apostle Paul was held prisoner in the grotto (see Baedeker Special).

In the Wignacourt College Museum, next to St Paul's Church, treasures of the order of the Knights are on display, including paintings from the school of Caravaggio, ancient maps, coins, majolicas and Roman and Carthaginian ceramics (open Mon.–Sat. 10am–3pm). The museum is housed in the former church college built by Grand Master Wignacourt at the beginning of the 17th century.

Wignacourt College Museum

The Catacombs of St Cataldus, diagonally opposite St Paul's Church, are a relatively small family burial-place underneath a chapel.

Catacombs of St Cataldus

South-west of the church, in St Agatha Street, are St Paul's Catacombs (open Oct.–mid-Jun. Mon.–Sat. 8.15am–5pm, Sun. 8.15am–4.15pm; mid-Jun.–Sep. daily 7.45am–2pm), the most extensive burial-place in the town. They are believed to have been used for burial between the 4th and the 6th century AD.

★St Paul's Catacombs

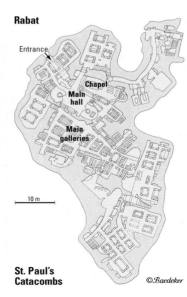

Rabat

Entrance

Chapel

Main hall

Main galleries

10 m

St. Paul's Catacombs

©*Baedeker*

A new flight of steps laid over the original one leads down to the **main hall** of the catacombs. In vaulted recesses in this room, as in many other Maltese catacombs, are two "agape tables" – round tables hewn from the rock, with raised rims, at which the mourners ate a funeral meal during the burial ceremonies or on the anniversary of a death, reclining on the sloping stone benches round the table. (Other scholars argue that because of the strong smell of dissolution in the catacombs the mourners could not stay underground for long, and believe that food and drink for the dead were set out on the tables).

From the main hall two steps lead down to a **chapel** on a lower level and numerous passages give access to the intricate network of **galleries**, on different levels,

The St Paul's Catacombs are the largest underground burial complex in Rabat

containing the tombs. The catacombs were apparently not systematically planned but extended as and when the need arose.

Sparse remains of colour on the walls indicates that the catacombs were once decorated with frescoes. The tombs presumably bore the names of the dead. The catacombs were supplied with air by air shafts and with light by oil lamps (traces of soot can still be detected on the walls of the galleries). When the catacombs were systematically excavated at the end of the 19th century they were found to be empty, having presumably been robbed many centuries before.

In a tour of the main galleries (some of the side galleries are closed for safety reasons) visitors will recognise different kinds of **tombs**. A common type is the loculus, a square recess in the wall which was closed by a stone; this type was mainly used for the burial of children. Also very common is the canopied tomb, in which the rock is hewn in an arc over the actual tomb. Usually one canopy covers two, three or four tombs, each of them with a stone support for the dead person's head. A very rare variant is the saddle-roofed tomb (or sarcophagus tomb), which was probably reserved for highly placed personages; there is also a canopy over this type of tomb. The opening of the burial chamber is in the base of the tomb.

St Agatha's Catacombs

Farther along St Agatha Street are other catacombs, a church dedicated to St Agatha and an associated museum (open Oct.–Jun. Mon.–Fri. 9am–noon and 1—5pm, Sat. 9am–1pm; Jul.–Sep. Mon.–Fri. 9am–5pm, Sat. 9am–1pm). The complex is famed for its frescoes.

In the **crypt** below the present church St Agatha is said to have hidden during the persecution of Christians in the time of the Emperor Decius. Here three layers of frescoes were found. The oldest of them (to left of the entrance, below) are dated to the 4th/5th century AD; three figures of saints in Byzantine style date from the 12th century; and the rest were painted by Salvatore d'Antonio in 1480. Many of them depict St Agatha.

From the crypt two passages leads to the **catacombs**. These have frescoes dating from the 4th–6th centuries, including a dove bearing an olive branch, peacocks, a laurel wreath and a shell. Here too is a representation of the menorah, the Jewish seven-branched candlestick, showing that the catacombs were used for the burial of Jews as well as Christians.

The **museum** attached to the catacombs has both religious and archaeological exhibits, including a large collection of pottery of the 4th and 3rd centuries BC and a collection of stone votive tablets of the medieval period which once formed a frieze in St Agatha's Church (built 1504).

The Augustinian church in north-eastern Rabat was built in 1571 by Gerolamo Cassar, the architect who two years later built the conventual church of the Order of St John. The nave, with four bays, has a gilded barrel vault.

St Augustine's Church

Santa Venera   H 6

Santa Venera (pop. 6200), 4 km south-west of Valletta, has now joined up with its larger neighbour, Hamrun (see entry). It has two sights of interest on the Hamrun–Attard road.

The Casa Leoni (or Palazzo Leoni) is a handsome country house built by Grand Master Manoel de Vilhena in 1730. Behind the house is a typical 18th century formal garden.

Casa Leoni

Wignacourt Aqueduct, near Santa Venera

Did Paul stay on Malta?

For the Maltese it is an irrevocable fact: in the autumn of AD 59 the apostle Paul landed on Malta and brought Christianity to the island. Their proof are chapters 27–28 of The Acts of the Apostles by St Luke.

For here it says that Paul was to be brought to Rome as a prisoner of the Romans in order to face the Emperor and answer to the accusations of the High Priests of Jerusalem. While travelling from Crete to Italy, his ship met with a heavy storm and, after two weeks of being lost at sea, it finally ran

St Paul's Church in Rabat: one of the numerous places on Malta connected with the supposed stay on the Mediterranean island by the Apostle Paul

aground on the reefs near the island of "Melita" where it shattered. The apostle, his fellow prisoners, the Roman soldiers and sailors managed to escape to land where the island's inhabitants (whom Luke calls "barbarians") gave them a friendly reception. The helpful islanders lit a fire for the shipwrecked crew to warm up in the rain and cold. "And when Paul had gathered a bundle of sticks, and laid them on the fire, there came a viper out of the heat, and fastened on his hand" (Acts of the Apostles 28.3). The

islanders were frightened and suspicious and said, "No doubt this man is a murderer, whom, though he hath escaped the sea, yet vengeance suffereth not to live" (Acts of the Apostles 28.4). When, however, nothing happened to Paul the superstitious islanders changed their minds and considered him to be a god.

Publius, the "first official of the island", had his estate nearby, and he extended his hospitality to the shipwrecked people for three days. Paul healed Publius' father who had fallen ill with swamp fever (malaria), and soon other sufferers came to be healed. After three months, the stranded crew boarded an Alexandrian ship and were supplied with all they needed by the islanders.

Until recently, theologians of both denominations were certain that "Melita" could only have been Malta (in the Middle Ages, at times, the southern Dalmatian island of Mljet was suggested). The Maltese believe that, after three months' stay, Paul had converted all islanders to Christianity and had declared the Roman governor Publius the island's first bishop. In St Paul's Bay, the presumed location of the shipwreck and the snake miracle, the grateful Maltese erected a white statue, 12 m high, on a tiny islet – one of numerous places on the island that commemorate the saint.

In the year 1987, the historian and geographer Heinz Warnecke published his book, "The real journey to Rome by Apostle Paul", in which he tried to prove that Paul did not land on Malta

Paul watches from his socket, as churches and streets are festively decorated for the patron saint's celebrations.

but on the island of Cephallonia in western Greece. He reckoned that Malta is ruled out as a candidate by the prevailing currents and climate of the southern Mediterranean (a ship sailing from Crete, driven by autumnal cyclones, would inevitably drift towards the islands of western Greece); that the Maltese had been granted Roman citizenship and would therefore not be described as "barbarians"; that Dike, the goddess of vengeance who was worshipped by the local population, had no Roman equivalent; and that the lack of standing water on Malta meant that there was no malaria on Malta which Publius' father was said to have suffered from; and that there were definitely no poisonous snakes on the island. Many professors described this Cephallonia theory as the "event of the century in theological terms". On Malta, however, there is little accep-

tance of this theory; for the Maltese are far too proud that their Christian faith dates back to the Apostle Paul himself, and there are just too many sacred places connected with these events for the inhabitants to want to let abandon their theory.

In the meantime – mainly Catholic – theologians have raised doubts about Warnecke's theory. Luke's geographical data applied to many Mediterranean coasts; at the time, all speakers of foreign tongues were described as "barbarians"; climatic change might have taken place in the course of the centuries, and so on. A solution to these religious disagreements is not in sight and, as long as the theologians cannot agree amongst themselves which island was described as "Melite", the Maltese, and especially the Maltese Tourist Office, are absolutely certain: Paul did stay on Malta.

Senglea

Wignacourt Aqueduct

Alongside the Santa Venera–Attard road runs a section of the Wignacourt Aqueduct, built by Grand Master Alof de Wignacourt, largely at his own expense, and brought into use in 1615. The water from a spring at Dingli was carried underground to Attard, from there to Hamrun on the aqueduct and finally underground again to Fort St Elmo in Valletta.

Senglea   J 6

Senglea (pop. 3500) lies on a promontory reaching out into the Grand Harbour opposite Valletta. Along with Vittoriosa and Cospicua (see entries), it is one of the "Three Cities" of Malta. It inhabitants are mainly workers in the nearby shipyards and factories.

History

After the Knights of St John established their headquarters in Birgu (now Vittoriosa) they were concerned to strengthen its defences on all sides. In 1554 Grand Master Claude de la Sengle, after whom the town is named (previously it was known as L'Isla), built Fort St Michael on the tip of the promontory next to Birgu. After the Great Siege of 1565 the town grew in size and was laid out on a strictly regular rectangular plan.

Lying so near the port and industrial installations round the Grand Harbour, Senglea was frequently the target of German and Italian air raids during the Second World War and was almost completely destroyed. Soon after the war it was rebuilt, preserving its original character.

The town

There are no buildings of major importance in Senglea. It is a town of relatively tall houses, plain to the point of austerity. It does not set out to attract tourists: there are no hotels and no restaurants of any size.

One feature, however, is worth visiting: the Vedette, a viewpoint at the extreme tip of the peninsula. On the way there you will pass, in the main square, the parish church of Our Lady of Victory, built after the Second World War. From the Vedette, once part of Fort St Michael and now in a small public garden, there are magnificent views of the Grand Harbour and Valletta on the far side. The watchfulness of the men once posted here is symbolised by carvings of two eyes and two ears; the pelican is a symbol of self-sacrificing Christian love.

Siggiewi   G 7

The little country town of Siggiewi (pop. 7100) lies in the south of Malta, 10 km south-west of Valletta.

St Nicholas

Prominently situated in the centre of the town is the parish church of St Nicholas, built by Lorenzo Gafà in the second half of the 17th century. It has a dome borne on a high drum. The neo-classical façade was added in the 19th century. The church preserves its original Baroque interior, in a style showing the influence of Roman and Sicilian architecture.

Laferla Cross

On the left of the road which runs south-west from Siggiewi to the Dingli Cliffs, on one of the highest points on the island (229 m above the sea), is the 12.5 m high Laferla Cross, erected in 1903. From here you can enjoy magic views over large parts of the island, with a particularly impressive view of Valletta in the setting sunlight.

Inquisitor's Palace

Farther along the Dingli road, on the hillside to the left, is the Inquisitor's summer palace (his main palace was in Vittoriosa: see entry), built between 1625 and 1627; the little chapel was added in 1760. The special attractions of the palace (which is not open to the public) are its beautiful setting and the wide views it enjoys.

A good road leads from Siggiewi southwards to Ghar Lapsi, a rocky bay with a short pebble beach and rocky shelves, popular with the locals for swimming, sunbathing and diving. A small restaurant, "Lapsi View", is above the bay.

Skorba

See Zebbieh

Sliema

Sliema lies on a peninsula reaching out into the sea to the west of Valletta, running into Gzira on the south and St Julian's on the north (see entries). With a population of over 12,500, it is one of Malta's largest towns. It is a residential area favoured by higher earners and

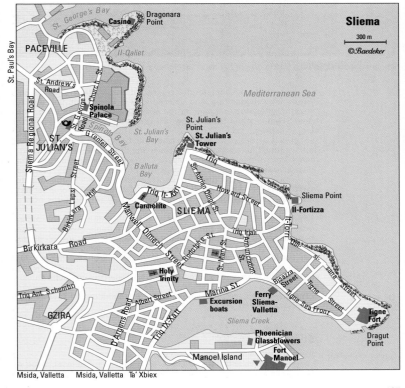

Msida, Valletta   Msida, Valletta   Ta' Xbiex

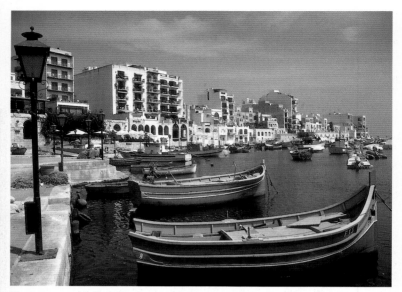

The area around Spinola Bay is one of the most attractive parts of St Julian's

also one of the leading tourist centres in the Maltese archipelago. Visitors who choose to spend their holiday in Sliema will find a wide range of entertainments and all the atmosphere of a large town. The name Sliema means "peace" – which is one thing they will have difficulty in finding.

Sliema is a modern town which came into being only at the end of the 19th century. Characteristic of the town and of the period are its apartment blocks of relatively sober aspect. The only historic buildings are St Julian's Tower, built by Grand Master Martin de Redin in 1657–60, and Tigné Fort, on the tip of the promontory, which was built by the Knights in 1761 to defend Marsamxett Harbour. On Sliema Point is another fort known as Il-Fortizza, built during the period of British rule; it is now a restaurant.

Tourism in Sliema is concentrated mainly on the seafront, along Tower Road and Marina Street, where there are numerous hotels in all price categories and innumerable bars and restaurants, souvenir shops and travel agencies. A pleasant promenade runs along Sliema Creek, with landing-stages where numerous excursion boats clamour for custom. Sliema has no sandy beaches. Those who are not put off by the constant traffic can sunbathe on rock terraces (particularly along Qui-si-sana Street.

The main shopping areas in Sliema are the south end of Tower Road and Bisazza Street.

St Julian's   H 5

6 km west of Valletta is St Julian's (San Giljan in Maltese), once a fishing village and now a town of 7000 inhabitants, which along with

neighbouring Sliema (see entry) to the south-east is one of Malta's main tourist centres. The town really comes to life only in the evening, particularly in the northern district of Paceville, where there are numerous restaurants, bars and discotheques, as well as a casino.

The ★**centre** of St Julian's, at the head of Spinola Bay, is exceedingly picturesque. Brightly coloured fishing boats bob up and down in the harbour, and round the seafront are restaurants with terraces on which visitors can relax and contemplate the scene.

In Spinola Street, at the corner of St George's Road, is the Spinola Palace of 1688, in front of which is a pretty little walled garden. The vaulted cellars of the palace now house a restaurant.

A favourite meeting-place for local people in the evenings is a square in Balluta Bay, on the boundary between St Julian's and Sliema. On the south side of the bay is a Carmelite convent with a neo-Gothic church.

St Julian's rocky beaches almost exclusively belong to the large hotels. Non-residents are usually welcome here, but at a hefty charge! There is a small sandy beach in the northern part of the town, in St George's Bay, but the very busy coastal road runs right next to it.

| Beaches

St Paul's Bay   F/G 4

A straggling built-up area runs round St Paul's Bay in northern Malta, extending from Xemxija (pronounced "shemshiya"), at the south end of the bay, by way of the township of St Paul's Bay (in Maltese San Pawl il-Bahar) and Bugibba to Qawra (pronounced "owra"), at the tip of the peninsula between St Paul's Bay and Salina Bay. This whole area (often lumped together as the resort of St Paul's Bay) is Malta's second major tourist centre, ranking after Sliema/St Julian's. The population of around 7000 is increased during the main holiday season by some 10,000 visitors. To meet this demand there are hotels in all price categories, innumerable restaurants, bars and pubs, as well as facilities for a wide range of sports. With its numerous discotheques and nightclubs, Bugibba counts as Malta's second hottest night spot after St Julian's.

The tourist resorts round St Paul's Bay are relatively modest assemblages of apartment houses and hotels. The only place with a real town centre is St Paul's Bay, which also has a small fishing harbour. Some parts of Bugibba and Qawra have a rather desolate air outside the main holiday season, and some of the apartment blocks, occupied only seasonally, look neglected and abandoned. There are few open spaces in the towns, into which the planners have been concerned to build ever new tourist ghettoes. The hub of the whole complex is the seafront square of Pjazza Tal-Bajja (Bay Square) in Bugibba.

There are no attractive sandy beaches in St Paul's Bay: only shelving rocks in San Pawl il-Bahar and a tiny sandy beach below Pjazza Tal-Bajja. Within easy reach, however, are the finest beaches in Malta – in Golden Bay, Ghajn Tuffieha Bay and Mellieha Bay (see Practical Information, Beaches).

| Beaches

In the centre of San Pawl il-Bahar (St Paul's Bay) is the parish church, which is dedicated to St Paul. 200 m away, on the coast, is the Wignacourt Tower, a watch-tower built by Grand Master Alof de Wignacourt (1601–22). It has been restored and is now open to the public (first Sunday of every month 10am–12 noon).

| Town

In the gardens of the New Dolmen Hotel are the remains of a small Neolithic temple, wrongly described as a dolmen. Part of the concave

| **Bugibba**

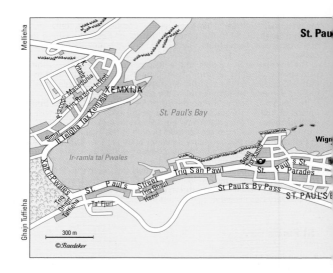

façade has survived, with a doorway formed by four orthostats leading into the temple, the ground-plan of which can be traced in part from the remains of the torba floor. The remains of the temple are particularly impressive in the evening, when they are floodlit.

Qawra

On the northern tip of the peninsula between St Paul's Bay and Salina Bay is the Qawra Tower, another watch-tower built by the Knights in the 17th century.

Salt has been won from the sea in **Salina Bay** since medieval times. During the summer months seawater is run into the salt-pans and left to evaporate, leaving a crust of salt.

Kennedy Memorial Grove

Near the south end of Bugibba and Qawra is the Kennedy Memorial Grove, planted to commemorate the murdered US President John F. Kennedy (1917–63). On a commemorative stone are inscribed Kennedy's words: "Ask not what your country can do for you – ask what you can do for your country". This little patch of woodland with its olive-trees and oleander bushes is a favourite picnic place at weekends.

Tal Qadi

Near the Kennedy Memorial Grove, a field track branches off the main road that skirts St Paul's Bay, signposted to St Michael's Chapel. After 500 m on this path, on the right, are the poorly preserved remains of the Neolithic temple of Tal Qadi (not signposted). There are only scanty traces to show that the temple consisted of two oval chambers.

St Paul's Islands

St Paul's Islands, two tiny bare islets at the north end of St Paul's Bay, are supposed to be the rocks on which the Apostle Paul's ship was wrecked during his voyage to Rome in AD 59. Recent research has shown, however, that Paul was never on Malta (see p. 28). The legendary event is commemorated by a 12 m high statue erected on one of the islands in 1845.

Mediterraneo

Continuing along the coastal road around Salina Bay in an easterly direction, you will reach, near the village of Bahar lc-Caghaq, the leisure

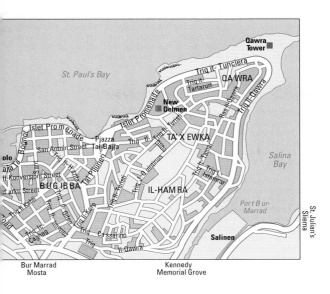

St. Paul's Bay

Qawra Tower

Triq It- Tuncierä

Triq it- Tartarun

QAWRA

New Dolmen

Triq It-Qawra

Triq il-Qawra

Islet Promenade

Islet Promenade

Bognor

Piazza Tal-Bajja

San Antnin Street

Triq Il-Turisti

TA' X EWKA

Triq It-Hamra

Triq il-Qntinar

Triq Il-Qntimar

Salina Bay

olo
ajja-Ta

Tt-Konversjoni Street

BUGIBBA

Trig Il-Kahli

Triq L- Istamrar

Trig It-Tramal

IL-HAMRA

Port Bur-Marrad

St arku Street

St. Julian's Sliema

Triq Ic-Caghaq

Triq It-Tnwwar

Trig Il-Gbejn

Trig Il-Koroj

Ca ssarino

Salinen

Triq Il-Qawra

Bur Marrad
Mosta

Kennedy
Memorial Grove

Dolphin show in the leisure park Mediterraneo

park Mediterraneo (open daily 10am–2pm and 3–6.30pm, Sun. and in summer daily until 7.30pm). It is situated directly by the sea, and as the name suggests, is all to do with water creatures. The climax of every visit are two (not overly spectacular) shows with dolphins and sea-lions. Other creatures of the sea can be seen in the aquarium.

Tarxien   J 7

The little town of Tarxien (pop. 7400), now joined up with Paola (see entry), lies 6 km south-east of Valletta. As the town's name (tirxa means a large stone slab) indicates, Tarxien's main feature of interest is a Neolithic temple, one of the most important in the Maltese archipelago. Only a few streets away from the Tarxien temple is the Hypogeum of Hal Saflieni (see Paola).

★★Tarxien Temples

The Tarxien temples are the best preserved Neolithic temple complex in Malta (opening times Jun. 16th–Sep. daily 7.45am–2pm, Oct.–Jun. 15th Mon.–Sat. 8.15am–5pm, Sun. 8.15am–4.15pm).

The latest temples in this area were built between 3000 and 2500 BC, the high point of megalithic architecture in Malta. The temples are notable for the richness of their decoration. Although all the decorated stone slabs, altars and smaller objects found by the excavators were removed for preservation in the Archaeological Museum in Valletta, they were replaced by excellent copies: a visit to the site, therefore, is still an impressive experience. The temple complex is entered through a small site museum displaying finds from the site – again mostly copies.

Tarxien

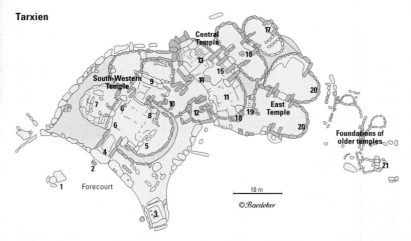

©Baedeker

1 Cistern	6 Altars with spiral motifs	10 Passage to Central Temple	16 Stone bowl
2 Slab with holes for tethering animals	7 Altars with processions of animals	11 Forecourt	17 Holy of holies of Central Temple
3 Altar for libations	8 Altar with blocked cavity	12 Chamber with animal reliefs	18 Passage to East Temple
4 Trilithon doorway	9 Threshold altar with spiral motifs	13 Carinated bowl	19 Steps
5 Colossal statue of Magna Mater		14 Bowl for burnt offerings	20 Oracle holes
		15 Slab with spiral motifs	21 Trilithon recess

South-Western Temple: looking into the holy of holies

The huge stones emerging from the ground on the site of the temple led archaeologists to carry out the first test excavations in 1915. On the uppermost level they found remains of an Urnfield cemetery of the Bronze Age, which were totally removed to reveal the important megalithic site below. Excavation came to an end in 1919, but between 1919 and 1964 various smaller excavations were undertaken.

The Tarxien temple complex consists of three well preserved temples which are connected with one another and three others of which there are only scanty remains. The three well preserved temples are dated to between 3000 and 2500 BC, the earliest being the East Temple, followed by the South-Western Temple and finally the Central Temple; the three others are older, dating from 3800–3000 BC. The size of the total complex and the monumentality of the buildings suggest that Tarxien was the religious and economic centre of the Maltese megalithic culture. It seems likely that there were other buildings here, forming a "temple city". The stones of these other buildings were no doubt removed in later centuries for re-use elsewhere.

Only the foundations of this once gigantic complex had been preserved, but a limestone model found at Tarxien gives some impression of how the temples must have looked.

The first temple encountered on entering the site is the South-Western Temple, the last but one to be built. In the forecourt in front of the temple are the remains of a cistern and several stone balls which served as rollers for transporting the immensely heavy megalithic slabs. The line of the concave temple façade is marked by the bench altars in front of it. At its east end is a recess paved by a slab in which five holes of varying size have been bored for the reception of libations. At the edge of the slab is a shallower depression, known as a potros, for offerings of fermented liquor. A reconstructed trilithon doorway, in front of which is a

South-Western Temple

143

slab pierced by two holes for tethering sacrificial animals, gives access to the first oval chamber of the temple. On either side are rows of altars separating the central part of the chamber from its apse-like rounded ends. On a low block of stone with ovoid ornament in the right-hand apse is the colossal statue of the Magna Mater (see History of Maltese Art) which the excavators found in situ. Only the lower part of the figure, which originally stood almost 3 m high, has been preserved. In the left-hand apse were found altars decorated with spirals and other motifs and others with processions of animals (goats, sheep and a pig), presumably sacrificial animals.

On both sides of the doorway into the second chamber are elaborately decorated altars. In the base of the altar on the right-hand side, which is decorated with spiral motifs, is a semicircular cavity blocked by a stone which fits exactly in place. In the cavity were found carbonised animal bones. Above the altar is a window stone, the opening in which matches the cavity below.

The central section of the second kidney-shaped chamber, unlike the apses, is paved with stone slabs. In front of the holy of holies lies a threshold altar over 3 m long with spiral decoration. It leads into the higher central chamber of the temple, which has a well preserved trilithon recess. On the inner surface of the two orthostats flanking the altar is carved ornament. The right-hand apse of the second chamber leads into the Central Temple. Before this was built there were probably altars here too.

Central Temple

In contrast to all the other temples excavated on Malta and Gozo, the Central Temple has three kidney-shaped chambers. There are indications that the first of the three served as a forecourt. Unlike the two chambers to the rear, it is paved with stone slabs; the outer walls were formed of orthostats of roughly uniform height. In the walls are several trilithon recesses. To the right of the entrance to the forecourt is a recess leading into a small chamber, on the rear wall of which is a carving of two bulls and a sow with her piglets (fertility symbols). In the centre of the forecourt is a stone bowl used for burnt offerings. In front of the entrance to the second kidney-shaped chamber is a stone slab 82 cm high, evidently marking the boundary between the forecourt and the temple proper. It is decorated with two spiral motifs, which are interpreted as the eyes of the Magna Mater, warding off all intruders. On either side of the entrance to the second chamber is an altar. In front of the left-hand (northern) altar is a large carinated bowl hewn from a single block of stone. Its function is not clear: it may have held water for ritual ablutions or possibly was a receptacle for the blood of sacrificial animals.

Beyond the slab with the two spiral motifs is a passage lined with huge orthostats leading to the first chamber of the temple proper, which is empty apart from a stone bowl in the middle. The rear chamber, beyond this, is much smaller, with a very shallow recess for the holy of holies. The orthostats which form the outer walls are inclined slightly inwards. With the transverse slabs above them, also projecting inwards, they look like the beginnings of a dome.

East Temple

From the forecourt of the Central Temple there is a passage into the East Temple, the oldest of the three linked temples. Between the two temples is a flight of steps which may have given the priesthood access to the cult chambers of the Central Temple.

The East Temple originally had two kidney-shaped chambers, but their western apses were destroyed during the building of the Central Temple, leaving only slight traces. The original torba floors, however, have been preserved. Both chambers have oracle holes in their eastern apses.

Other temples

To the east of the three linked temples are the scanty remains of three older temples. It is difficult for non-archaeologists to make sense of the surviving foundations and thresholds.

Valletta   J 6

Valletta (officially Il-Belt Valletta), capital of the Republic of Malta, is strategically situated on the Sciberras peninsula on Malta's north-east coast, surrounded by what are surely the most powerful fortifications in the world. The Sciberras peninsula, 3 km long and up to 700 m across, with a maximum height of 60 m above sea level, lies between Malta's two largest and economically most important harbours, Marsamxett Harbour and the Grand Harbour, the best and most beautiful natural harbours in Europe, which enclose the town on the north, east and south.

Valletta itself has a population of only 7200, but it is surrounded by a ring of small towns which along with the capital form the Valletta conurbation. Strangers usually cannot tell where one town ends and another begins but the locals know the differences. Along the east and south sides of the Grand Harbour, running into one another, are the towns of Kalkara, Vittoriosa, Cospicua, Senglea, Paola and Marsa; to the northwest, round Marsamxett Harbour, are Pietà, Msida, Ta'Xbiex, Gzira and Sliema; and on the Sciberras peninsula is Valletta's suburb of Floriana.

As Malta's capital Valletta is the seat of government, with Parliament, the Supreme Court, government offices and other institutions. It is also the country's cultural centre (operatic and dramatic performances, concerts), the see of a bishop and the seat of the University of Malta (founded 1769), the Malta College of Arts, Science and Technology, the Malta Cultural Institute, the Agrarian Society, the Observatory and several higher educational institutions.

The Valletta region, with its two harbours, is also the economic centre of the Maltese islands. The biggest employer of labour is the naval dockyard, with five dry docks in which passenger ships are built and refitted and tankers of up to 300,000 tons can be repaired and cleaned. It has a

Valletta is attractive not only in this view from the sea. The former residence of the Knights of the Order St John is just like an open-air museum.

total labour force of over 5000. The Grand Harbour, which handles almost all the country's freight and passenger traffic, has a deep-water wharf which can take ships up to 92,000 GRT, with a grain silo (capacity 12,500 tons) and numerous transit sheds.

Although the two harbours play a dominant role in Malta's economic life it has a variety of other industries, particularly foodstuffs, chemicals, textiles and mechanical engineering. Most industrial establishments are in Marsa, at the head of the Grand Harbour.

History

The foundation of Valletta was a consequence of the Great Siege from May to September 1565. Although the Knights of St John had withstood the attacks of Turkish forces which were numerically far superior, they realised that the rebuilding of the defences which had been destroyed or badly damaged – Fort St Elmo, at the tip of the Sciberras peninsula, then unbuilt-on; Fort St Angelo, on the promontory occupied by Birgu (now Vittoriosa), the Knights' headquarters; and Fort St Michael, on the promontory now occupied by Senglea – would not be sufficient to withstand a further Turkish attack. Accordingly on March 28th 1566 Grand Master Jean Parisot de la Valette founded the town which now bears his name in order to provide better protection for the Grand Harbour. The best strategic position was Mount Sciberras, above Fort St Elmo, and plans for a town on that site were drawn up by Francesco Laparelli da Cortona (1521–70), one of the leading military engineers of the day. Pope Pius IV had sent him to Malta for this purpose in order to demonstrate his appreciation of the Knights' defence of Malta. Thanks to the money which now flowed in from all over Europe Laparelli was able to revert to an earlier plan which had been turned down on grounds of expense. First parts of the Sciberras peninsula were levelled, and then work began on the construction of fortifications round the site of the town. Since a further Turkish attack was feared the work was carried out with the utmost speed, around 8000 slaves and other workers being regularly employed. When Laparelli left Malta three years later the fortifications were largely completed but there were no houses or public buildings within the walls, though plans and guidelines for their construction existed. In order to ensure that the town was developed as quickly as possible it was laid down that building must begin on a site within ten months of its purchase and must be completed within three years. Houses or their front gardens were not allowed to project on to the street, and each house was required to have its own cistern and to be connected with the public water supply and drains. A major part in the development of the town was played by Gerolamo Cassar, who had been Laparelli's assistant. He was responsible, among other work, for the design of the seven Renaissance-style auberges (lodgings) for the langues of the Order, of which only four now survive, as well as the Grand Master's Palace and St John's Co-Cathedral.

Most of the buildings of old Valletta, however, were in the Baroque style which reached Malta from Italy around 1650. The best known architects of the Baroque period were Lorenzo Gafà (1630–1704), Giovanni Barbara (1660–1730), Giuseppe Bonnici (1707–c. 1780) and Domenico Cachia (1710–90). Cachia rebuilt Cassar's Auberge de Castille, whose sumptuous façade reflects the prosperity of Valletta in the final century of the Order of St John. This period of splendour came to an end in 1798, when the French fleet sailed into the Grand Harbour and Grand Master Ferdinand von Hompesch surrendered the town to Napoleon without a fight; and on June 18th the Knights left Malta. French rule lasted only two years: in 1800 British forces occupied Valletta, and in 1814, under the treaty of Paris, the Maltese islands became a British colony. Until the middle of the 20th century the Grand Harbour was a major British naval base. During the Second World War Valletta came under heavy attack in German and Italian air raids, some 85% of its buildings being destroyed.

Street in Valletta, with the characteristic oriel windows ▶

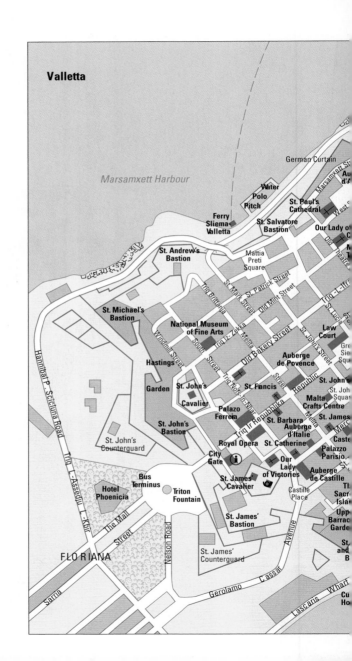

Valletta

Marsamxett Harbour

German Curtain

Au d'A

West

Water Polo Pitch

St. Paul's Cathedral

Ferry Sliema Valletta

St. Salvatore Bastion

Our Lady of C

St. Andrew's Bastion

Mattia Preti Square

St. Michael's Bastion

National Museum of Fine Arts

Old Mill Street

St. Patrick Street

St. Mark Street

Triq Britannia

Triq L-Ifr

St. Lucie

Law Court

Gre Sie Squ

Hastings

Old Bakery Street

St. John's Street

Auberge de Povence

Windmill Street

South Street

Triq Iz-Zekka

Triq Mons in Miar

Garden

St. John's Cavalier

St. Fancis

Republic

St. John's

St. Joh Squa

Palazo Ferreta

Malta Crafts Centre

St. James

St. John's Bastion

St. Barbara

Merc

St. John's Counterguard

Triq Ir Repubblika

Auberge d'Italie

Caste

Royal Opera

St. Catherine

Palazzo Parisio

City Gate

Our Lady of Victories

Auberge de Castille

Bus Terminus

Hotel Phoenicia

Triton Fountain

St. James Cavalier

Castille Place

Tl Sacr Isla

Upp Barrac Garde

The Mall

Street

Nelson Road

St. James' Bastion

Avenue

St. and B

FLORIANA

St. James' Counterguard

Sarna

Gerolamo C. Cassar

Lascaris

Wharf

Cu Ho

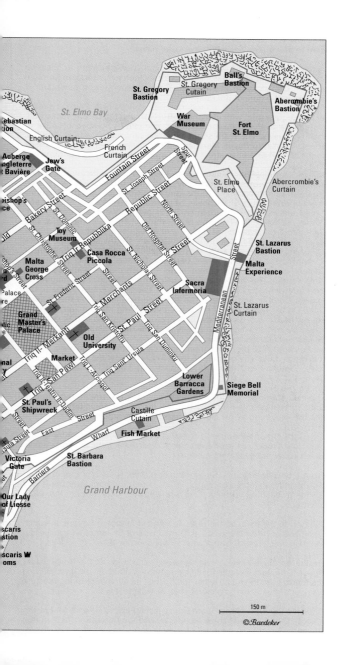

St. Elmo Bay

Ball's Bastion

St. Gregory Bastion

St. Gregory Cutain

Aberombie's Bastion

War Museum

Fort St. Elmo

ebastian ion

English Curtain

French Curtain

St. Elmo Place

Abercrombie's Curtain

Auberge ngleterre t Bavière

Jew's Gate

Fountain Street

Spur Street

St. Joseph Street

Bishop's ce

Bakery Street

Republic Street

North Street

St. Lazarus Bastion

Old

St. Domini

Toy Museum

Casa Rocca Piccola

Old Hospital Street

St. Nicholas Street

Malta Experience

Malta George Cross

St. Christopher Street

Striq il-Repubblika

Street

Sacra Infermeria

St. Lazarus Curtain

Bishop's Street

rd

St. Frederic Street

Merchants Street

Mediterranean

Palace re

Grand Master's Palace

Triq il-Merkanti

Triq San Kristofri

St. Paul Street

Triq San Dumnku

Old University

Street

Market

Triq San Pawl

Triq Sant Ursula

Triq l-Acisqof

Lower Barracca Gardens

Siege Bell Memorial

nal y t

St. Paul's Shipwreck

Triq il-Batrirl-Daun

Street

Castille Cutain

East

Wharf

Fish Market

sula Street

Victoria Gate

St. Barbara Bastion

Bartiera

Our Lady of Liesse

Grand Harbour

scaris stion

scaris W oms

150 m

©Baedeker

Valletta

After the war, with British help, almost all the town's major buildings were rebuilt on the basis of the original plans.

Town

Valletta has preserved much of its original character. With its massive fortifications and its numerous palaces and churches, mostly in Baroque style, it still gives an impression of the prosperity and splendour it enjoyed in the time of the Knights.

The first planned town of modern times, Valletta is laid out on a regular rectangular grid, with nine main streets traversing it from end to end, crossed by twelve transverse streets, sometimes stepped because of their steepness. The main shopping street and promenade is Republic Street. Parallel to this is Merchants Street, where there are also many shops as well as a busy street market held every morning but Sunday.

Fortifications

Valletta's fortifications, built between 1566 and 1571, with their elaborate system of outworks, bastions, cavaliers and curtain walls, were long regarded as impregnable. On the landward side there are four bastions (from north to south St Michael's, St John's, St James's and St Peter and Paul's) linked by short curtain walls. Below the walls is a deep moat. Within the walls, flanking one of the three openings in the walls, City Gate, are two cavaliers, St John's and St James's – tall towers with a good view over the approaches to the town. On the south side, above the Grand Harbour, are a series of fortifications – the Lascaris Bastion, St Barbara's Bastion, the Lower Barracca Bastion and the St Lazarus Bastion, again linked by curtain walls – which make skilful use of the rocky terrain. The various curtain walls are named after the langues of the Order whose duty it was to defend them (the French Curtain, the English Curtain, and so on). The entrance on this side is the Victoria Gate. On the north side of the town, overlooking Marsamxett Harbour, are the bastions of St Andrew, St Salvator, St Sebastian and St Gregory, linked by curtain walls, with a sally port, the Jews' Gate. The tip of the peninsula is guarded by the star-shaped Fort St Elmo. In the late 16th century some 150 bronze cannon with a considerable range were posted round the walls. The cannon on the two cavaliers at the west end of the town commanded the whole of Valletta as far as Fort St Elmo and beyond.

Sightseeing

The best starting-point for a tour of Valletta is the square outside City Gate. Passengers travelling by bus will arrive at the bus terminus here and those coming by car can find parking in the square.

City Gate

City Gate, the main entrance to Valletta, is a modern structure dating only from 1968. It replaced an earlier and narrower gate, the Porta Reale, which could not cope with modern traffic.

Republic Street

From City Gate Republic Street runs east. This is Valletta's main street, with many handsome public buildings. During shopping hours it is a scene of bustling activity; cars are allowed only during the early afternoon.

Freedom Square

Just inside the gate, on the right, is arcaded Freedom Square, in which is the tourist information office. On the wall of St James's Cavalier is a fountain erected by Grand Master Wignacourt in 1614.

Royal Opera House

On the north-east side of the square are the ruins of the Royal Opera House. Originally built in 1566, it was burned down in 1873, rebuilt and then destroyed in an air raid in 1942. Since its neo-classical architecture was out of line with the general style of Valletta it was not rebuilt.

Palazzo Ferreria

Opposite the ruins of the Opera House is the Palazzo Ferreria (or Francia Palace), built by the Maltese architect Giuseppe Bonavia in 1877 on the site of the Knights' gun foundry. It is now occupied by shops and offices.

Along Republic Street, on the right, is St Barbara's Church, on an oval plan, which was built by Giuseppe Bonnici in 1739 as the church of the langue of Provence.

On the opposite side of the street is the church of St Francis, built in 1598, remodelled in Baroque style in 1681 and subsequently much altered. It has a ceiling painting by the 19th century Maltese artist Giuseppe Cali.

The next block on the left is occupied by the Auberge de Provence (built by Gerolamo Cassar from 1571–76 to accommodate the Knights of the Provençal langue), a handsome building which since 1960 has housed the National Museum of Archaeology (open Jun. 16th–Sep. daily 7.45am—1.30pm, Oct.–Jun. 15th Mon.–Sat. 8.15am—5pm, Sun. 8.15am–4.15pm). The central section of the façade is given emphasis by a projecting portico of paired columns, contrasting with the engaged pilasters on the wings. The portico is flanked by windows with triangular and segmented pediments. The rusticated corner-stones are a borrowing from military architecture.

The Museum collections, covering a time span of 5000 BC to the 17th century, are at least as impressive as the building itself. In the mid-1990s, major renovation and rebuilding work took place, and today the collection of artefacts from the Neolithic period on the ground floor of the museum has been reopened to the public. The collections from the Phoenician, Carthaginian and Roman times on the first floor of the museum are set to be reopened at the end of 1999, while the rooms on the lower floor that are set aside for changing exhibitions will not open again before the end of the year 2000.

Almost all the material recovered from Megalithic temples all over Malta have been brought together on the ground. The oldest finds are from Ghar Dalam and are dated to 5200 BC, while the most recent exhibits from the Megalithic culture date back to 2500 BC. The National Museum has an expansive collection of large-sized architectural fragments and altar pieces from various temples of the Neolithic period. One of the most important exhibits is the famous pillared altar from Hagar Qim, which is covered with pecked holes and has on all four sides carvings of flowerless plants like trees of life growing out of jars.

Of special interest is the large collection of figures of the **Magna Mater**, including the probably oldest colossal figure found anywhere in the world, the over-lifesize Magna Mater found in Tarxien. Originally this figure was 3 m high, but today only the lower part is preserved. This figure, like many of the smaller ones displayed here, are all of very generous proportions and mostly headless. Although they have no distinctive sexual characteristics they are clearly female. Some of them have a hole in the neck area into which a head could be fitted. In a side chamber is the "Sleeping Lady", a small Magna Mater figure reclining on a couch which was found in the Hypogeum of Hal Saflieni, is Malta's best known Neolithic find. The figure, only 7 cm high and 12 cm long, shows traces of ochre paint. Almost equally famous is the "Venus of Malta", a 12.9 cm high headless clay figure, beautifully modelled. Other exhibits include many pottery and fragments of pottery, jewellery, tools and implements, and models of temples.

On the reopened upper floor a votive cippus will be exhibited, dedicated to the god Melkart, one of a pair found at Marsaxlokk in the mid 17th century; the other is now in the Louvre in Paris. On the base is an inscription, in both Greek and Phoenician characters, which enabled the Phoenician alphabet to be deciphered.

★★St John's Co-Cathedral

Off Republic Street to the right, in St John's Street, is St John's Co-Cathedral (open Mon.–Fri. 9.30am–12.45pm and 1.30–5.15pm, Sat. 9.30am–12.40pm and 4–5pm), built between 1573 and 1577 by the Maltese architect Gerolamo Cassar. It was founded by Grand Master Jean l'Evàque de la Cassiäre as the conventual church of the Order of St John and dedicated to the Order's patron saint, John the Baptist. The church has a simple rectangular plan, 58 m long by 39 m wide. The sacristy was added in 1598, the oratory in 1603, the two-storey side wings in the mid-17th century, the corridors flanking the nave in 1736. After the departure of the Knights, in 1816, Pope Pius VII granted it the status of Co-Cathedral, co-equal with Mdina Cathedral.

The Renaissance façade, flanked by twin towers, is relatively plain. Above the doorway is a balcony on which newly elected Grand Masters showed themselves to the knights.

In sharp contrast to the austere exterior is the sumptuously decorated interior. For the Grand Masters and the individual langues of the Order it was a matter of pride to deck their church with valuable works of art. It was thoroughly looted by Napoleon in 1798, and only a fraction of the stolen pictures and sculpture could later be bought back; but what remains is still impressive enough.

The floor of the church is covered with 375 gravestones in marble intarsia work, which record not only the name, arms and dates of the dead knights but frequently also their deeds of valour. Here too (by the first pier to the left of the entrance) is buried Mattia Preti, who painted the ceiling paintings for Grand Masters Raphael and Nicola Cotoner between 1662 and 1667, but at his own expense in gratitude for his admission to the Order. The paintings in the six bays of the barrel vaulting depict 18 scenes from the life of John the Baptist. Preti used the unusual technique of painting in oil directly on the limestone, giving the colours a stronger glow than in fresco painting. He also designed the gilded reliefs on the walls and piers, most of them motifs connected

Valletta   **St. John's Co-Cathedral**

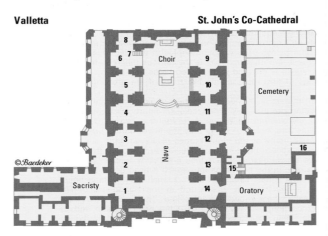

©Baedeker

1 Entrance to Sacristy	8 Chapel of English- Bavarian Langue	13 Chapel of Castile and Portugal
2 Chapel of Germany	9 Chapel of Blessed Sacrament	14 Entrance to
3 Entrance to north corridor	10 Chapel of Auvergne	Oratory
4 Chapel of Italy	11 Chapel of Aragon, Catalonia	15 Stairs to other
5 Chapel of France	and Navarre	rooms
6 Chapel of Provence	12 Entrance to Museum	16 Souvenir shop
7 Stairs to Crypt		

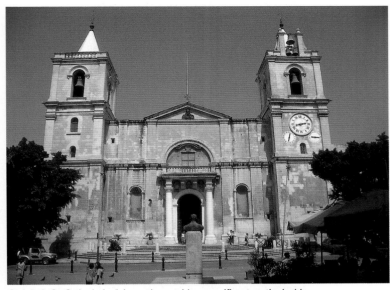

St John's Co-Cathedral: plain on the outside, magnificent on the inside

with the Order (helmets, weapons, Maltese crosses), together with plant ornament and fabulous animals.

The raised chancel is marked off from the nave by a balustrade of coloured marble (17th c.). Behind the sumptuous high altar of marble and lapis lazuli (1688) is an over-lifesize white marble group depicting the Baptism of Christ. The sculptor, Melchiore Gafà (1636–67) intended it to be in bronze, but he died soon after undertaking the commission and the work was completed in marble by Giuseppe Mazzuoli (1644–1725). The choir-stalls (late 16th c.) are decorated with gilded carving.

In 1604 a side chapel in the church was allotted to each of the langues of the Order; but since at that time the English langue was not actively represented in the Order it had no chapel until 1754, when it was allotted the Chapel of the Holy Relics, to be shared with the Bavarian langue. The various langues competed with one another in accumulating valuable works of art in their chapels. The tombs of the Grand Masters were also richly decorated. Among the most impressive are the tomb of Manuel de Vilhena (1722–36) in the chapel of Castile and Portugal and that of Nicola Cotoner in the chapel of Aragon, Catalonia and Navarre. The latter chapel, which is dedicated to St George, also has an altarpiece by Mattia Preti depicting the saint on his horse, painted in 1656, shortly before Preti's arrival in Malta. The chapel of the German langue, dedicated to the Three Kings, survived the Second World War almost unscathed and thus preserves its original Late Baroque furnishings.

In the crypt are the sarcophagi of twelve Grand Masters, including Philippe Villiers de l'Isle Adam, who led the Order from Rhodes to Malta, and Jean Parisot de la Valette, founder of Valletta. The only non-Grand Master buried in the crypt is an English knight, Sir Oliver Starkey, who was secretary to Grand Master de la Valette.

★**Cathedral Museum** The oratory of the Cathedral and a number of rooms in its south wing form the Cathedral Museum, which is entered from the interior of the church (open Mon.–Fri. 9.30am–12.30pm and 1.30–4.30pm, Sat. 9.30am–12.30pm; admission ticket also covers admission to Mdina Cathedral Museum).

In the oratory is a masterpiece by Caravaggio (1571/3–1610), "The Beheading of John the Baptist". The artist, who had fled from Rome to Malta in 1607, presented it to the conventual church in 1608 in gratitude for his admission to the Order. It is an impressive and dramatic work. The observers in the background stare down at the Baptist, lying bleeding on the ground, as do the active participants in the scene standing in a semicircle on the left, their outstretched arms pointing to the head, which the executioner is about to cut off with a knife. It is a work of harsh realism and vigorous colour (the Baptist's red loincloth directing the eye to his execution) combined with a striking play of light and shadow. Here too are some fine works by Mattia Preti, including his "Crucifixion", "Ecce Homo" and "Crowning with Thorns".

Notable items in the other rooms of the Museum include Caravaggio's "St Jerome", relics, vestments, choir books and above all 28 Flemish tapestries (1697–1700) depicting allegories of the Christian faith, some of them after cartoons by Rubens and Poussin.

Malta Crafts Centre

Opposite the Cathedral is the Malta Crafts Centre, where a wide range of Maltese arts and crafts is on view (see Practical Information, Arts and Crafts).

Great Siege Square

The west front of the Cathedral looks on to Great Siege Square, in which is a neo-classical monument by Antonio Sciortino commemorating the siege. The figures on the monument symbolise Valour, Freedom and Faith – the ideals of the Knights of St John.

Law Courts

Opposite the north front of the Cathedral are the neo-classical Law Courts, erected in the 1960s on the site of the Auberge d'Auvergne, which was almost completely destroyed during the Second World War.

Republic Square

A few yards beyond this Republic Street runs into Republic Square – the real centre of Valletta with its charming street cafés. It was formerly called Queen's Square, and still has a statue of Queen Victoria to recall the period of British rule.

National Library

On the south side of Republic Square is the National Library, usually referred to as the Biblioteca. The building was erected in the late 18th century, but the library was originally founded in 1555 for the use of the chaplains of the Order of St John and was housed in premises adjoining the conventual church. It was opened to the public in 1750. Its stock of books was rapidly increased by donations, and by the end of the 18th century it possessed some 80,000 volumes. Like other institutions in Valletta, it suffered from the plundering activities of Napoleon's troops, and after the departure of the French the library was left with only some 30 000 volumes. It was reopened in its new building in 1812.

The National Library now has around 300,000 volumes, including some 10,000 manuscripts and documents on the history of the Order of St John and of Malta. A number of particularly important documents are on permanent display in the main hall of the Library on the upper floor. The hall, 41 m long by 12.5 m wide, has survived in its original state. Among the documents on show are Pope Paschal II's Bull of February 15th 1113 recognising the Order of St John as an independent organisation and a document signed by the Emperor Charles V in 1530 granting Malta to the Knights of St John as a perpetual fief.

★Grand Master's Palace

Immediately north-east of Republic Square is the Grand Master's Palace. It was originally intended to build the palace on the site now occupied by the Auberge de Castille, the highest point in Valletta, but it was decided instead to site it in the centre of the town. Building began

The Council Chamber or Tapestry Hall in the Grand Master's Palace, where the Knights of the Order of St John held their council meetings

in 1571 to the design of Gerolamo Cassar, who was required to incorporate an existing building into the palace, and by 1574 it was ready for occupation. It was given its present appearance in the mid-18th century, when the two Baroque doorways and the wooden balconies on the main façade were added. All Grand Masters of the Order resided in the palace until 1798. Under British rule it became the residence of the governor. It is now the seat of the Maltese Parliament and the official residence of the President. Much of the palace, however, is open to the public.

The palace is rectangular in plan, measuring 96 m by 81 m. There are four entrances, one in the middle of each side and two, with Baroque doorways, on the main front facing Republic Street. The one on the left leads into Neptune's Court. Until the end of the 19th century this was occupied by stables, with a wall fountain bearing the arms of Grand Master Perellos y Roccaful (1697–1720) serving as a horse-trough. The court takes its name from a statue of Neptune, modelled on an original by Giambologna, which Grand Master Alof de Wignacourt (1601–22) originally set up in the fish market; it was moved to its present site in 1861. A passage on the right-hand side of the court leads into Prince Alfred's Court, named after Queen Victoria's second son, who visited Malta in 1858. In this court is a clock installed by Grand Master Manuel Pinto de Fonseca (1741–73) on which the hours are struck by two figures in Turkish dress.

In one corner of Prince Alfred's Court is a doorway from which a narrow staircase leads up to the **State Apartments** on the upper floor. These rooms are used by the President of Malta for receptions and other official occasions, but when not required for these purposes are open to the public on conducted tours (open Mon.–Sat. 9am–3pm, in summer only until 1pm). Visitors are taken along the Armoury Corridor, at the far end of which is the former Armoury, now the chamber of the Maltese

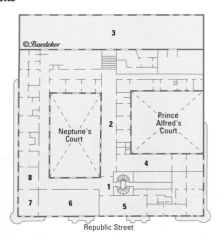

1 Entrance corridor
2 Armoury corridor
3 Parliament
   (former Armoury)
4 Council Chamber
5 State Dining Room
6 Supreme Council Chamber
7 Hall of the Ambassadors
   (Red State Room)
8 Yellow Room

Republic Street

Parliament. On the inner wall are portraits of Grand Masters. Off the Armoury Corridor is the former Council Chamber of the Order, now known as the Tapestry Hall, which was the meeting-place of the Maltese Parliament until it moved to the Armoury in 1976. The Tapestry Hall is so called after the ten valuable 18th century Gobelins tapestries depicting exotic scenes from Africa, the then little known Caribbean and South America which hang on its walls. They were commissioned by Grand Master Perellos y Roccaful (1697–1720) from the Gobelins manufactory at the court of King Louis XIV. Above the tapestries is a frieze depicting naval battles fought by the Order.

In the Supreme Council Chamber or Hall of St Michael and St George is a frieze of twelve frescoes depicting in chronological order events in the Great Siege of 1565. They were painted by Matteo Perez d'Aleccio in 1576–81 on the basis of eyewitnesses' accounts. From the Supreme Council Chamber a door leads into the Hall of the Ambassadors, also known as the Red State Room after the red damask which covers its walls. This room has a frieze depicting eight scenes from the history of the Order, as well as a number of portraits of European monarchs. The Yellow Room also has a series of scenes from the early history of the order and two pictures by José de Ribeira, "Jacob with his Sheep" and "Joseph's Dream". In the Dining Room are portraits of British monarchs.

The **Palace Armoury** (open Jun. 16th–Sep. daily 8.30am–2pm, Oct.–Jun.15th Mon.–Sat. 8.30am–5pm, Sun. 8.30am–4pm) has been housed since 1976 in the former stables of the Grand Master's Palace (entrance from Neptune's Court). Under a decree of 1555 a knight's arms and armour became the property of the Order on his death, so that within a short time the Order acquired enough equipment to arm tens of thousands of men. The Armoury now has only some 5800 weapons and suits of armour from many European countries, as well as booty taken by the Knights (Turkish weapons and shields). Perhaps the most impressive exhibit is Grand Master Alof de Wignacourt's gold-plated parade armour, made in Milan.

The 17th century **Main Guard** was given its present aspect, with a neo-classical portico, in the 19th century. In the time of the Knights it housed the Grand Master's bodyguard.

The **multi-vision show "Malta George Cross"** (Mon.–Fri. 11am, 1 and 3 pm, Sat. and Sun. 11am), in a building facing the side of the Main Guard, illustrates the story of Malta during the Second World War. The Maltese were awarded the George Cross in 1942 in recognition of their valour. Alternating with this show is "the Valletta Experience", a nostalgic trip through the history of the town (Mon.–Fri. 12 noon and 2pm, Sat. and Sun. 10am and 12 noon), on the history of Valletta.

At 74 Republic Street is the Casa Rocca Piccola (open Mon.–Sat. 10 and 11am, 12 and 1pm), a private house dating from the 16th century which gives a unique impression of the life-style of a noble Maltese family. The de Piro Family lives here, but it is open to the public with entertaining guided tours.

Casa Rocca Piccola

Diagonally opposite the Casa Rocca Piccola is the toy museum with exhibits on three floors.

Toy Museum

Turning right off Republic Street into St Dominic Street, we come to Old Bakery Street (the second cross street), named after the Order's bakery which once stood here. It is a charming little street, mainly of old houses with the characteristic Maltese balconies.

Old Bakery Street

Old Bakery Street cuts across Old Theatre Street, in which is the Manoel Theatre, built for Grand Master Manoel de Vilhena in 1731 and thus one of the oldest theatres still showing regular performances in Europe. Originally known as the Public Theatre and later as the Theatre Royal, it was given its present name in 1866. After the Second World War the state acquired the theatre, which had become increasingly dilapidated since the opening of the Royal Opera House and was then in private ownership. After thorough restoration it was reopened in 1960. It has a

Manoel Theatre

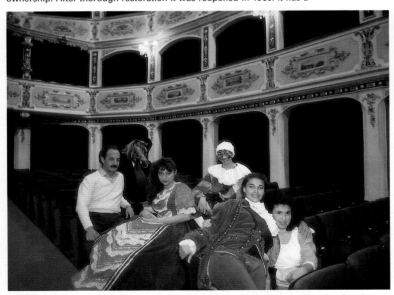

The Manoel Theatre hides a magnificent theatre space behind an unassuming façade. Both plays and concerts are performed here.

sumptuous interior with seats for 720 in four tiers of boxes. (Conducted tours through the theatre and a small theatre museum Mon.–Fri. 10.30 and 11.30am, Sat. 11.30am).

Our Lady of Mount Carmel

A short distance to the north-west is the Carmelite church of Our Lady of Mount Carmel (open daily 6am–12 noon and 4–7.30pm), whose tall dome makes it a striking feature in Malta's skyline. It stands on the site of an earlier church built by Gerolamo Cassar in 1570 which was so badly damaged during the Second World War that it was decided in the late 1950s to replace it by a new building.

St Paul's Anglican Cathedral

In Independence Square, on a site once occupied by the Auberge d'Allemagne, is St Paul's Anglican Cathedral (open Mon.–Fri. 8am–12 noon), with a tall spire which is one of Valletta's landmarks. It was built in 1839–42 at the expense of the dowager Queen Adelaide who during her visit in 1839 could not find a church in Malta that catered for her own denomination of faith. It has a pleasantly harmonious interior in neo-classical style.

Auberge d'Aragon

Across the square from St Paul's is the Auberge d'Aragon (1571), the oldest of the seven auberges built by Gerolamo Cassar and apart from the Auberge de Provence the only one which has largely been preserved in its original condition; the Doric portico was a later addition. Today the Auberge houses the Ministery of Economics.

Archbishop's Palace

In Archbishop's Street, on the left, is the imposing Archbishop's Palace. The ground floor was built in 1624; the upper floor and the present façade date only from the mid-20th century. The reason for this is that while the bishops of Malta had the right to reside in Valletta the Knights allowed them no further privileges; the bishops preferred, therefore, to have their main residence in Mdina.

Auberge d'Angleterre et Bavière

To the north-west, along Old Mint Street, is the Auberge d'Angleterre et Bavière, with its main front looking on to St Elmo Bay. This large, plain Baroque building dating from the late 17th century was acquired in 1784 by the Anglo-Bavarian langue.

Fort St Elmo

From here it is a short walk along the walls of Valletta to Fort St Elmo, at the tip of the Sciberras peninsula. This strategic position was occupied in Phoenician times by a fortification which was later taken over by the Romans. In the 14th/15th century there was a fort with a small chapel dedicated to St Elmo, the patron saint of seafarers. The Knights built a fort here in 1552 to guard the entrance to the Grand Harbour. It was taken by the Turks in 1565 after a month of heavy fighting in which the knights held out to the last man and inflicted heavy losses on the enemy. After the foundation of Valletta the fort was rebuilt, and in the 17th century its defences were still further strengthened. Held by the French from 1798 to 1800, it then passed into British hands and was used as a barracks. During the Second World War it was of strategic importance for beating off attacks by Italian submarines.

Today, the fort, which is occupied by The Malta Police Academy, is open to the public with guided tours (open Sat. 1–5pm, Sun. 9am–5pm).

Every second Sunday of the month a historical parade (In Guardia) takes place inside the fort, a one-hour spectacle where about 90 participants parade wearing the costumes and armour of the Order of the Knights.

National War Museum

A small part of the fort has been occupies since 1975 by the National War Museum (open Oct.–Jun. 15th Mon.–Sat. 8.45am–5pm, Sun.

The historical parade "in Guardia" in the Fort St Elmo, a colourful ▶ spectacle in uniform, with the armoury from the time of the knights

Service to Sir Patient

Cynically, a traveller observed that the splendid marble floor was no substitute for the windows which were too small and thus could not make one forget the nauseating stench. Other visitors to the island, however, admired the architecture of the hospital in Valletta and the cleanliness prevailing there, for example the British ship's priest Henry Teonge who stayed on Malta in 1674, "the hospital is a spacious building in which lie the sick and the wounded. It is so wide that in the centre, without any difficulty, twelve men could be accommodated next to each other. On both sides are beds with iron posts, they are equipped with white curtains, sheets and bed covers and are kept extremely clean, neat and fresh . . ."

Although, over time, the order of the knights of St John developed more and more into a military order, and the masters of the order increasingly asked to be represented in royal attire when they had their portraits painted, the knights nevertheless continued to follow the strict founding rules and never forget their true raison d'être: to serve the sick, the "sir patients". Soon after landing on Malta in 1530, and although the order's coffers were severely depleted after their long odyssey, they built a small hospital in Birgu (now Vittoriosa). Two years later they began with the construction of a new hospital, using hospitals in Jerusalem and on Rhodes as models. Dedicated in 1578 as "Sacra Infirmeria di Malta", it was one of the largest hospitals of the time. The hospital was built into the cliffs of Monte Sciberras which fell away towards the

harbour. To accommodate the topography of the land they terraced the cliffs; one part of the building was broken out of the soft rock, and these rocks were used to build the upper storeys. The lowest floor was linked with the Grand Harbour via a covered walkway so that the sick and wounded could be transported directly from the ship to the treatment rooms.

The largest ward, enlarged in 1662–68, was 165 m long, 11 m wide and almost 10 m high. The ceiling height was important – with summer temperatures of up to 40°C rooms could only be kept cool by raising the ceiling as high as possible. The floor was covered with marble slabs; high windows allowed for fresh air and brightness without blinding the patients; and the gobelins that decorated the walls made the rooms warmer on cold days, while its pictures told the history of the order. Eventually, the hospital had 800 beds, the 300 in the largest ward all had canopies which in summer were replaced by mosquito nets. The islanders were amazed to find that the patients all had their own beds, an unheard-of luxury up until the 19th century, and that they were eating from silver plates, not for reasons of pomp but hygiene; at times when the Knight's finances were not too rosy, zinc was used instead of silver. The Knights themselves served the food to the patients; this way, every knight had to do one day's service in hospital per week, "personally to serve the sirs patients", as required by a decree of 1629, with each langue having its own fixed week day in the rota. Even the

Grand Master was not exempt from this duty, and entered the hospital, always on a Friday, as a plain caring brother – after laying down all signs and symbols of his position first.

The building had several departments: the very sick were separated from those with minor diseases, while the dying were accommodated in a few small rooms; there were isolation wards for communicable diseases; there was even, unusual at the time, a department for the mentally ill who were lovingly cared for. After 1700, the hospital was enlarged by the creation of a women's hospital, an ophthalmic clinic and a quarantine sick bay. Hospital care was not reserved for Catholics; members of other Christian denominations as well as Jews and Muslims were equally entitled to expect treatment. A class system did, however, exist: only members of the order and those of a higher social standing were entitled to specialist treatments.

qualifications. Initially, the Knights paid out of their own pockets for young Maltese men to attend university, usually in Italy. In 1676, the leadership of the order decided to build its own medical school which, because of its good reputation, was attended by many students from other countries. In western countries, medicine was then still of a fairly low standard, and anaesthesia, too, was only in its beginnings. Before an operation, patients were anaesthetised with the fumes of alcohol, opium, poppies and other drugs or – in emergencies – with a simple, but effective means: a hammer. One of the most important remedies for treating wounds, bleeding and dysentery was a black fungus which grew on Fungus Rock by Gozo's coast. In 1968, however, the British Naval Hospital in Bighi on Malta, found as a result of their scientific investigations that this fungus was medically completely without value. Its dark colour, resembling dried blood, was probably the reason why it had been considered a panacaea.

The Knights of St John did not restrict their care of the sick to the hospital. The large hospital also sent doctors to serve for a while at the smaller hospitals of Malta and Gozo. None of the Knights' ships left the harbour without doctor and medical personnel; especially on the narrow galleys the Knights were keen to observe strict cleanliness and hygiene rules. And finally, the Knights also felt obliged to pro-

A reproduction of the large ward is exhibited on the lower floor of the Sacra Infirmeria in Valletta

The sick were professionally cared for by three doctors and three surgeons, each of whom had two assistants, as well as three pharmacists. Nursing care was provided by the knights and by women, while the heavy and dirty work was done by slaves. Any doctor who wanted to work at the Valletta hospital needed to possess medical

vide hospital services outside their own realm. Thus they supplied, for example, the town of Augusta on Sicily with medicines, clothes and food when it had been hit by an earthquake. In short, they were to the Mediterranean region what today might be called "international aid troops".

8.15am–4.15pm; Jun. 16th–Sep. daily 7.45am–2pm) with a display of weapons and other miltary equipment of the 19th and 20th centuries. Numerous photographs and other documents tell the story of Malta's "second siege" in 1940–43. The pride of the museum, however, is the George Cross awarded to Malta by King George VI in 1942 for its valour in withstanding enemy attack.

In front of the fort are a number of circular stone slabs. They cover the entrances to underground grain stores.

★Sacra Infirmeria

A little way south of Fort St Elmo is the Sacra Infirmeria, the Hospital of the Order, built in the time of Grand Master Jean l'Evàque de la Cassiäre by an unknown architect. Its main front is in Mediterranean Street, facing the Grand Harbour, so that the sick and wounded could be brought quickly from ships anchored in the harbour to the Hospital. The Hospital of the Order was famed throughout Europe, and visitors came from far and wide to admire the light and welcoming atmosphere of the wards and standards of hygiene which were uniquely high for their time (see Baedeker Special). Used during the period of British rule as a military hospital and later as police headquarters, the Hospital suffered heavy damage during the Second World War. After rebuilding it was opened in 1979 as the Mediterranean Conference Centre. The main hall was almost completely destroyed by fire in 1987, but after repair, modernisation and enlargement the conference centre reopened two years later. There are six conference rooms accommodating any number of participants from 70 to 1500.

On the lower floor of the Sacra Infirmeria is the exhibition "The Knights Hospitaliers" (open Mon.–Fri. 9.30am–4.30pm, Sat. and Sun. 9.30am–1.30pm) with the history of the Order represented by life-sized figures.

Malta Experience

In a building opposite the Hospital is housed the Malta Experience (Mon.–Fri. at 11am, 12 noon and 1, 2, 3 and 4pm, Sat. and Sun. 11am, 12 noon and 1pm), a multi-vision show which in 45 minutes gives visitors a quick survey of Maltese history, with over 1000 slides, background music and an explanatory commentary.

★Lower Barracca Gardens

South of the Hospital are the Lower Barracca Gardens, which in the time of the Knights were a training ground. Beautifully laid out, they offer a fantastic view of the Grand Harbour. In the centre of the gardens is a building in the style of a Greek temple, erected in honour of Rear Admiral Sir Alexander Ball, commander of the British naval force which blockaded the French occupying force on Malta in 1798–1800 and later the first British high commissioner on Malta. He died on the island in 1809 and was buried in Fort St Elmo.

Siege Bell Memorial

Below the Lower Barracca Gardens is a monument, inaugurated by Queen Elizabeth II and the President of Malta in May 1992, commemorating those who died in the Second World War and the 50th anniversary of the award of the George Cross to Malta.

Old University

From the Lower Barracca Gardens St Dominic Street runs north-west, cutting across Merchants Street. Along this street to the left, on the left-hand side, is the Old University. The University of Malta was founded in 1592 as a Jesuit college teaching theology, philosophy and literature. After the expulsion of the Jesuits in 1769 Grand Master Manuel Pinto de Fonseca added other faculties to the college and raised it to the status of a university. In 1969 the main part of the University was transferred to Msida (see entry), but some departments are still housed in the old building. Within the complex is the Chiesa del Gesó, built between 1596 and 1604; the façade dates in its present form from the mid-18th century.

St Paul Shipwrecked

Farther along Merchants Street is the Valletta Market (1859), and beyond this, on the left, is the church of St Paul Shipwrecked , originally built by

Gerolamo Cassar and remodelled by Lorenzo Gafà in 1629. The façade in its present form dates only from the end of the 19th century. The altar-piece depicts Paul's shipwreck on the shores of Malta (see Baedeker Sepcial); the carved wooden figure of the saint is attributed to Melchiore Gafà (1657).

At 15 Merchants Street is the Castellania, the courthouse of the Order, with prison cells in the basement, which was built by Giuseppe Bonnici in 1748 for Grand Master Manuel Pinto de Fonseca. A symmetrical two-storeyed building, it is now occupied by the Ministry of Health. Over the doorway are allegorical figures of Justice and Truth by the Sicilian sculptor Maestro Gian.

Castellania

Diagonally opposite the Castellania is St James's Church, the chapel of the langue of Castile, which was built in 1710 on the site of an earlier church of 1612. The altarpiece, with a figure of St James, was painted by the 16th-century artist Palladini.

St James's Church

Farther along Merchants Street, on the same side, is the Auberge d'Italie, built in 1574 by Gerolamo Cassar. It was much altered in later centuries; the Baroque features on the façade, for example, were a 17th century addition. The top storey may have been added as late as the reign of Grand Master Gregorio Caraffa (1680–90), of whom there is a bronze effigy above the rusticated doorway.

Auberge d'Italie

Opposite the Auberge d'Italie is the Palazzo Parisio, with a marble tablet on the façade recording that Napoleon stayed here for a few days in 1798. The palace, laid out round an inner courtyard, was built in 1760. It is now occupied by the Foreign Ministry.

Palazzo Parisio

Adjoining the Auberge d'Italie, with its west front on Victory Square, is St Catherine's Church, the church of the Italian langue. It was built by Gerolamo Cassar in 1576; the façade was remodelled in the early 18th century. Over the high altar is a painting by Mattia Preti of the martyrdom of St Catherine.

St Catherine's Church

On the opposite side of Victory Square is the church of Our Lady of Victories (Ta Vittoria). The first building erected after the Great Siege of 1565, it stands on the exact spot where the foundation stone of Valletta was laid. The façade dates in its present form from the late 17th century. The bust of Pope Innocent XI on the pediment of the church was set there by Grand Master Ramon Perellos y Roccaful in gratitude to the Pope for his mediation in a dispute with the bishop of Malta.
  Beside the church is a monument to Sir Paul Boffa (d. 1966), the first Labour Party prime minister after the Second World War.

Our Lady of Victories

Immediately south of these two churches is Castile Place, which is dominated by the Auberge de Castille, Léon et Portugal. It was originally built by Gerolamo Cassar but was magnificently remodelled in Baroque style by Domenico Cachia for Grand Master Pinto de Fonseca (1741–73). The dominant feature of the two-storey façade is the imposing doorway, flanked by paired columns, surmounted by old canons and approached by a broad flight of steps. Over the central window is the coat of arms of Grand Master Pinto de Fonseca, and his bust is above the entrance. The building, laid out round an inner courtyard, was formerly the British military headquarters; it is now the office of the prime minister.
  In the gardens in front of the auberge is a statue (1975) of Manwell Dimech (1860–1921), a pioneer of the socialist movement in Malta.

★★Auberge de Castille, Léon et Portugal

Farther south-east, on St Peter and Paul's Bastion, are the Upper Barracca Gardens. From the terrace there is a superb view of the Grand Harbour and the Three Cities. Originally an exercise ground for knights

★Upper Barracca Gardens

The former Auberge de Castille, Léon et Portugal is today the office of the Maltese prime minister

of the Italian langue, this has been a public garden since the 18th century. The arcades, which date from 1661, were originally roofed, but in 1775, after the priests' rebellion (see History), Grand Master Ximenes had the roof removed in order to prevent the arcades from being used as a meeting-place for subversive groups. Among the many statues and monuments in the gardens is a fine group, "Les Gavroches", by the Maltese sculptor Antonio Sciortino.

The Sacred Island	In a building next to the entrance to the Upper Barracca Gardens the multi-vision show "The Sacred Island" tells of the religious history of the Maltese (Mon.–Fri. 10 and 11.30am, 1, 2.30 and 4pm, Sat. 10 and 11.30 am, 1pm, Sun. 10 and 11.30 am).
Our Lady of Liesse	The red dome below the Upper Barracca Gardens belongs to the church of Our Lady of Liesse. Built in 1620, it was renovated in 1740. It contains a much revered image of Our Lady of Liesse.
Lascaris War Rooms	Below the Upper Barracca Gardens are the Lascaris War Rooms. During the Second World War these were the headquarters and operations rooms of British forces in the Mediterranean. The commander's rooms are preserved with their original furnishings, and life-sized figures tell of the years of the Second Great Siege (open Mon.–Fri. 9.30am–4pm, Sat. and Sun. 9.30am–1pm).
Custom House	Farther south, still below the Upper Barracca Gardens, is the Custom House (by Giuseppe Bonnici, 1774). The walls are up to 4 m thick.
★National Museum of Fine Arts	From the Custom House it is a short distance to the starting-point of the tour outside City Gate. But before leaving Valletta a visit should be paid to the National Museum of Fine Arts in South Street (open Oct.–Jun.

15th Mon.–Sat. 8.15am–5pm, Sun. 8.15am–4.15pm, Jun. 16th–Sep. daily 7.45am–2pm). The Museum is housed in a palace built in 1761–63, originally a guest-house of the Order and during the Order's last years in Malta the residence of the Grand Master's secretary. From 1821 it was the headquarters of the commander of the British fleet in the Mediterranean, under the name of Admiralty House. After it became the property of the Maltese government in 1961 it was thoroughly restored and in 1974 became the home of the National Museum of Fine Arts.

The collection is arranged in chronological order, beginning on the upper floor. The first two rooms are devoted to Florentine and Tuscan painting of the 14th and 15th centuries. The other rooms on the upper floor contain mainly works of the 16th and 17th centuries, including "Portrait of a Lady", of the school of Jan van Scorel, Tintoretto's "Man in Armour", Guido Reni's "Christ with the Cross" and several paintings by Mattia Preti. A special room is devoted to the Maltese sculptor Antonio Sciortino (1879–1947). The tour continues on the ground floor, beginning with Room 14, which contains works by the French artist Antoine de Favray (1706–98), who painted many portraits of Grand Masters and other high dignitaries of the Order. In room 19 are views of Valletta and harbour scenes by Louis du Cros (1748–1810) which are of great historical interest. Rooms 20 to 24 are devoted to Maltese artists of the 17th–20th centuries.

In the basement are objets d'art and everyday objects connected with the life and work of the Order. Of particular interest are a collection of 18th century silver in which meals were served to patients in the Hospital, models of the Order's vessels, coins, weights and measures and a small collection of weapons.

To conclude the tour a visit can be paid to the Hastings Garden, just within the walls at the west end of Valletta, from which there is a good view of the suburb of Floriana (see entry). The garden is named after the Marquis of Hastings, governor of Malta 1824–26.

Hastings Garden

From here it is a short distance, passing St John's Cavalier (now occupied by the embassy of the Sovereign Order of Malta), back to City Gate.

Vittoriosa   J 6

The promontory reaching into the Grand Harbour between Kalkara Creek and Dockyard Creek is occupied by the town of Vittoriosa (pop. 3000), which along with Senglea and Cospicua (see entries) is one of the "Three Cities" which the Maltese often refer to under the collective name of the Cottonera. Unlike its two neighbours, it is not merely a residential district but has many features of interest for visitors. There are no hotels or restaurants – only a few modest bars to offer refreshment. Most visitors, therefore, only come to Vittoriosa for a brief tour of the old town.

Before the Knights of St John came to Malta there was a village on the site of Vittoriosa called Birgu – a name by which the people of Vittoriosa often still refer to their town. The origins of the settlement go far back in time. There is believed to have been a temple here in Phoenician times. When the Knights came to Malta in 1530 Birgu was a modest little fishing village, but it was so well situated that they moved the headquarters of the Order from Mdina to Birgu. They built auberges for the various langues of the Order, a hospital and above all massive fortifications. These fortifications were put to the test during the Great Siege of 1565, and after the Turkish attack was finally repelled Birgu was renamed Vittoriosa in honour of the victory. A few years later, however, in 1571, the headquarters of the Order were transferred from Birgu to the new town of Valletta. But the Knights recognised the continuing strategic

History

Numerous historical buildings in Vittoriosa still remind us today that the town used to be the first seat of the Knights on Malta

importance of the town and, like Senglea and Cospicua, it was protected by massive bastions. Dockyard Creek, on the south side of the town, served as a harbour for the Order's fleet of galleys, and along its shores were built warehouses, workshops and accommodation for harbour workers and soldiers.

During the Second World War Vittoriosa, with its port installations and shipyards, was exposed to constant air attack. Nevertheless some of its historic buildings survived the war unscathed.

Town

In the narrow streets visitors will encounter a variety of interesting buildings dating from the time of the Knights (though with the exception of the churches and the Inquisitor's Palace they are private property and are not open to the public), and they will find themselves in a typically Maltese atmosphere well away from the swarms of tourists.

The town is protected on the landward side by a moat (now public gardens) and massive ramparts and watch-towers. The east side of the peninsula is also fortified. The knights of the various langues were responsible for the defence of particular sections of the fortifications (see town plan).

From the Main Gate of the town Main Gate Street (Triq il-Mina il-Kbira) runs through the centre of the town and soon comes to the Inquisitor's Palace, on the right.

★Inquisitor's Palace

The Inquisitor's Palace (open Oct.–Jun. 15th Mon.–Sat. 8.15am–5pm, Sun. 8.15am–4.15pm; Jun. 16th–Sep. daily 7.45am–2pm) contains a small folk museum and is also occasionally used for special exhibitions. A visit to the palace – the only one of its kind in Europe – is worth while mainly for the opportunity of seeing the Inquisitor's public and private apartments.

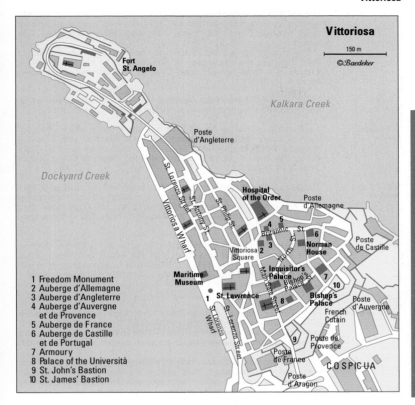

Vittoriosa

150 m

©Baedeker

Fort St. Angelo

Kalkara Creek

Dockyard Creek

Poste d'Angleterre

Hospital of the Order

Poste d'Allemagne

Poste de Castille

St. Lorenzo Street

Vittoriosa Wharf

St. Antony St.

St. Philip St.

Britannic St.

North St.

Vittoriosa Square

Norman House

Maritime Museum

Inquisitor's Palace

Bishop's St.

Main Gate Street

St. Lawrence

Bishop's Palace

Poste d'Auvergne

French Cutain

Poste de Provence

Poste de France

Posta de Aragon

Posta de France

COSPICUA

St. Lorenzo Wharf

1 Freedom Monument
2 Auberge d'Allemagne
3 Auberge d'Angleterre
4 Auberge d'Auvergne et de Provence
5 Auberge de France
6 Auberge de Castille et de Portugal
7 Armoury
8 Palace of the Università
9 St. John's Bastion
10 St. James' Bastion

The building of the palace began in 1535, but it was much altered in later centuries. It was given its present aspect in 1767. From 1574 to 1798 the Inquisitors appointed by the Pope had their residence here. Although there were never any persecutions of heretics or mass executions in Malta the Inquisitors represented a significant counterweight to the authority of the Order.

Behind the plain façade of the palace is a labyrinth of rooms and passages laid out round three inner courtyards. Opposite the main doorway is a staircase leading to the upper floor. The principal rooms are the Council Chamber, decorated with the coats of arms of the Inquisitors (including two who later became Pope), and the Court Room. On the far side of this is an unusually low door through which the accused person was brought in, so that he was forced to bow down when appearing before the Inquisitor. Through this doorway is a staircase leading down to the dungeons. Narrow openings in the wall give a view of the Gallows Yard. The Inquisitor's private apartments are reached on another staircase.

From the Inquisitor's Palace various narrow lanes run west to a square on Dockyard Creek. Before the Knights came to Malta there stood here a church dedicated to St Lawrence which became the

St Lawrence's Church

Order's first conventual church. A new church was built on the site by Lorenzo Gafà between 1681 and 1697; the west front in its present form, however, dates only from 1913, when the second tower was added.

The church, on a Latin cross plan, has an altarpiece by Mattia Preti depicting the martyrdom of St Lawrence. In the Chapel of the Crucifix is a cross brought from Crete in 1657 as one of the spoils of war.

Freedom Monument

In the square in front of the church is the Freedom Monument, which commemorates the withdrawal of the last British troops in 1979.

St Joseph's Oratory

To the north-east of the church is St Joseph's Oratory, which was originally a Greek Orthodox church. It has been restored and is now a museum, which in addition to many mementoes of the siege of Malta during the Second World War possesses the sword of Grand Master Jean de la Valette.

National Maritime Museum

The National Maritime Museum on Vittoriosa Wharf was opened in 1991 in the former naval bakery. It illustrates the history of Maltese shipping with a variety of shop models, documents and paintings (open Jun. 16th–Sep. daily 7.45am–2pm, Oct.–Jun. 15th Mon.–Sat. 8.15am–5pm, Sun. 8.15am–4.15pm).

Fort St Angelo

St Anthony Street leads to Fort St Angelo, at the tip of the promontory. There was an Arab fort here as early as 670, which the Knights rebuilt and strengthened. From 1912 to 1979 it was the headquarters of the Royal Navy. A hotel was opened in the fort in 1984, but the whole complex is now empty (conducted tours Sat. 10am–2pm, in summer only until 1pm).

Vittoriosa Square

From Fort St Angelo St Philip Street leads back to Vittoriosa Square (Misrah ir-Rebha) in which are a monument erected in 1705 to commemorate the victory over the Turks in 1565 and a stone cross marking the spot on which public executions were carried out until the 16th century.

On the east side of the square is the Auberge d'Allemagne, which was destroyed in an air raid in 1942 and rebuilt after the war without its former watch-tower. Like the other auberges in Vittoriosa, it is privately owned and is not open to the public.

Hospital of the Order

In St Scholastica Street, to the north of Vittoriosa Square, is the Hospital of the Order, built in 1530. After the Sacra Infirmeria was built in Valletta the building was made over to an order of Benedictine nuns, which still occupies it.

Other sights

From Vittoriosa Square Britannic Street runs north-east. On the left-hand side of this street are the Auberge d'Auvergne et de Provence (No. 17–23) and the Auberge de France (Nos. 24–27). In North Street, which goes off Britannic Street on the right, is the Norman House, a 16th century building which owes its name to some 11th century architectural features it preserves from an earlier building on the site. Farther along Britannic Street are the Auberge de Castille (No. 57) and the Auberge de Portugal (No. 59). To the south of this is the former Armoury of the Order, and opposite it, in Bishop's Palace Street, the Bishop's Palace (now occupied by a school), which dates in its present form from 1615. A few yards east of the Bishop's Palace, in Convent Street, is the Palace of the Università (1538), Malta's self-governing body in the time of the Knights.

The east end of Convent Street runs into Main Gate Street, which returns to the starting-point of the tour.

Zabbar   J 6/7

On the eastern edge of the built-up area surrounding Valletta is the town of Zabbar (pop. 14,000). There is archaeological evidence that the site was occupied in the Neolithic period and the Bronze Age. After the building of a number of watch-towers in the 17th century to provide protection against pirate raids the town developed rapidly.

Zabbar was granted its municipal charter and the honorific title of Città di Hompesch by the last Grand Master of the Order, Ferdinand von Hompesch (1797–98).

The last Grand Master is commemorated by the neo-classical Hompesch Gate through which the road from Paola enters the town.

Hompesch Gate

In the centre of the town is the imposing parish church of Ta' Grazzia (Our Lady of All Graces), built on a Latin cross plan between 1641 and 1696 to the design of Tommaso Dingli. The Baroque façade dates from 1737, the dome only from 1928, when it replaced a lower dome destroyed by a cannonball in 1798. It has an interior of great sumptuousness for a parish church, having been decked by the Order with valuable works of art and furnishings. The altarpiece of the Virgin on the high altar is by Alessio Erardi, the son of Stefano Erardi (1650–1733).

Ta' Grazzia

The Sanctuary Museum (open Sun. 9am–12 noon) beside the church contains votive offerings dating from the time of the Knights. In addition

Sanctuary Museum

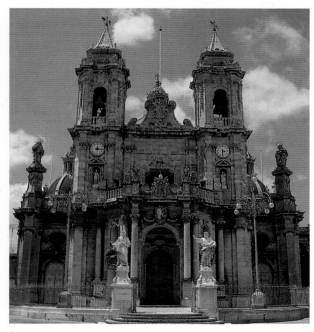

Zabbar: parish church of Ta'Grazzia

to models of galleys, a number of pictures and banners and standards captured during the Turkish siege the exhibits include an early 17th century coach which belonged to Grand Master Alof de Wignacourt.

Zebbieh   E 5

The little town of Zebbieh, a few kilometres north of Mdina, made news in the early 1960s when the Skorba temples were brought to light.

Skorba

On the northern outskirts of Zebbieh a signpost on the Mdina-Ghajn Tuffieha road points left to the Skorba excavation site. Although the site is enclosed by railings there is a good view of it through the railings.

To the non-expert eye the remains are not impressive, but to the archaeologists they yielded important information. Remains of a wall and foundations dating from the earliest phase of megalithic culture (c. 5200–4100 BC) were discovered. These are believed to be the oldest remains of human settlement in Malta. No trace of this earliest level is now to be seen, since above it lay two Neolithic temples of a later period and the foundations of Bronze Age huts.

The site is also important because of the pottery found here – grey and later red ware dated to between 4600 and 3800 BC after which this period of megalithic culture is known as the Skorba phase.

Zebbug   G 6/7

Zebbug is a little town of 10,000 inhabitants 9 km south-west of Valletta. It was granted its municipal charter by Grand Master Emmanuel de Rohan de Polduc (1775–97).

Zebbug was the home town of the sculptor Antonio Sciortino, one of the few major Maltese artists.

De Rohan Gate

At the entrance to the town on the road from Qormi is a triumphal arch erected by the second-last Grand Master of the Order.

St Philip's Church

The parish church of St Philip, on a Latin cross plan, was built by Vittorio Cassar in 1599. The main doorway is reminiscent of the doorway of St John's Co-Cathedral in Valletta, which was designed by Vittorio Cassar's father, the famous architect of the Order of St John, Gerolamo Cassar.

Zejtun   J 7

In eastern Malta, half way between Paola and Marsaxlokk, is the little town of Zejtun (pop. 11,500). As its name ("place where there is oil") indicates, there were olive-groves here at an early period, and agriculture is still the main occupation of the inhabitants.

The Zejtun area has been settled at least since the Bronze Age. Until early modern times the area was frequently raided by pirates, and since Zejtun, lying in a plain, was not easily defensible the inhabitants fortified their own houses. Many of the older farms in the area have a fortress-like appearance.

Zejtun is a modest little country town whose main features of interest for visitors are its two churches. The imposing parish church of St Catherine stands in the centre of the town; the little church dedicated to St Gregory is on the outskirts of the town on the road to Tas-Silg.

St Catherine's Church

The parish church of St Catherine was begun by Lorenzo Gafà in 1692,

St Gregory's Church

but it took almost a century for the nave, transepts and side chapels to be completed. The dome was added in the early 20th century. The façade is divided into two storeys by a projecting cornice and flanked by two tall, slender bell-towers. The central section has a segmented pediment.

The paintings in the interior of the church date from the late 17th to the end of the 19th century. The altarpiece was painted by Stefano Erardi (early 18th c.). In one of the side chapels is a Madonna attributed to Botticelli.

From the parish church St Gregory's Street (Triq San Grigor) runs south-east for some 300 m to the fortress-like St Gregory's Church, one of the oldest in Malta. An older chapel on the site was enlarged in 1436, when an adjoining watch-tower was incorporated in the church as the south transept The nave and transepts were given saddle roofs in the late 16th century; the Renaissance doorway dates from the 17th century. It was originally planned to demolish St Gregory's after the completion of the new parish church. This plan was finally abandoned, but the choir was demolished and replaced by a wall to the rear of the altar, to which the sacristy was later built on.

St Gregory's is now a cemetery chapel and is normally opened only for funerals.

St Gregory's Church

Zurrieq   H 8

Zurrieq (pop. 8700), in southern Malta, is one of the oldest towns on the island. It was one of the original ten parishes into which Malta was divided in 1436. It is usually visited only by tourists on their way to the Blue Grotto (see entry).

This long straggling town has no sights of outstanding importance, but the parish church of St Catherine (built in the first half of the 17th century but later much altered) is worth visiting for the sake of its collection of works by Mattia Preti, who lived in Zurrieq for some years and painted the altarpiece depicting the martyrdom of St Catherine, one of his finest works.

The Armeria is a plain 17th century palace which was used by the Knights in the 18th century as an armoury.

At the north end of the town is the little Chapel of the Annunciation, which, after several restorations, ranks as the best preserved medieval church in Malta. It has a cycle of 15th century frescoes.

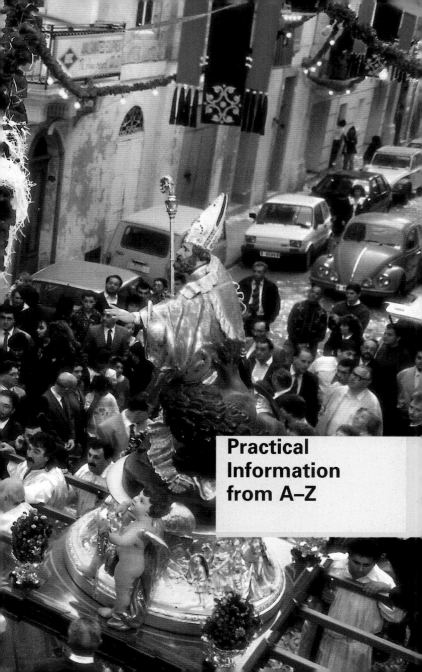

**Practical
Information
from A–Z**

Practical Information from A to Z

Accommodation

See Hotels; Youth Hostels

Airlines

Air Malta

In Malta:
Luqa Airport; tel. 690890; fax 882912 (head office)
Freedom Square, Valletta; tel. 240686
Air Malta offices also make reservations for Malta Air Charter helicopter flights to Gozo.

In the United Kingdom:
36–38 Piccadilly, London W1V 9PA
Tel. (020) 72924949, fax (020) 77341836
Also at Birmingham, Glasgow and Manchester Airports

In the United States:
Rockefeller Centre
630 Fifth Avenue, Suite 2662
New York NY 10111
Tel. (212) 2457768, fax (212) 245 7758

Malta Air Charter runs a scheduled service between Malta and Gozo with 20-seater helicopters

◀ *Procession in Floriana. The climax of every patron saint's festival is on the Sunday, when the life-size statue of the saint is carried through the town.*

In Malta:
World Aviation Systems, 20/2 Republic Street
Valletta; tel. 242233; fax 242237
Malta Air Charter also offers excursion flights over the island (see Excursions); booking at travel agents or Air Malta.

British Airways

Airports

Luqa Airport, Malta's only international airport (for information tel. 249600), lies only 6 km south of Valletta. In recent years it has been steadily enlarged and modernised (tourist information, car rental desks, post office, banks, duty-free shop). There is a shuttle bus service (Nos. 8) between the airport and the town terminal at City Gate, Valletta, where there are connecting services to all parts of the island.

Gozo has only a short airstrip for helicopters at Xewkija, although with an ultra-modern terminal. In summer, there are several scheduled flights a day in 20-seater helicopters to and from Luqa Airport. The journey takes about 15 minutes.

Gozo Heliport

Arts and Crafts

In the larger towns and tourist centres there are plenty of shops selling Maltese arts and crafts and souvenirs. The largest selection, however, is to be found in the craft centres of Ta'Qali on Malta and its smaller counterpart, Ta'Dbiegi, on Gozo, where, in hangars on a disused military airfield in the one case and in plain barrack-like buildings in the other, visitors can not only buy souvenirs but also watch the craftsmen making them. The range is wide: pottery and ceramics, gold and silver filigree work, mouth-blown coloured glass, articles carved from Maltese stone, woven and embroidered fabrics, wrought-iron objects and much else. An old-established traditional craft is pillow-lace making; glass-blowing, on the other hand, was introduced to Malta only in the mid-1960s. It needs a good deal of luck to find anything really unusual, such as a traditional door-knocker in the form of a dolphin.

Souvenirs

Malta Government Crafts Centre
St John's Square (facing the Cathedral), Valletta
Opening times from October to mid-June: Mon.–Fri. 9am–12.30pm and 3–5pm; from mid-June to September: Mon.–Fri. 9am–1.30pm
  The exhibition displays the whole range of Maltese arts and crafts. The exhibits are not for sale but prospective purchasers are given the addresses of suppliers.

Exhibition of arts and crafts

Phoenician Glassblowers
Manoel Island, Gzira
Tel. 313606
Opening times: Mon.–Fri. 8am–4.30pm, Sat. 9am–12.30pm
  Visitors can watch the glassblowers at work and can buy the finished products. From the Strand, Sliema's seafront promenade, there is a free boat service (an appointment must be made by telephone).

Glass-blowing

Ta'Qali Crafts Village (Malta)
Below Mdina. The access road goes off on the left of the Mdina-Attard road.
  The opening times of the individual craftsmen vary: most of them are open Mon.–Fri. 9.30am–4pm and Sat. 10am–1pm.

Craft centres

Ta'Dbiegi Crafts Village (Gozo)
On the Victoria–San Lawrenz road, soon after the turn-off for Gharb.

Automobile Club

Touring Club
Malta (TCM)

Philcyn House
Ursuline Sisters Street
G'Mangia MSD 09
Tel. 320349, fax. 238226
There is no breakdown service on Malta, but in case of emergencies a towing away service can be hired under tel. 333332 and 248116.

Banks

Bank of Valletta
15 Islet Promenade, Bugibba
Dragonara Road, St Julian's
85 Main Street, St Paul's Bay
Republic Street, Valletta
It-Tokk, Victoria (Gozo)
Mgarr (Gozo)

Mid-Med Bank
High Street, Sliema
Republic Street, Valletta

Normal banking hours are: October 1st to June 15th, Mon.–Fri. 8.30am–12.30pm, Sat. 8.30am–12 noon; June 16th to September 30th, Mon.–Fri. 8am–12.30pm, Sat. 8–11.30am. On Tuesdays and Fridays many banks are also open in the afternoon.

With a Eurocheque card or credit card and PIN, money can be drawn at any time from the **cash dispensers** with which many bank branches are now equipped.

Changing money outside normal banking hours: there are foreign exchange bureaux at Luqa Airport. There are also two banks which are open round the clock, though this service is available only to passengers arriving or departing.

Thomas Cook, Bureau de Change
Il-Pjazzetta, Tower Road
Sliema
Open Mon.–Fri. 9am–6pm, Sat. 9.30am–12.30pm

W. and J. Coppini and Co., Exchange Bureau
58 Merchants Street, Valletta
6 Ross Street, Paceville
Open Mon.–Sat. 9am–12.30pm and 3–6pm

Beaches

Bathing in the Mediterranean is possible, with pleasant water temperatures, from May to October. But a holiday in the Maltese archipelago cannot be unreservedly recommended for those who want to spend most of their time on the beach. Malta, Gozo and Comino have only relatively small beaches, and although some of them are very beautiful they are hopelessly overcrowded during the main holiday season.

Nude bathing or sunbathing is prohibited in Malta. Even going topless is frowned on, though it is tolerated in some places.

Beaches on Malta

Although there is a sandy beach in Pretty Bay, to the south of **Birzebbuga**, it cannot be recommended for bathing, being dominated by the port installations of the Kalafrana deep-water harbour.

There are a number of charming bathing beaches with rock terraces on the east side of the **Delimara** peninsula which bounds Marsaxlokk Bay. Peter's Pool is a particular favourite.

The finest sandy beaches on Malta are at **Ghajn Tuffieha**, in the north-west of the island. The one best equipped with facilities for holidaymakers (restaurants, hire of recliners, sun umbrellas and equipment for water sports) is Golden Bay. Ghajn Tuffieha is quieter and unspoiled by over-building. Just to the south of it is Gnejna Bay, which has only a small beach of reddish sand and a shingle beach.

At **Ghar Lapsi**, on the south coast of Malta near the Neolithic temples of Hagar Qim and Mnajdra, is a rocky cove with a shingle beach and concrete platforms.

Marfa Ridge There are a number of attractive bathing beaches at the north-western tip of Malta. The most beautiful is Paradise Bay, which has a small beach of light-coloured sand. Runners-up are Ramla Bay and Armier Bay. All the beaches have snack bars, sun umbrellas and recliners, and equipment for water sports can be hired.

Mellieha Bay in the north-west of the island has one of the longest sandy bays on Malta. Unfortunately, however, the main road runs just above the beach.

Sliema/St Julian's There are no sandy beaches in this area, Malta's main tourist centre. Sunbathers must make do with the shelving rocks on the foreshore.

There are no sandy beaches in **St Paul's Bay** apart from a tiny one below Pjazza Tal-Bajja in Bugibba. Apart from this there are the rock terraces at San Pawl il-Bahar and the swimming pools of the hotels.

St Thomas Bay, on the east coast of Malta, has a short sandy beach and a longer one of shingle, neither of them particularly well cared for.

Beaches on Gozo

In **Hondoq Bay** near Qala right in the south-eastern tip of Gozo a new sand beach has been created. There are toilets and a kiosk, and good views towards Comino and Malta.

The shingle beaches round the **Inland Sea** on the west coast of Gozo are shared by fishermen and visitors. A few hundred metres south rather quieter spots can be found on the rocks round **Dwejra Bay**, against the romantic backdrop of Fungus Rock.

Marsalforn, Gozo's principal tourist centre, has only a tiny sandy beach in the town centre. Most visitors prefer the rock terraces on the west side of Marsalforn Bay and at Qbaijar.

The long fjord-like inlet of **Mgarr ix-Xini**, south-east of Xewkija, is fringed with rocks, but is nevertheless a popular bathing area both with local people and with visitors.

Gozo's finest beach, at Ramla Bay

Ramla Bay Gozo's finest beach, some 500 m long and 50 m wide, is on the north coast, a few kilometres east of Marsalforn. During the season sun umbrellas and recliners are available for hire, and refreshments are provided by two or three improvised bars.

San Blas Bay, also on the north coast, has a small sandy beach which before and after the main holiday season has a less well cared for look than Ramla Bay. There are no tourist facilities.

Xlendi, the largest tourist area on Gozo after Marsalforn, has no sandy beaches. Sunbathers must be content with the rock terraces which run round Xlendi Bay.

Beaches on Comino

Comino's main attraction is the **Blue Lagoon**, between the main island and the rocky islet of Cominotto. The water of the lagoon shimmers in every shade of blue and green. There are usually numbers of boats and excursion ships in the lagoon. There is only a tiny sandy beach, and most visitors must fall back upon the surrounding rocks and rock terraces. There is no shade.

Santa Marija Bay, on the north coast of Comino, has a small sandy bay.

Business Hours

Normal **banking hours** are: October 1st to June 15th, Mon.–Fri. 8.30am–12.30pm, Sat. 8.30am–12 noon; June 16th to September 30th, Mon.–Fri. 8am–12.30pm, Sat. 8–11.30am. Some banks and exchange offices are also open outside these hours (see Banks).

Chemists' shops are open Mon.–Fri. 9am–1pm and 3.30–7pm, Sat. 8.30am–12 noon. An emergency service is available on Sunday mornings (see Chemists).

Churches are frequently open both in the morning and afternoon.

Museums: see entry

Petrol stations are open Mon.–Sat. 7am–7pm (in winter many petrol stations close at 5.30pm). On Sundays and public holidays almost all petrol stations are closed.

Post offices are open Mon.–Sat. 8am–12.45pm. The General Post Office in Valletta (Merchants Street) is open in summer Mon.–Sat. 7.30am–6pm, in winter Mon.–Sat. 8am–6.30pm.

Many **restaurants** are open between 11am and 2pm and between 7pm and midnight; some are open only in the evening. Pizzerias and snack bars often open as early as 5pm.

Most **shops** are open Mon.–Fri. 9am–7pm, Sat. 9am–8pm; on Gozo shops close on Saturday at 12 noon. Many shops close for two or three hours at lunch-time.

Bus Services

Buses are the most important means of transport on Malta and Gozo. Many of them are old-stagers which have seen good service, but whether old or new they are all easily distinguished by their colour – yellow with dark orange stripes (grey on Gozo).

Fares are low. Single tickets cost between 11c and 30c. A new ticket is required for every journey. Tickets are bought on the bus; day tickets cost LM1.25 and are available from various sales points in Sliema and Bugibba; a 7-day ticket can be bought at all branches of the Bank of Valletta (a 3-day ticket costs LM3, a 7-day ticket LM4).

Timetables

At the busiest times of day the buses run at intervals of between 5 and 30 minutes. After 9pm buses run from Valletta only to the main tourist centres on Malta. At weekends the last buses to towns throughout Malta are usually at 7pm.

On Gozo bus services are less frequent; on many routes there are no more than four buses a day (and outside the holiday season sometimes none at all). The last bus to some places leaves at 6pm.

Bus routes

On Malta almost all bus routes start from Valletta. The central bus station is outside City Gate, round the Triton Fountain. There are few local connections: to get from one place to another in a different part of the island it is usually necessary to change in Valletta. The situation on Gozo is similar.

The Valletta Tourist Office has a free brochure with the most important bus routes.

Bus stops

Bus stops are marked by red or blue signs. Buses only stop on request; on the bus, a button needs to be pushed or a line pulled to indicate to the driver that one wishes to get off.

179

Camping

There are no camping sites in Malta, and "wild" camping is prohibited.

Car Rental

Car rental charges in Malta are government-controlled and are remarkably low (from about LM11 per day including comprehensive insurance; weekly rates are particularly good value); they usually include unlimited mileage. Most firms ask for flat fee of LM6 or 7 for petrol; you receive a car with a half-full tank and can return it almost empty.

To hire a car you must be at least 25 (or 21 if you take out comprehensive insurance) and not more than 70 and must have held a driving licence for at least two years. All drivers are separately listed in the contract, and a fee for every extra driver is usually charged.

Make sure that the hire car has a spare tyre: punctures are a regular occurrence in Malta!

International car hire firms usually offer a car delivery to Gozo, and cars hired on Malta can normally be taken across to Gozo.

Cars can be hired before leaving home through one of the big international rental firms.

Malta

Avis
50 Seafront, Msida; tel. 246640 and 225986
Offices also in Bugibba, Floriana, Luqa Airport, Mellieha and St Julian's.

Budget
Mexico Buildings, Zimelli Street, Marsa; tel. 247111
Offices also in Bugibba, Luqa Airport, Qawra and Sliema.

Europcar/InterRent
Alpine House, Naxxar Road, San Gwann; tel. 337361
Offices also at Luqa Airport and in Sliema.

Hertz
Tower Road, Sliema; tel. 319939
Offices also in Gzira, Luqa Airport and Qawra.

Chemists

Most internationally used drugs are available in Malta. If you are on some particular drug, however, it is advisable, for safety's sake, to take a supply with you.

Chemists' shops are open Mon.–Fri. 8.30 or 9am to 1pm and 3.30–7pm, Sat. 8.30am–12 noon.

A list of chemists open at weekends is published in the weekend editions of newspapers.

Cinemas

On Malta there are cinemas in Valletta and Sliema. On Gozo the Astra and Victoria Theatres in Victoria sometimes show films. Films are shown in the original English (or sometimes Italian) version.

Conferences and Congresses

The state-owned **Mediterranean Conference Centre** in Valletta (housed in the Sacra Infirmeria, the old Hospital of the Order of St John), has six conference rooms with the most modern equipment which can accommodate conferences with anything from 70 to 1500 participants.

Information: Conference and Incentive Travel Bureau, 280 Republic Street, Valletta; tel. 234448 or 225048/9, fax 220401.

In recent years many **hotels** have increased their conference capacity. The Oracle Conference Centre in the New Dolmen Hotel, Qawra, can accommodate up to 1100 participants. Other hotels with conference facilities include the Suncrest Hotel in Qawra, the Phoenicia Hotel in Floriana and the Corinthia Palace Hotel in Attard.

Conversions

To convert metric to imperial multiply by the imperial factor; e.g. 100 km equals 62 mi. (100 x **0.62**).

1 metre	**3.28** feet, **1.09** yards	Linear measure
1 kilometre (1000 m)	**0.62** mile	
1 square metre	**1.2** square yards, **10.76** square feet	Square measure
1 hectare	**2.47** acres	
1 square kilometre (100 ha)	**0.39** square mile	
1 litre (1000 ml)	**1.76** pints (**2.11** US pints)	Capacity
1 kilogram (1000 grams)	**2.21** pounds	
1 metric ton (1000 kg)	**0.98** ton	

°C	°F	°C	°F	Temperature
-5	23	20	68	
0	32	25	77	
5	41	30	86	
10	50	35	95	
15	59	40	104	

Currency

The Maltese unit of currency is the lira (LM), which is divided into 100 cents (c). There are banknotes for 2, 5, 10 and 20 LM and coins in denominations of 1, 2, 5, 10, 25 and 50 cents.

The maximum amount of Maltese currency that can be brought into the country is LM50; the maximum amount that can be taken out is LM25.

There are no restrictions on the import or export of foreign currency, though for safety's sake very large sums should be declared on arrival in Malta.

Outside banking hours, money can be changed in exchange bureaux, some travel agencies and the receptions of larger hotels. Money is exchanged at the same rate everywhere, but the commission charges can vary widely. At the airports, money can be changed 24 hours a day,

Changing money

and in Valletta and the main tourist centres, machines will exchange foreign paper money into Maltese Lira.

Bancomats are the easiest and cheapest way of obtaining Maltese currency. These issue currency, usually up to LM70, against several credit cards and EC cards and PIN number.

Eurocheques can be cashed for amounts not exceeding LM70. If you lose your Eurocheque card you should report the loss immediately by telephone to the bank which issued it.

Credit cards Banks, the larger hotels, restaurants in the higher categories, car rental firms and many shops accept most international credit cards.

The loss of a credit card should be reported at once to the issuing agency.

Customs Regulations

Personal belongings and clothing intended for the visitor's own use are not liable to duty. The duty-free allowance for adults is 200 cigarettes, 50 cigars or 250 grams of tobacco, 0.75l spirits, 0.75l wine and a reasonable quantity of perfume and toilet water. Duty needs to be paid on all gifts. Mobile telephones have to be declared on entry.

Diplomatic and Consular Offices

United Kingdom

High Commission
7 St Anne Street, Floriana
Tel. 233134, fax 292001

United States

Embassy
Development House
St Anne Street, Floriana
Tel. 235960, fax 256917

Canada

Consulate
Demajo House
103 Archbishop Street, Valletta
Tel. 233121 and 243127

Dress

In summer light cotton clothing is best. In spring and autumn it can be quite cool, particularly in the evening, so something warmer is required. In winter warm clothing is essential, and above all protection against rain.

In general dress in Malta is rather more formal than in other holiday areas in the Mediterranean. Bathing suits should be confined to the beach or the swimming pool. In restaurants of the better sort men are expected to wear jackets in the evening.

In churches there are rather stricter rules. Ladies should cover their shoulders and décolleté (scarves can sometimes be hired at the entrance to the church), and men should not wear shorts.

Electricity

Electricity is 240 volts AC. The square-fitting standard three-pin British plugs and sockets are used.

Emergencies

Ambulance Malta and Gozo: dial 196
Fire Malta and Gozo: dial 199
Police Malta and Gozo: dial 191

Events

Details of events in Malta, as well as much other information, are given in the fortnightly publication "What's On" and in the brochure "Welcome – A Holiday Guide", which appears monthly.

Throughout the year, particularly in the summer months, there are patronal festivals all over Malta (see Baedeker Special), when towns and villages celebrate the day of their patron saint with services of thanksgiving in the parish church, musical events and fireworks. The celebrations usually go on for five days. The high point of the festival is on Sunday, when a life-size figure of the saint is carried in procession through the streets. The church is elaborately decorated, as are many houses. The following list includes only a selection of such festivals.

Patronal festivals

Malta Marathon: an event, first held in 1986, which attracts runners around the world.

February

Carnival. Towns and villages on Malta and Gozo all have their own parades and other celebrations. The main centre of activity, however, is Valletta (see Art and Culture, Music, Festivals and Customs).

February/March

Holy Week, celebrated with processions. Particularly interesting for visitors are the ceremonies on Easter Saturday in Vittoriosa and Cospicua.

March/April

Flower, Fruit, Vegetable and Pot Plant Show, organised by the Horticultural Society in the San Anton Gardens on a weekend in May.
Fur and Feather Show: a show of furry animals and birds in the San Anton Gardens.

May

Film and Video Competition, organised by the Amateur Cine Circle (beginning of June).
International Air Rally: an annual event in which some 75 aircraft take part.
St Philip: in Zebbug on the second Sunday in June.
Mnarja, the Festival of Lights, held on June 28th/29th: one of the most popular events of the year, particularly interesting for visitors (see Art and Culture, Music, Festivals and Customs).
St George: in Qormi on the last Sunday in June.
St Nicholas: in Siggiewi on the last Sunday in June.

June

International Fair of Malta: a trade fair (industry, agriculture, imports, service industries) held at Naxxar from July 1st to 15th.
St Joseph the Worker: in Birkirkara on the first Sunday in July.
St Paul: in Rabat on the first Sunday in July.

July

Il-Festa

Every year in summer, all hell breaks loose at the weekend in one of the villages on Malta and Gozo – this is when the local communities celebrate the festivals of their local patron saints. No matter whether this community is a town, a village or just a tiny hamlet – a "festa" lasting several days is the most important

The Maltese know how to celebrate

annual event, and the Maltese know how to celebrate it.

Preparations for the "festa" have been going on for weeks, nay months. Money is collected, decorations crafted, costumes sewn, musical pieces are studied by the band clubs, the local brass bands. For you owe it to your saint, and besides it just won't do to have your villages festival shown up by a much grander event in the other villages! And so a regular competition develops between the villages. The preparations are organised by the so-called Partit, the local representatives, leading citizens, dignitaries, members of the church youth group, the sports club, the brass band and so on.

The actual saints day, as fixed in the church calendar, however, is not of paramount importance here: all the saints festivals take place in the nice-weather period between April and September. And to ensure that the celebrations can last for at least two full days, the festivals have all been moved to a weekend (in the past, many communities celebrated them in the middle of the week which, however, was not very conducive to work).

Some days before the "festa" commences, people start to decorate streets and village squares as well as the doors, windows and balconies of each house with flags, ribbons, bunting, flowers, pictures of the saints, colourful light bulbs and lanterns. Many houses are freshly painted for the festa, and gleam in sparkling new white-wash. Colourfully decorated wooden sockets with statues of the saint made from wood and papier-mâché line the main roads along the route of the procession. The parish church is illuminated from the outside and bedecked with strings of fairy lights. The church interior is cloaked in red damask, and all the church's treasures such as relics, chasubles and precious gifts are on display, neatly spruced up and the silver polished. All the families help with the floral decorations, each one presenting one bouquet – with the name of the family prominently displayed on a sign.

Probably the most important part of each festa are the fireworks. In order to impress the neighbouring village also in this respect, a village may produce some of its own bangers and rockets, using ammunition from guns if nothing else is at hand. But even if the bangers can be heard going off in the streets for days before the actual festa, the celebrations themselves will run to perfection, to a very strict and orderly schedule.

The celebrations begin with the first few events on the Wednesday, but it is the Saturday morning when the festa really gets going. Starting signal are the bangers which wake up the village as early as 7am. Some time later, the band club, the village brass band, consisting of at least 30 members, will march through the streets, while confetti rains down from the balconies, onto their uniforms and

this day. Afterwards, many villagers invite friends and family for a festive meal in their own homes, while others crowd into the local bars and restaurants, or they just take a snack from one of the numerous booths and stalls offering all sorts of delicious foods. Much drink is also consumed amidst animated discussions.

The procession in the early evening is the festa's highpoint. Strong, hand-picked men, dressed in black-and-white servers' robes, carry the life-size, richly decorated figure of the saint through the village streets, followed by church dignitaries and leading members of the community. The procession is loud and colourful. Thundering brass music, loud cheering from the spectators, cracking bangers

Festive crowds in Zabbar: nobody wants to miss out on the festival in honour of the patron saint

and whistling rockets as well as the cries of the street merchants who are offering nougat, hot dogs and ice-cream for sale all combine in an almighty cacophony of noises with the ceaseless ringing of the church bells. The noise level rises even further when the statue returns to the church, where it is received with ear-shattering noise. The firework display with flaming

brass instruments. And if the band is too small, "guest players", that is trumpeters and trombonists from neighbouring villages, are loaned to make sure that a good show is put on.

The real festival day is the Sunday. In the morning, a mass is read in honour of the patron saint. The entire village attends this mass. It is as much a social as a religious event, and even those Maltese who normally won't be seen near a church, will be there on

Catherine's wheels and hundreds of rockets lighting up the night sky above the village is the official end to the festa. Unofficially, however, the celebrations continue right through the night.

In the summer half year it is impossible to escape from the numerous festas (or festi, the correct plural in Maltese). There are 161 churches on Malta, and every saints' day is honoured in this way.

Excursions

Our Lady of the Sacred Heart: in Bur Marrad and Sliema on the first Sunday in July.
St Andrew: in Luqa on the first Sunday in July.
Our Lady of Pompeii: in Marsaxlokk on the second Sunday in July.
Our Lady of Mount Carmel: in Gzira on the second Sunday in July.
St Joseph: in Kalkara on the second Sunday in July.
St Dominic: in Sliema on the third Sunday in July.
St Sebastian: in Qormi on the third Sunday in July.
St George: in Victoria (Gozo) on the third Sunday in July.
Our Lady of Mount Carmel: in Balluta on the last Sunday in July.
Our Lady of Sorrows: in St Paul's Bay on the last Sunday in July.
St Anne: in Marsaskala on the last Sunday in July.
St Venera: in Santa Venera on the last Sunday in July.
St Lawrence: in San Lawrenz (Gozo) on the last Sunday in July.
St Dominic: in Valletta on the Sunday before August 4th.

July/August
Maltafest: the most important event in Malta's cultural calendar, a month of open-air cultural activities with the participation of local and foreign artistes.

August
St Peter: in Birzebbuga on the first Sunday in August.
St Joseph: in Qala (Gozo) on the first Sunday in August.
St Gaetan: in Hamrun on the Sunday after August 7th.
Our Lady of Lourdes: in Paola on the Sunday after August 15th.
Stella Maris: in Sliema on the Sunday after August 18th.
St Dominic: in Vittoriosa on the last Sunday in August.
Maria Regina: in Marsa on the last Sunday in August.
St Paul: at Safi on the last Sunday in August.

September
Our Lady of Victories: a national holiday on the first weekend in September, commemorating the lifting of the Great Siege in 1565 and the end of the siege by the Axis powers in 1942, celebrated by a boat race in the Grand Harbour and other aquatic events.
St Catherine: in Zurrieq on the first Sunday in September.
St Gregory: in Sliema on the first Sunday in September.
Our Lady of Graces: in Zabbar on the Sunday after September 8th.
St Leonard: in Kirkop on the third Sunday in September.

October
Tour of Malta, an international cycling event (beginning of month).
International Book Fair (different venues).
November
St Catherine: in Zejtun on the second weekend in November.

Excursions

By bus
Tour operators and local travel agencies offer a wide range of English-language bus tours to the sights of Malta and Gozo. In service buses (see Bus Services) the journeys take longer, but travel in these typically Maltese and sometimes rather antiquated vehicles has its own particular charm – as well as being cheaper.

By car
A hired car is a good way of exploring the islands at your own pace. Three round trips taking in all the major sights are described in the Suggested Routes chapter of this guide.

By boat
Numerous organised boat trips are on offer on Malta and Gozo. Particularly popular are cruises round Malta and/or Gozo, trips to the Blue Lagoon between Comino and Cominotto, with plenty of time for bathing, a sailing tour with a catamaran and underwater safaris, on which Malta's marine fauna and flora can be observed through windows

Arrival and departure point for many excursion boats: the marina in Sliema

under the waterline. There are also special evening cruises, including a meal and sometimes dancing. Most cruises start from Sliema or Bugibba.

Harbour cruises offer an opportunity of seeing Valletta from a different viewpoint. There are cruises round Marsamxett Harbour and the Grand Harbour, with explanatory commentary, starting from the Strand in Sliema several times daily.

The largest cruise operators are Captain Morgan (tel. 343373 and 331961) and Jylland Cruises (tel. 332684).

You can also organise an excursion for yourself. There are ferries at one- or two-hour intervals between Malta (Cirkewwa) and Gozo (Mgarr), and smaller boats shuttle between Cirkewwa or Mgarr and Comino (see Ferries and Shipping Services). From Malta it is only an hour and 40 minutes by hovercraft to Sicily, and the timetables are so arranged as to allow time for a brief stay on Sicily.

Sightseeing flights are on offer from Luqa Airport. Another attractive possibility is a helicopter trip to Gozo, offered by the Malta Air Charter company, a subsidiary of Air Malta.

By air

Ferries and Shipping Services

There are passenger ferries at 40–60 minute intervals between Sliema (the Strand) and Valletta (Marsamxett Harbour); the trip takes between 5 and 10 minutes. Information: Marsamxett Steam Ferry Service (tel. 338981 and 335689).

Sliema–Valletta

Car ferries operate throughout the year between Cirkewwa on the north

Malta–Gozo

Ferries and Shipping Services

Ferries shuttle all day between Malta and the harbour of Mgarr on Gozo

coast of Malta and Mgarr on Gozo. The crossing takes about half an hour. In July and August there are ferries round the clock at roughly 45-minute intervals; at other times of year the ferries operate between 6am and 10pm at 2-hour intervals. There is also a ferry several times weekly between the Gozo Ferry landing-stage on the south side of Marsamxett Harbour (Sa Maison) and Mgarr; the journey takes about 75 minutes. Between July and September (daily except Sunday) there is an express service by hovercraft (35 minutes) between Gozo, Sliema and Sa Maison.

All the ferry services between Malta and Gozo are run by the Gozo Channel Company, Hay Wharf, Sa Maison, Pietà (tel. 243964) and Mgarr, Gozo (tel. 556114).

Gozo–Comino	During the season small boats ply at roughly 2-hour intervals between Mgarr (Gozo) and Comino (landing-stage near hotels). The first boat to Comino departs about 6.30am, the last one about 9.30pm.
Malta–Comino	From Cirkewwa, on the north coast of Malta, boats sail according to demand to the Blue Lagoon on Comino.
Malta–Sicily	Virtu Rapid Ferries Ltd run an express ferry service between Malta and Sicily (daily in summer, at other times of year 4 times weekly). The ferries sail between Valletta (Grand Harbour, Marina Pinto) and Pozallo, Syracuse and Catania on Sicily. The crossing by catamaran from Valletta to Pozallo takes about 1 hour 40 minutes, to Catania about 3 hours. Information: Virtu Ferries, 3 Princess Elizabeth Street, Ta'Xbiex (tel. 345220; fax 345221).

Throughout the year, a twice-weekly ferry service runs between Catania and Valletta; the trip takes eleven hours (company ma.re.si.).
The Gozo Channel Company (address, see above) also runs a service several times every week in summer between Malta and Pozallo (Sicily).

The Italian ma.re.si. line runs a weekly ferry service throughout the year between Reggio di Calabria and Valletta (14 hours).

The Italian shipping line Grandi Traghetti runs a weekly service between Genoa and Malta (42 hours). Information and tickets from SMS Travel in Valletta (tel. 232211, fax. 240097).

Food and Drink

Most hotels and restaurants in Malta offer an international cuisine showing clear British influence and, not surprisingly, Italian features: pizzas and pasta dishes feature on many menus. While in the past culinary standards in Malta were unremarkable, there are now increasing numbers of restaurants serving fine Italian cuisine (at correspondingly high prices).

Breakfast in Malta, as in other Mediterranean countries, is a fairly spartan meal – though a traditional British breakfast can also be had at additional cost. Those who take their breakfast in a bar will do well to content themselves with a cappuccino or espresso and a croissant.

Lunch is usually taken between 12 noon and 2pm, dinner between 7 and 10pm. In the better class restaurants it is quite common to have your aperitif at the bar or in the lounge and move into the restaurant when the waiter tells you that the first course is ready.

There are no restaurants or hotels serving exclusively Maltese dishes, though the menu will frequently include some Maltese specialities. Maltese cuisine shows clear parallels with Italian cooking, while the use

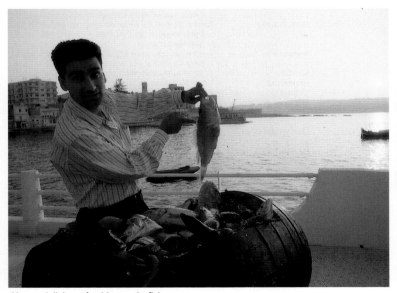

Always delicious: freshly caught fish

of spices in particular betrays North African influence. The ingredients are mainly those which the Maltese have used from time immemorial. The traditional Sunday meal is a joint of beef or pork. The meat is put in a casserole, covered with potatoes and other vegetables, herbs and oil; stock is then poured over it and it is cooked slowly in the oven. This method of preparation is known as patata il-forn. At Easter lamb replaces beef or pork.

Many restaurants offer a wide choice of fish dishes. Most of the fish sold in Malta, however, do not come from the waters round the archipelago: over 60 per cent are imported. The fish that most frequently appear on menus are swordfish, tunny, sea-bass and red mullet. Also to be recommended in lampuka (dolphin fish), a species of mackerel with firm white flesh which is available freshly caught from the middle of August to the end of November.

The standard accompaniment to fish and meat dishes is chips. Boiled potatoes are also served if desired. Vegetables vary according to the season.

The dessert course is frequently confined to a choice between ice-cream, fruit and various kinds of cake. Many Maltese prefer heavy, very sweet tarts made with almonds.

Aljotta	A clear fish soup with garlic.
Bragioli	A beef olive made with minced meat (or egg and ham), steamed in red wine.
Brugiel mimli	Aubergines stuffed with minced meat, olives and capers, usually flavoured with mint.
Bzar andar mimli	Peppers stuffed with minced meat, olives and capers.
Fenek	Rabbit – roast, baked or in a pie.
Fenek stuffat	Rabbit braised with tomatoes, red wine and capers.
Gbejna	A goats'-milk or ewes'-milk cheese made on Gozo, spiced with peppercorns.
Hobz biz-zejt	Bread dipped in olive oil and spread with tomtoes, capers and spices – a popular snack between meals.
Kappunata	A stew of courgettes, aubergines, capers, garlic, paprika, tomatoes and onions.
Kawlata	A vegetable soup with pork or sausages.
Minestra	Vegetable soup.
Mqaret	A pastry with a filling of dates and aniseed.
Mqarrun fil-forn	Macaroni and minced meat in a béchamel sauce.
Pastizzi	Pastries with a filling of purée'd peas and ricotta cheese.
Qaghaq tal-ghasel	A pastry ring filled with syrup, semolina, and candied fruit – a favourite winter sweet.
Ravjul	A variant of ravioli with a filling of ricotta cheese.
Ross fil-forn	Baked rice with minced meats, eggs and a strong flavouring of saffron.
Soppa tal-armla	Vegetable soup with a small round gbejna cheese.
Timpana	A case of flaky pastry filled with ricotta cheese, macaroni, minced meat, tomato purée, aubergines, onions and eggs.
Torta tal-Lampuka	Lampuka pie: fried slices of lampuka, covered in pastry and baked, along with a variety of vegetables.

Drinks

Refreshing drinks Although Maltese tapwater has a slightly salty taste, it is perfectly safe to drink. Mineral waters are available, both still and carbonated.

A refreshing Maltese soft drink is kinnie. Made from water, unpeeled oranges and wormwood herbs and other ingredients, it is carbonated and has a slightly bitter taste.

Maltese wines are mainly dry, relatively strong and of middling quality. They are good table wines, to be drunk young. The Marsovin company's red Cabernet-Sauvignon and white and rosé Verdala and Special Reserve and Lachryma Vitis's Green Label wines are widely available. The best-known Gozo wineries are Ggantija and Citadella. Imported wines are subject to high duties and are therefore relatively expensive.

Beer The local brewery, Farson's, produces several good brands of beer. Cisk lager is like a German lager, Blue Label is a dark, slightly sweet beer, Hop Leaf a light-coloured mild ale, Clipper a light beer. Draught beer is relatively rare. Imported beers can also be found but are dearer than local brands.

Spirits The usual international brands of spirits are available in Malta. The only locally produced spirit is anisette, an aniseed liqueur.

Getting There

British Airways fly several times weekly from London Heathrow to Luqa International Airport. Flying time is just over 3 hours. Air Malta has flights from Heathrow and Gatwick, and also from Birmingham, Glasgow and Manchester. There are also numerous charter flights from these and other British airports.

For passengers travelling to Gozo the onward journey can be either by ferry (see Ferries and Shipping Services) or by air. During the summer months the Malta Air Charter company flies regular services by helicopter from Luqa to Gozo (flying time about 10 minutes).

There are ferry services to Malta from Sicily and the Italian mainland throughout the year (see Ferries and Shipping Services).

Hotels

There are about 45,000 beds of all categories on Malta. In the last few years, the number of top-class hotels especially has markedly increased, and some attractive apartment complexes have also been built.

Maltese hotels are officially classified in five categories according to their comfort and amenities. They range from luxury hotels with five stars to modest establishments with one. This classification (which does not always match international standards) is shown in the following list of hotels.

Special to Gozo is accommodation in so-called farm houses. These former farms and country houses, lovingly restored in their original style as typical on the island. Every house has its own individual character and is individually furnished; many have their own swimming pool. Accommodation can be booked with many travel agents.

Farm houses

Hotels on Malta

★★★★★Corinthia Palace
De Paule Avenue
Tel. 440301, fax 465713

Attard

Hotels

This hotel is situated in the centre of Malta, in one of the best residential districts on the island, near the San Anton Gardens. Good bus services to all other Maltese towns. 158 luxurious rooms. Two restaurants offering international cuisine; rather more formal dress expected in the evening. The Athenaeum, a beauty centre, has 50 different therapies for the well-being of body, mind and spirit on offer. There is also a beauty salon, a pool and a sauna landscape.

Bugibba

★★★★Topaz
Triq Ic–Chaghaq
Tel. 572416, fax 571123
Modern apartment hotel with 246 apartments. 10 minutes from seafront promenade. Good bus connections. Almost all apartments have a balcony. Family atmosphere. Swimming pool.

★★★Mediterranea
Bugibba Road
Tel. 572273
A medium-range hotel with relatively good prices. 55 spacious rooms, some with balcony. Rooms with seaview only have a side-view of the sea. Sun terrace with pool on the roof.

Floriana

★★★★★Le Meridien Phoenicia
The Mall
Tel. 225241, fax 235254
A luxury hotel with a long tradition, right in front of Valletta's town gates. After thorough restoration in the early 1990s it has 136 air-conditioned rooms with every comfort and amenity. The outdoor pool, in terraced gardens, is heated in winter.

Ghajn Tuffieha

★★★Golden Sands
Golden Bay
Tel. 573961, fax 580875
Special thanks to its situation on Malta's most beautiful sandy beach, but the 313-room hotel does not offer a high degree of comfort. The rooms are plain, and guests who are looking for night-time entertainment are restricted to the events on offer in the hotel (disco and occasional live music).

Marsaskala

★★★★Jerma Palace
Dawret It–Torri
Tel. 633222, fax 639485
One of the largest hotels on Malta, with 326 rooms. A middle-range hotel which attracts an international clientele. Most rooms have a view of the sea. Wide range of leisure and entertainment facilities. Facilities for disabled.

★★★Etvan
Triq Il-Bahhara
Tel. 633265, fax 684330
A popular family-run hotel with very reasonable prices. Some of the 36 rooms have a view of the sea. Programme of entertainments on some evenings.

★★Cerviola
Triq Il-Qaliet
Tel. 633287, fax 632056
A modest but friendly hotel (32 rooms) in a new district of the town.

Mellieha

★★★★Grand Hotel Mercure Selmun Palace
Tel. 521040, fax 521060
Incorporated in the modern hotel complex is the 18th century Selmun

Palace. Remote from the nearest town, it offers absolute peace and quiet and magnificent panoramic views of the Mediterranean and picturesque bays and inlets. For sightseeing purposes it is advisable to have a hired car, but there is a hotel bus to the nearest beach. The 148 rooms are luxuriously appointed; some suites are furnished in medieval style. Wide range of sporting and leisure activities.

★★★Mellieha Holiday Centre
Mellieha Bay
Tel. 573900, fax 575452
Under Danish management. Only a few minutes' walk from the sandy beach. Extensive gardens. Very suitable for children (programme of play and entertainments). 150 bungalows for 2–6 persons, furnished in Scandinavian style. Good sports facilities.

★★★Continental   Msida
St Louis Street
Tel. 339620, fax 319034
Middle-range hotel with 43 rooms and view of yachting harbour. Sun terrace, unheated swimming pool, restaurant. A good centre from which the island can be explored by bus.

★★★★New Dolmen   Qawra
St Paul's Bay
Tel. 581510, fax 581081
Large medium-range hotel (387 rooms) situated on the sea. Extensive gardens and private bathing beach (rocky). Almost all rooms have balcony or terrace. Four restaurants. Wide range of sporting activities. Diving school. Facilities for disabled.

★★★★Suncrest
Qawra Coast Road
Tel. 577101, fax 575478
Malta's largest hotel complex (413 rooms), separated from the sea only by the coast road, with its own bathing beach (rocky); sandy beaches 15 minutes away by car. Most rooms have view of sea. Five restaurants. Wide range of sporting and leisure activities (including diving school).

★★★★Inter-Continental   Rabat
Inguanez Street
Tel. 451700, fax 451708
Large hotel (200 rooms) in quiet situation on outskirts of Rabat, well away from tourist centres. Top price category.

★★★★★ Crowne Plaza Malta   Sliema
Tigné Street
Tel. 343400, fax 311292
Luxury hotel in a quiet part of the town. 182 spacious and elegantly appointed rooms, some with view of sea. Sports facilities. Two restaurants.

★★★★Fortina
Tigné Seafront
Tel. 343380, fax 339388
A not particularly attractive hotel (194 rooms) on the seafront promenade with a magnificent view of Valletta. Daily programme of activities and entertainment.

★★★Metropole
Sir Adrian Dingli Street
Tel. 330188, fax 336282

Hotels

Tourist hotel with 160 rooms in a quiet side street. Well furnished rooms; roof terrace.

★★Caprice
G. Muscat Azzopardi Street
Tel. 340459, fax 330524
Small pleasant hotel (25 rooms) in relatively quiet part of town; reasonable rates. Well furnished rooms of varying size, some with small balcony. Roof terrace with recliners; bar and restaurant.

St Julian's

★★★★Cavalieri
Spinola Road
Tel. 336255,
fax 330542
Well situated, only a few minutes walk from the centre but away from the tourist bustle. Seawater pool and large sun terrace, sauna, gym, Restaurant and bar.

★★★Alexandra Palace
Schreiber Street
Tel. 341151,
fax 341157

Hotel Cavalieri in St. Julian's

In centre of St Julian's, 500 m from sea. 125 pleasantly appointed rooms.

★★Tropicana
Ball Street
Paceville
Tel. 337557, fax 342890
Not quiet, but very much in the centre of things; ideal for night owls. 60 rooms; middle-range price category.

St Paul's Bay

★★★★Mistra Village
Xemxija Hill
Tel. 580481,
fax 582941
Spacious apartment complex (255 apartments), about 1 km above Xemxija (a district of Sta Paul's Bay), with fine view of whole bay. 600 m to rocky beach. Modest but well furnished apartments in older part of complex, large and elegantly appointed apartments and suites in newer part.

Mistra Village in Xemxija

Several restaurants and bars in the newer part – all of which close surprisingly early! Two swimming pools and children's paddling pool; recliners. Sports facilities and varied programme of entertainments.

★★★Castille
                                                        Valletta
348 St Paul Street
Tel. 243677, fax 243677
Middle-range hotel adjoining the Auberge de Castille, refurbished in 1994. 38 rooms with rather old-fashioned appointments but full of atmosphere. Restaurant with Maltese, French and Italian specialities. Breakfast served on roof terrace.

★★British
267 St Ursula Street
Tel. 224730, fax 239711
Modest hotel in quiet situation near the Grand Harbour. 46 rooms of varying size, some with view of harbour.

Hotels on Gozo

★★★★Grand Hotel
                                                   Ghajnsielem
St Anthony Street
Tel. 556183, fax 559744
On the site of the Grand Hotel which dated back to 1897, this new terraced complex was built, incorporating some of the architectural elements of the former hotel. High above the Bay of Mgarr. 46 rooms, each with a specious seating area, air-conditioning and satellite TV.

★★★Atlantis
                                                   Marsalforn
Qolla Street
Tel. 554685, fax 555661
Small family hotel (46 rooms) in middle range. Relatively quiet situation in new part of town. Rooms of varying size and amenity, most of them with balcony or terrace.

Elegant accommodation on Gozo: Ta' Cenc

★★★★★Ta'Cenc
                                                   Sannat
Tel. 561522, fax 558199
A luxury hotel with a very special atmosphere. The complex consists of several bungalows and flat-roofed buildings which, surrounded with lush vegetation, blend beautifully into the landscape. 82 tastefully and comfortably furnished rooms. Very attractive restaurant area, shaded by trees (although the service is not always up to a standard expected of a five-star hotel!) Hotel bus to private beach in rocky cove (2.5 km and to Victoria. Sports facilities.

★★★★Cornucopia
                                                   Xaghra
10 Gnien Imrik Street
Tel. 556486, fax 552910
Country-style hotel in upper middle range with 44 large rooms. Restaurant, also in rustic style.

Information

Xlendi	★★Serena Upper St Simon Street Tel. 553719, fax 557452 Situated above the old part of the town, with magnificent views over the bay and the sea. 12 spacious apartments with 1, 2 or 3 bedrooms.
Hotel on Comino	Comino Tel. 529821, fax 529826 Attractive hotel complex, directly on the sea. A small sandy beach is only 100 m away. Regular boat transfer from hotel to Gozo and Malta. Wide range of sporting facilities: tennis courses, diving school, water skiing, surfing, sailing etc. Double bedrooms and spacious bungalow-style apartments (the latter in an adjacent bay).

Information

Internet	http://www.tourism.org.mt
United Kingdom	Malta National Tourist Office Malta House, 36–38 Piccadilly London W1V 0PP Tel. (020) 72924900, fax (020) 77341880
North America	Malta National Tourist Office Empire State Building 350 Fifth Avenue, Suite 4412 New York NY 10118 Tel. (212) 6959520, fax (212) 6958229
On Malta	National Tourism Organisation Malta 280 Republic Street, Valletta Tel. 224444, fax 220401 Tourist Information Office Malta International Airport Tel. 249600 Tourist Information Office 1 City Gate Arcade, Valletta Tel. 237747 Tourist Information Office Bisazza Street, Sliema Tel. 313409 Tourist Information Office Bay Square, Bugibba Tel. 577382
On Gozo	Tourist Information Harbour, Mgarr Tel. 553343 Gozo Tourist Office Republic Street, Victoria Tel. 558106

Karrozzini

The Maltese horse-drawn cab, the karrozzin, is now mainly used for sightseeing. In Valletta they are to be found in Palace Square, in Mdina outside the Main Gate, in Sliema on the promenade. The drivers point out the principal sights.

The fare (usually not less than LM4) should be agreed with the driver before setting out.

Language

Malta has two official languages, Maltese and English. Since English is learned from the early school years almost every Maltese speaks it.

Maltese is a Semitic language (see Art and Culture, Language and Literature), the only one written in Latin characters. The alphabet has 5 vowels and 24 consonants.

The consonants include four modified characters – c (pronounced ch), g (soft g), h (a hard h) and z (pronounced like English z); the combination gh is generally silent. For the sake of simplicity these four characters are replaced in this guide by the unmodified letters, the pronunciation being specially indicated where necessary.

The consonants b d f k l m n p r t v w are pronounced more or less as in English; g is a hard g as in "go"; j is pronounced y as in "yes"; q is a kind of glottal stop; s is always unvoiced, as in "so"; x is pronounced sh; and z is pronounced ts.

Maltese vowels are pure, not diphthongised as in English.

Leisure Parks

Mediterraneo (see entry, St Paul's Bay)
Dinosaurs in Ta Qali National Park
There is a small "dinosaur park" next to Ta Qali Crafts Village. A hefty admission charge permits you to experience how several fearsome dinosaurs used to turn their heads! Open Oct.–May daily 11am–3.30pm; Jun.–Sep. Mon.–Sat. 10am–5pm.
Popeye Village, see entry Mellieha
Rinella Movie Park, see entry Kalkara
Playmobil Fun Park
Bulebel Industrial Estate, Zejtun
The Playmobil company runs a fun park where children can enjoy its products (open Oct.–Jun. Mon.–Fri. 9am–6pm, Sat. and Sun. 3–6pm; Jul.–Sep. Mon.–Fri. 9am–6pm, Sat. 6–9pm).
Splash & Fun Park
Bahar lc-Caghaq (on the coast, between St Julian's and St Paul's Bays)
Water slides, large pool and playground next to the sea (open daily from 9.30am).

Markets

Valletta The market held in Merchants Street on Monday–Saturday mornings offers a wide range of clothing, linen and domestic equipment.

Market in Marsaxlokk: lacy tablecloths and all kinds of souvenirs . . .

A similar market, on a larger scale, is held on Sunday mornings below St James's Bastion.

A wide choice of fresh fruit and vegetables, fish, meat and poultry is to be found in the Market Hall in Merchants Street.

Other markets on Malta The market held daily by Marsaxlokk harbour is specially aimed at tourists. The goods on offer include clothing, leather goods, linen, embroidery and lace. In many towns there are smaller markets selling fruit and vegetables; often the traders sell direct from their lorry.

On Gozo a market, selling clothing, domestic requirements and foodstuffs, is held every morning in It-Tokk, Victoria's central square.

Medical Care

Facilities for medical care in Malta and Gozo are fully adequate. Most doctors speak English.

Malta has a reciprocal agreement with the United Kingdom under which British citizens holidaying in Malta for a period of not more than a month can receive medical treatment free of charge in some cases and subject to charges in others. Immediately necessary treatment in a government hospital, area health centre (polyclinic) or district dispensary is provided free of charge on production of a British passport. Charges are, however, payable for treatment in a non-governmental hospital dispensary or polyclinic, treatment at a private doctor's surgery and prescribed medicines. It is still advisable to take out short-term insurance covering any costs for treatment and transport home if required.

St Luke's Hospital
Gwardamanga (Msida), Malta
Tel. 241251 and 247860

Gozo General Hospital
Victoria, Gozo
Tel. 561600

Ambulance on Malta or Gozo: dial 196

Motoring

In Malta, as in Britain, traffic goes on the left, with overtaking on the right. At the intersection of two roads of equal importance traffic coming from the left has priority.

In general traffic regulations and traffic signs are in line with European practice. The Maltese, however, sometimes take a fairly relaxed view of the regulations. You must always be prepared for the driver who does not recognise your priority or overtakes on the left. Due caution is required, therefore, when driving in Malta.

The maximum permitted **speed** is 40 km an hour in built-up areas and 65 km an hour on the open road.

There is an absolute ban on driving after taking alcohol.

There are few traffic lights in Malta, and at road junctions traffic is often regulated by **roundabouts**. Unless traffic signs indicate otherwise, vehicles entering a roundabout must give way to vehicles already on it.

Even on relatively good **roads** there are likely to be potholes and other obstacles. In the remoter country areas the roads tend to be narrow and bumpy.

Leaded **petrol** (premium, 98 octane) and lead-free petrol (95 octane) and diesel fuel are available in Malta. There are petrol stations in all the larger towns and villages; it is important to note, however, that they are closed on Saturday and Sunday.

Traffic conditions Malta is a densely populated island, and traffic is correspondingly heavy. Particularly at the rush hours there are likely to be hold-ups and tailbacks in the built-up area centred on Valletta. At weekends many Maltese make for the beaches in the north-west of the island or on Gozo. On Saturday and Sunday mornings there is usually a long trail of cars heading for Cirkewwa, with a similar trail back in the evening. In and around St Julian's, particularly on Saturday evenings, the roads are crowded with traffic drawn by its numerous bars and discos.

There is a great shortage of **parking** in the towns. Outside the walls of Valletta, in the larger towns and at the major sights there are guarded car parks; the custodians expect a tip (about 10–25 c). Parking is not allowed on sections of road marked with a yellow line.

Even in minor **accidents** or in the event of minor damage to your car where no other vehicle is involved you must inform the police and, in the case of a hired car, the car rental firm: if you do not you will not be covered by insurance.

Museums

State-run museums have standard opening times: October 1st to June 15th, Mon.–Sat. 8.15am–5pm; June 16th to September 30th, daily 7.45am–2pm. Visitors are often not admitted in the last 30 minutes before closing. Opening times for other museums vary: see the appropriate entry in the Sights from A to Z section of this guide. Museums and all excavation sites are closed on public holidays.

Archaeological museums

National Museum of Archaeology
See Sights from A to Z, Valletta

Roman Villa
See Sights from A to Z, Rabat

Gozo Museum of Archaeology
See Sights from A to Z, Gozo: Victoria

Natural history museums

Natural History Museum
See Sights from A to Z, Mdina

Natural Science Museum
See Sights from A to Z, Gozo: Victoria

Folk museums

Casa Rocca Piccola
See Sights from A to Z, Valletta

Folklore Museum
See Sights from A to Z, Gozo: Victoria

Gharb Folklore Museum
See Sights from A to Z, Gozo: Gharb

Gozo Heritage
See Sights from A to Z, Gozo

Inquisitor's Palace
See Sights from A to Z, Vittoriosa

Medieval Times
See Sights from A to Z, Mdina

Norman House
See Sights from A to Z, Mdina

Ta' Kola Windmill Museum
See Sights from A to Z, Gozo: Xaghra

History of the Knights
The Knights Hospitaliers (in the Sacra Infermeria)
See Sights from A to Z, Valletta

The Knights of Malta
See Sights from A to Z, Mdina

Wignacourt College Museum
See Sights from A to Z, Rabat

Art museum

National Museum of Fine Arts
See Sights from A to Z, Valletta

Manoel Theatre Museum
See Sights from A to Z, Valletta

Toy Museum
See Sights from A to Z, Valletta

Pomskizillious Museum of Toys
See Sights from A to Z, Gozo: Xaghra

St John's Co-Cathedral Museum
See Sights from A to Z, Valletta

Cathedral Museum
See Sights from A to Z, Mdina

Sanctuary Museum
See Sights from A to Z, Zabbar

Cathedral Museum
See Sights from A to Z, Gozo: Victoria

Grand Master's Palace Armoury
See Sights from A to Z, Valletta

National War Museum
See Sights from A to Z, Valletta

Lascaris War Rooms
See Sights from A to Z, Valletta

Mdina Dungeons
See Sights from A to Z, Mdina

Armoury
See Sights from A to Z, Gozo: Victoria

National Maritime Museum
See Sights from A to Z, Vittoriosa

Malta Experience
See Sights from A to Z, Valletta

Malta George Cross
Valletta Experience
See Sights from A to Z, Valletta

Mdina Experience
See Sights from A to Z, Mdina

Tales of the Silent City
See Sights from A to Z, Mdina

The Sacred Island
See Sights from A to Z, Valletta

Island of Joy
See Sights from A to Z, Gozo: Victoria

Theatre Museum

Toy museums

Church museums

Armouries, war
museums

Maritime museum

Multi-vision
shows

Newspapers and Periodicals

The only English-language daily is the "Times". There are three English-language weeklies: the "Weekend Chronicle", the "Democrat" and the "Sunday Times".

Newspapers published in the United Kingdom are available in Malta on the day of publication.

Night Life

Maltese night life, in so far as it exists, is concentrated mainly in St Julian's and Sliema and to a lesser extent in St Paul's Bay and Bugibba. Gozo is quiet in the evenings.

At the casinos of St Julian's (Dragonara Palace) and Bugibba (New Dolmen Hotel) you can try your luck every evening. French and American roulette, baccarat and blackjack are played under international rules.

Opening Times

See Business Hours

Parks and Gardens

On a bare and waterless island like Malta there are, understandably, only a few parks and public gardens, and those listed below are almost without exception are quite small, though often very beautifully laid out.

On Malta

Argotti Botanic Gardens
See Sights from A to Z, Floriana

Buskett Gardens
A small wood rather than a park
See Sights from A to Z, Buskett Gardens

Hastings Garden
See Sights from A to Z, Valletta

Kalkara Gardens
See Sights from A to Z, Floriana

Lower Barracca Gardens
See Sights from A to Z, Valletta

Maglio Gardens
See Sights from A to Z, Floriana

San Anton Gardens
A park of some size, with animal enclosures
See Sights from A to Z, Attard

Upper Barracca Gardens
See Sights from A to Z, Valletta

The numerous bars and discos of St Julian's on Saturday night

Rundle Gardens
Victoria's municipal park, with old trees and aviaries
See Sights from A to Z, Gozo: Victoria

On Gozo

Police

Emergency calls on Malta and Gozo: dial 191
Police General Headquarters
Harper Lane, Floriana (Malta)
Tel. 224001

Police Headquarters
113 Republic Street, Victoria (Gozo)
Tel. 556011 and 556430

Post and Telephone

The postage on a letter (up to 20 grams) or postcard to Europe is 16 cents.

Post-boxes (pillar-boxes) on Malta and Gozo are red.

Post offices on Malta and Gozo are open Mon.–Sat. 8am–12.45pm. The General Post Office in Valletta (Merchants Street) is open in summer Mon.–Sat. 7.30am–6pm, in winter Mon.–Sat. 8am–6.30pm.

Malta's telephone service is run by Maltacom. Overseas calls can be made to nearly all parts of the world from public payphones (operated by coins or telephone cards respectively, for LM2, 3 and 5, obtainable from Maltacom offices, all branches of the Mid Med Bank, at post offices and some shops). From Maltacom offices you can make calls abroad (payment is made on completion of the call) and send faxes. The head office of Maltacom in St Julian's (St George's Road) is open 24 hours. Other offices (open daily from 8am–10.30pm) are at the following addresses: South Street, Valletta (Mon.–Sat. 8am–6.30pm); Bisazza Street and Plaza Shopping Complex, Sliema, St Paul's Street, St Paul's Bay, Triq il-Fliegu, Qawra, and at the airport. The Gozo office of Maltacom office is in Republic Street, Victoria, open daily 8am–11pm. There are reduced charges on Sundays and public holidays and between 6pm and 6am. Calls from hotel rooms are often considerably dearer.

International dialling codes

From the United Kingdom to Malta or Gozo: 00356
From the United States or Canada to Malta or Gozo: 011356

From Malta or Gozo to the United Kingdom: 0044
From Malta or Gozo to the United States or Canada: 001

From Gozo to Malta: 8

Directory enquiries for Maltese numbers: dial 190

Public Holidays

January 1st	New Year's Day
February 10th	St Paul's Shipwreck
March 19th	St Joseph
March 31st	Freedom Day
March/April	Good Friday
May 1st	Workers' Day
June 7th	Anniversary of the rising on June 7th 1919
June 29th	SS. Peter and Paul
August 15th	Assumption
September 8th	Feast of Our Lady of Victories (commemorating the end of the Great Siege of 1565)
September 21st	Independence Day
December 8th	Immaculate Conception
December 13th	Republic Day
December 25th	Christmas

Religious festivals: see Events

Radio and Television

The two radio channels of the state broadcasting corporation Xandir Malta broadcast programmes in Maltese, with news bulletins in English. There are also a number of local radio stations.

The BBC World Service, and usually also the Voice of America, can be heard on short waves.

Television Malta (the television department of Xandir Malta) produces programmes in both Maltese and English, but also shows many British and American films and programmes.

Italian television and various satellite and cable programmes are also received in Malta.

Religious Services

Many churches on Malta and Gozo have several masses daily, usually in Maltese. On Sundays and special feast days mass is sometimes celebrated in English.

Roman Catholic

In St Barbara's Church, Republic Street, Valletta, mass is celebrated in English at 12 noon. Other places where mass can be heard in English are St Max Kolbe's Church in Bugibba (10am); Our Lady's Shrine in Mellieha (10am); St Dominic's, Rabat (11.15am); Casa Leoni in St Julian's (11am); Our Lady of Sorrows, St Paul's Bay (11am); St Patrick's, Sliema (8, 9 and 10am, 6.30 and 7.30pm); and St John of the Cross Church, Ta'Xbiex (10am).

There are two Anglican churches in Malta: St Paul's Cathedral in Valletta (tel. 225714) and Holy Trinity Church, Rudolph Street, Sliema (tel. 330575).

Protestant

St Andrew's Church, South Street, Valletta (tel. 222643), serves both Church of Scotland and Methodist congregations.

Restaurants

The snack bars and pizzerias listed below are usually open from 12 noon to 2pm and from 5 or 6pm in the evening. The better-class restaurants are often open only in the evening from 7pm to midnight. Most restaurants are closed on one day in the week. Hotel restaurants and cafés are only exceptionally included in the following list.

The service charge is usually not included in the price. A tip of 15–20 per cent is generally appropriate.

Service charge

Restaurants on Malta

Portobello Restaurant, St Luke's Road; tel. 571661

Bugibba

About 200m east of St Paul's Chapel, in a road parallel to the coastal road. Excellent fish dishes, delicious pizza and pasta. Small terrace with excellent views over St Paul's Bay. Very friendly service.

Lapsi View; tel. 821608

Ghar Lapsi

A modest, plain restaurant on the coast, popular with locals and busy at weekends.

Escoffier, Triq il-Butar; tel. 684429

Marsaskala

French cuisine; good helpings.The fish dishes are especially worth recommending.

Fishermen's Rest, St Thomas Bay; tel. 822049

A modest but good fish restaurant in rustic style; popular with locals. Service sometimes not as friendly as it might be.

Hunter's Tower, in harbour; tel. 871792

Marsaxlokk

Higher category, with modest pizzeria attached; fish specialities.

Bacchus, Inguanez Street; tel. 454981

Mdina

Stylish restaurant with international cuisine.

Clappetti, 5 St Agatha's Esplanade; tel. 459987

A snug café on the fortifications, with good snacks; terrace with superb view.

Restaurants

Fontanella, 1 Bastion Street; tel. 454264
  Café and snack bar on the walls of Mdina, with magnificent view of surrounding country; home-made cakes.
The Medina, Holy Cross Street; tel. 454004
  Higher category restaurant in an old palace; international cuisine.

Mellieha

Il Mithna, Triq il-Kbira; tel. 570404
  "Il Mithna" means "the windmill", and this luxury class restaurant is actually in a building attached to an old windmill. Expensive.
The Arches, 113 Main Street; tel. 573436
  Luxury class, elegant setting; international cuisine with something of an Italian flavour.

Qawra

The Village Square Restaurant, Sunny Coast Resort Club, Qawra Coast Road; tel. 572945
  International cuisine (mainly fish and steak dishes) at surprisingly reasonable prices. Very friendly service.
Ta'Cassia, Triq il-Fugass; tel. 571435
  In the southern part of town, not far from the football pitch. The menu includes Maltese specialities. The garden with its trees is attractive in the summer.
Ta'Fra Ben, Qawra Tower; tel. 573405
  Higher-category restaurant in an old watch-tower.

Rabat

Stazzjon, Mtarfa Road; tel. 451717
  An unusual restaurant in the old Mdina/Rabat railway station. Medium price range.

There are numerous restaurants around Spinola Bay in St Julian's. Many afford excellent views of the harbour

A pleasant ambience in the restaurant Ta' Frenc on Gozo

Il-Fortizza, Tower Road; tel. 336908
    Inexpensive pizzeria and elegant (but pricey!) Italian restaurant in an
    old British fort.
Mangal Turkish Restaurant, Tigné Seafront; tel. 342174
    Turkish specialities.
Ta'Kolina, 151 Tower Road; tel. 335106
    Named after a Maltese girl named Nicole or Kolina. Maltese and inter-
    national cuisine. Stylishly and comfortably furnished, with friendly
    service. Middle-range price category.

Sliema

The Rendez-vous, 55 Dingli Street; tel. 337468
    French and Maltese cuisine.

Barracuda, 194 Main Street; tel. 331817
    Higher category; beautiful terrace on Spinola Bay. Italian-style cuisine;
    mainly fish dishes.
Caffe Raffael, on Spinola Bay; tel. 332000
    Terrace with beautiful view. Pizzas and pasta dishes of medium qual-
    ity. Ideal for a quick snack between meals.
China House, 8 Spinola Road; tel. 311709
    Chinese cuisine; wide selection.
L-Ghonella, St George's Road; tel. 341037
    Stylish restaurant in the Spinola Palace. In summer you can eat in the
    garden. Only open in the evening. Italian and French cuisine as well as
    Maltese specialities.

St Julian's

Da Rosi, 44 Church Street; tel. 571411
    Middle-range category; pleasant atmosphere and friendly service. Fish
    specialities.

St Paul's Bay

Restaurants

Gillieru, Il-Knisja Street; tel. 573480
Luxury category; fish specialities. Terrace directly on sea.
Il Veccja, St Paul's Bay Street, Tel. 582376
At the western exit from St Paul's Bay. Small, slightly isolated restaurant with a lot of atmosphere. Excellent fish dishes and salads!. Medium price range.

Valletta

Bologna, 55 Republic Street, Tel 246149
On upper floor, middle-range Italian restaurant; on ground floor pizzeria.
Cordina, 244 Republic Street, Tel. 234385
Old-established café, with tables on the pavement.
Giannini, St Michael's Bastion, 23 Windmill Street, Tel. 237121
Luxury caregory; fine view of Marsamxett Harbour and Sliema. Maltese and international cuisine.
Pappagall, 174 Melita Street, Tel. 236195
Italian restaurant, good fish dishes; higher price category.
Scalini, 32 South Street, Tel. 246261
Italian cellar restaurant.

Xemxija

Porto del Sol, Xemxija Road; tel. 573970
Higher price category; beautiful view of St Paul's Bay. Lunch only if ordered in advance.
Shaukiwan, Xemxija Road, Tel. 573678
Good Chinese restaurant on the main road. Especially delicious dishes cooked and served on a stone. Friendly service.

Restaurants on Gozo

Gharb

Auberge Chez Amand, on main road to Ta'Pinu; tel. 551197
Luxury category. French cuisine, with some Maltese specialities; good wine cellar. Terrace (closed in winter).
Jeffrey's, Gharb Street, Tel. 561006
Restaurant in a former country house. In summer you can sit on the terrace. Only open in the evening. Good Maltese cuisine (steaks and fish dishes).

Marsalforn

Castello, Obaijar Bay, Tel. 551197
French-Belgian cuisine at moderate prices. Open lunchtime and evening.
Ta'Frenc, on Victoria-Marsalforn road; Tel. 553888
Stylish restaurant in an old farmhouse; French cuisine. Open lunchtime and evening.

Victoria

Citadello, Castel Hill Road, Tel. 556628
Café/restaurant with attractive inner courtyard, directly above the citadel. Ideal for coffee breaks or a meal when you are exhausted after sight-seeing in the old town of Victoria.

Xajhra

Gesther Restaurant, next to the church
Down-to-earth restaurant run by two sisters. Large selection of Maltese dishes at lunchtime.

Xlendi

Churchill, Xlendi Bay; tel. 555614
Modest restaurant with some tables on the sea; solid food, delicious pizzas, inexpensive.

Shipping Services

See Ferries and Shipping Services

Shopping

Malta is not a shopping paradise. The best shopping streets in Malta are Republic Street and Merchants Street in Valletta and round the southern part of Tower Road in Sliema. Fresh food is best bought in street markets (see Markets). For souvenirs see Arts and Crafts.

Most shops are open Mon.–Fri. from 9am to 12 noon or 1pm and from 4 to 7pm, Sat. 8am–12 noon.

Souvenirs

See Arts and Crafts

Sport

Visitors who want to pursue their particular sporting interests in Malta should get in touch with the Marsa Sports Club, which they can join on a daily or weekly basis. This private club, open daily from 9am to 9pm, has an 18-hole golf course, 18 tennis courts, 5 squash courts, a cricket field, a minigolf course and a large swimming pool.

Marsa Sports Club
Aldo Moro Street, Marsa
Tel. 233851 and 230664

There are no special cycle paths on Malta and cycling on the roads amongst the heavy traffic can be dangerous. On the side streets, however, an exploration of the island by bike or mountain-bike is ideal because of the limited distances and low heights. Bikes can be hired in all larger tourist centres.

Cycling
Mountain Biking

Malta offers excellent conditions for scuba diving and snorkelling: a varied marine flora and fauna, interesting underwater landscapes, with caves, grottoes and clefts, and good visibility up to 50 m under water. Since the water temperature off Malta's coasts hardly ever falls below 13°C, diving is possible all year round. If you want to dive on your own you must have a diving permit (C card), obtainable from the Department of Health (Merchants Street, Valletta; tel. 224071) or from a diving school. Visitors taking a course at a diving school under the supervision of a licensed diving instructor need produce only a medical certificate of fitness. A leaflet produced by the National Tourism Organisation of Malta, "Malta – a Paradise for

Diving

All three Maltese islands offer excellent diving conditions

Divers", gives a list of diving schools and detailed information about diving in Malta.

Malta's only **golf** course is that of the Marsa Sports Club (see above), which can be played on all year round.

There are **riding** school in Marsa (at the trotting course), Mellieha Bay, Golden Bay, Naxxar and elsewhere.

Sailing Visitors can become temporary members of the Royal Malta Yacht Club (Gzira, Manoel Island; tel. 331131), and can then hire a sailing boat or perhaps help to crew one. The Club can supply information about moorings and repair facilities.

Surfboards can be hired at many beaches during the summer.
Many of the large hotels have their own **tennis** courts. Of the Marsa Sports Club's 18 courses two are floodlit.

Walking The barren countryside of the main island of Malta is not exactly a walkers' paradise, but there is some attractive walking country in the north and west of the island, though strangers to the area will usually do well to confine themselves to the narrow and unfrequented country roads. The best walking is to be had on the Marfa Ridge in the north, along Ghajn Tuffieha Bay and the Dingli Cliffs on the south coast and, in the west, the still very isolated area bounded by Mgarr, Mosta and Rabat/Mdina. For shorter walks there are the Buskett Gardens.
   On the smaller and more rural island of Gozo there is magnificent walking country.

On many beaches there are facilities for **water-skiing**.

The favourite Maltese **spectator sports** are football (season from September to May; National Stadium at Ta'Qali) and trotting races. At Marsa there is a trotting course on which there are races every Sunday afternoon, starting at 1pm, from mid October to the beginning of June (for information tel. 233851).
   Water polo is a popular sport in many places. At some points on the coast you will see the enclosed basins on which local teams train for the national championships.

Taxis

Taxis have meters, and fares are at rates fixed by the government. If the meter is not switched on you should agree the fare before getting in. There are taxi ranks at Luqa Airport, at harbours, in front of the large hotels and outside City Gate in Valletta. There is no single number for calling a radio taxi: you should, therefore, ask at your hotel's reception desk.

Water taxis (dghajsas) ply for custom in the Grand Harbour and Marsamxett Harbour: the fare is a matter for negotiation. From the landing-stage at the Custom House in Valletta the boats cross to Senglea and Vittoriosa.

Telephone

See Post and Telephone

Theatres and Concerts

Malta has no theatre company of its own. Performances in the Manoel Theatre in Valletta (Old Theatre Street) and the Astra and Aurora theatres in Victoria (Gozo) are by visiting international companies and artistes.

The theatre season is from October to May. The box office for productions in the Manoel Theatre is open Mon.–Fri. 10am–12 noon and 4–7pm, Sat. 10am–12 noon.

Time

Malta time is an hour ahead of Greenwich Mean Time. Summer Time is in force from the last Sunday in March to the last weekend in October, when Malta is two hours ahead of GMT.

Tipping

Tipping is generally in line with European practice. In restaurants where the bill does not include a service charge the tip should be at least 15 per cent. Chambermaids in hotels expect something like LM1.50 per person per week. Porters at airports get about 50 cents per item of luggage.

Transport

See Bus services; Car Rental; Ferries and Shipping Services; Taxis

Travel Documents

Visitors from the United Kingdom, Ireland, Commonwealth countries and the United States require only a valid passport for a stay of not more than three months in Malta; no visa is needed. Children under 16 must either have their own passport or be entered in their parents' passport. Visitors intending to stay for more than three months should obtain a visa before leaving home from the nearest Maltese embassy or high commission.

National driving licences and car registration documents are recognised. Visitors taking their own car must have an international insurance certificate (green card).

When to Go

Malta is particularly beautiful in spring, when even on this barren island the countryside is green and spangled with blossom. In April and May temperatures during the day are very agreeable; but at this time of year you should still be prepared for spells of bad weather. This is compensated for by the fact that the islands are not yet overcrowded, so that the scenery, the sights and the beaches can be enjoyed in peace. Bathing in the Mediterranean is pleasant from May onwards, with water temperatures averaging 18.4°C.

Spring

Climatic Table	Temperatures in °C		Hours of sunshine per day	Days with rain	Rainfall in mm
Months	Average maximum	Average minimum			
January	14.4	10.2	5.5	12	90
February	14.7	10.3	6.3	8	60
March	16.1	11.2	7.3	5	39
April	18.3	13.1	8.8	2	15
May	21.6	15.9	9.9	2	12
June	25.9	19.4	11.5	0	2
July	28.9	22.1	12.4	0	0
August	29.3	22.9	11.4	1	8
September	27.1	21.6	9.4	3	29
October	23.8	18.9	7.5	6	63
November	19.7	15.6	5.8	9	91
December	16.1	12.0	5.0	13	110
Year	20.3	16.1	8.4	61	519

Summer

Although in summer there are frequently temperatures of 30°C or more, the heat is not too oppressive. There is almost always a refreshing breeze, and the sea also has a moderating influence. But this is the time when most Maltese people take their summer holiday, so that the beaches tend to be crowded.

Autumn

The first banks of cloud appear in September, but the weather is mostly fine until well into October. Sea bathing is still possible in November, with water temperatures of around 19°C. There is little colour left in the landscape, now dry and brown.

For those mainly interested in Malta's cultural and artistic treasures winter is also a good time for a visit. Even in January, the coldest month, temperatures seldom fall below 10°C and may be as high as a pleasant 15°C during the day. During the winter months, however, an umbrella is an essential requisite.

Youth Hostels

There are two organisations in Malta which run youth hostels and youth guest-houses. The overnight charge ranges between LM1 and 3 according to season and hostel.

NSTS – Student and Youth Travel
220 St Paul's Street, Valletta
Tel. 244983, fax 230330
Guest-houses in Sliema, St Julian's and Fgura.

Malta Youth Hostels Association (MYHA)
17 Triq Tal-Borg, Paola
Tel. and fax 693957

To stay in a youth hostel you must be a member of the MYHA. Visitors can join by applying to the above address and paying a small membership fee; a passport photograph is required. There are youth hostels in Paceville/St Julian's, Sliema and Senglea and on Gozo.

Index

Index

Picture Credits

Archiv für Kunst und Geschichte: p. 32, 35, 123
Baedeker-Archiv: p. 45 (2x), 47
Bareth: p. 88
Borowski: p. 3 (top), 6 (top), 7 (bottom l), 13, 24, 52 (2x), 71, 73, 77, 79, 82, 85, 90, 92, 94, 97, 100, 103, 104, 106, 107, 111, 118, 133, 134, 138, 141, 143, 153, 161, 164, 166, 169, 171, 174, 178, 179, 187, 188, 194 (2x), 195, 198, 206
Fabig: p. 114, 147
Fotoagentur Lade: p. 3 (bottom), 5, 6/7
Fotoagentur laif: p. 7 (top), 81, 135, 151, 159, 172/173, 189, 207
Friedrichsmeier/Gronau: p. 15, 23, 41, 65, 98/99, 109, 155, 209
Friedrichsmeier/Hackenburg: p. 6 (bottom), 7 (bottom r), 8/9, 17, 18, 25, 55, 57, 58, 60, 86, 117, 122, 132, 157, 184, 185
Otto: p. 50, 68/69, 125, 145
Roth: p. 119, 203

Imprint

99 illustrations, 21 maps and plans, 1 large country map

German text: Birgit Borowski, Reinhard Strüber
General direction: Baedeker-Redaktion
Cartography: Franz Huber, Munich; Ingenieurbüro für Kartographie Harms (large map of Malta)

Editorial work English edition: g-and-w PUBLISHING
English translation: James Hogarth

Front cover: Pictures Colour Library. Back cover: AA Photo Library (P. Enticknap)

2nd English edition 2000
Reprinted 2001, 2002 ($\times$ 2)

© Karl Baedeker GmbH, Ostfildern
Original German edition 1999/2000

© Automobile Association Developments Limited 2002
English language edition worldwide

Published by AA Publishing, a trading name of Automobile Association Developments Limited, whose registered office is Millstream, Maidenhead Road, Windsor, Berkshire SL4 5GD. Registered number 1878835.

Distributed in the United States and Canada by:
Fodor's Travel Publications, Inc.
1745 Broadway
New York, NY 10019

All rights reserved. No part of this publication may be reproduced, stored in a retrieval system or transmitted in any form by any means – electronic, photocopying, recording or otherwise – unless the written permission of the publisher has been obtained.

The name Baedeker is a registered trade mark.

A CIP catalogue record of this book is available from the British Library.

Licensed user: Mairs Geographischer Verlag GmbH & Co., Ostfildern

Typeset by Fakenham Photosetting Ltd, Fakenham, Norfolk, UK

Printed in Italy by G. Canale & C. S.p.A., Turin

ISBN 0 7495 2411 1

A01648